Bloom's Modern Critical Interpretations

Modern Critical Interpretations

Arthur Miller's
THE CRUCIBLE

Edited and with an introduction by
Harold Bloom
Sterling Professor of the Humanities
Yale University

CHELSEA HOUSE PUBLISHERS

Bloom's Modern Critical Interpretations: The Crucible

© 1999 Infobase Publishing

Introduction © 1999 by Harold Bloom

Chelsea House
An imprint of Infobase Publishing
132 West 31st Street
New York NY 10001

Library of Congress Cataloging-in-Publication Data

The crucible / edited and with an introduction by Harold Bloom.
    p. cm. — (Modern critical interpretations)
  Includes bibliographical references and index.
  ISBN 0-7910-4775-X (hc)
    1. Miller, Arthur, 1915–   Crucible. 2. Politics and literature—United States—History—20th century. 3. Historical drama, American—History and criticism. 4. .Salem (Mass.)—History—Colonial period, ca. 1600–1775.
5. Salem (Mass.)—In literature. 6. Witchcraft in literature.
  I. Bloom, Harold. II. Series.
  PS3525.I5156C7334   1998
  812'.52—dc21   98-15482

Printed in the United States of America

Lake 10 9 8 7 6

This book is printed on acid-free paper.

Contents

Editor's Note

My Introduction considers some of the aesthetic limitations of *The Crucible*, while joining in the general judgment that the play is redeemed by its social and theatrical effectiveness.

Sheila Huftel defends Miller against some aspects of the critique of Eric Bentley, whose stance I largely endorse in my Introduction. Miller is praised by Stephen Fender for showing us that Salem's "evil is not positive," its ethic being not mistaken but non-existent.

Thomas E. Porter investigates *The Crucible* as courtroom drama, and finds it lacks a ritual basis for ascribing a moral triumph to its protagonist, John Proctor, while Robert A. Martin explores the historical sources of the play.

John Proctor's playfulness and imaginative qualities are stressed by William T. Liston, after which William J. McGill Jr., finds in Proctor's fate an essential historicity.

For Michael J. O'Neal, Proctor's affirmation of his good name is the decisive element in his becoming a tragic protagonist, while E. Miller Budick subtly argues that moral arrogance is at once the heart of the American temperament and of Miller's play.

June Schlueter and James K. Flanagan, in an overview of *The Crucible*, judge it to be a vision of communal guilt, after which Iska Alter, in a feminist rereading, emphasizes "female power" that subverts patriarchal society in Salem.

In a Jungian analysis, Michelle I. Pearson traces the pattern of John Proctor's individuation, while Wendy Schissel gives us another feminist interpretation, which faults Miller for his male blindness in centering upon Proctor, and not upon the women that Proctor in no way merited.

This book concludes with Stephen Marino's argument that Proctor, at last a moral hero, dies for truth and for his name's honor.

Introduction

Forty years ago, in his introduction to his *Collected Plays*, Arthur Miller meditated upon *The Crucible*, staged four years before, in 1953. A year after that first production, Miller was refused a passport, and in 1956-57 he endured the active persecution of the American witch-hunt for suspected Communists. The terror created in some of his former friends and associates by the possibility of being branded as warlocks and witches "underlies every word in *The Crucible*," according to Miller. "Every word" necessarily is hyperbolical, since *The Crucible* attempts to be a personal tragedy as well as a social drama. Miller, Ibsen's disciple, nevertheless suffers an anxiety of influence in *The Crucible* not so much in regard to Ibsen's *An Enemy of the People* but in relation to George Bernard Shaw's *Saint Joan*. The frequent echoes of *Saint Joan* seem involuntary, and are distracting, and perhaps fatal to the aesthetic value of *The Crucible*. For all its moral earnestness, *Saint Joan* is enhanced by the Shawian ironic wit, a literary quality totally absent from Miller, here and elsewhere. Though a very well-made play, *The Crucible* rarely escapes a certain dreariness in performance, and does not gain by rereading.

This is not to deny the humane purpose nor the theatrical effectiveness of *The Crucible*, but only to indicate a general limitation, here and elsewhere, in Miller's dramatic art. Eric Bentley has argued shrewdly that "one never knows what a Miller play is about: politics or sex." Is *The Crucible* a personal tragedy, founded upon Proctor's sexual infidelity, or is it a play of social protest and warning? There is no reason it should not be both, except for Miller's inability to fuse the genres. Here he falls short of his master, Ibsen, who concealed Shakespearean tragic purposes within frameworks of social issues, yet invariably unified the two modes. Still, one can be grateful that Miller has not revised *The Crucible* on the basis of his own afterthoughts, which have emphasized the absolute evil of the Salem powers, Danforth and Hathorne. These worthies already are mere facades, opaque to Miller's understanding and our own. Whatever their religious sensibility may or may

1

not have been, Miller has no imaginative understanding of it, and we therefore confront them only as puppets. Had Miller made them even more malevolent, our bafflement would have been even greater. I am aware that I tend to be an uncompromising aesthete, and I cannot dissent from the proven theatrical effectiveness of *The Crucible*. Its social benignity is also beyond my questioning; American society continues to benefit by this play. We would have to mature beyond our national tendency to moral and religious self-righteousness for *The Crucible* to dwindle into another period-piece, and that maturation is nowhere in sight.

SHEILA HUFTEL

The Crucible

C ry *witch*! The Salem witch-hunt marked a time when "long-held hatreds of neighbors could now be openly expressed, and vengeance taken, despite the Bible's charitable injunctions. Land-lust . . . could now be elevated to the arena of morality; one could cry witch against one's neighbor and feel perfectly justified in the bargain. Old scores could be settled on a plane of heavenly combat between Lucifer and the Lord."

Its climate of terror is the first we know of this play. The slave Tituba's initial fright is followed by the Reverend Parris' fear—and the fear is of witchcraft. He has discovered some girls "dancing like heathen in the forest," and, shaken, he tells his niece Abigail (who led them) what he saw: "I saw Tituba . . . and I heard a screeching and gibberish coming from her mouth. She were swaying like a dumb beast over that fire!" In the shock of discovery a child has fallen sick, and the town leaps to cry witchcraft. Abigail, to escape whipping, embraces the excuse, and in the general hysteria vengeance breaks out.

Fear and guilt were in the air of Salem, heightened by the prim order of life. Children were regarded as young adults. "They never conceived that the children were anything but thankful for being permitted to walk straight, eyes slightly lowered, arms at the sides, and mouths shut until bidden to speak." Once this rigidity was broken the people found themselves prey to

From *Arthur Miller: The Burning Glass.* © 1965 by The Citadel Press.

fantastic terrors never felt before. Ann Putnam, "a twisted soul of forty-five, a death-ridden woman, haunted by dreams," chillingly confesses to sending her young daughter Ruth to conjure up the dead and discover who murdered her brothers and sisters—all of whom had died at birth. Avidly the neighbors gather to inquire into Betty Parris' strange illness. "How high did she fly?" Complacently they assure one another that "the Devil's touch is heavier than sick." The fear in the Reverend Parris is greater than in all the rest. He will be hounded out of Salem for the witch-craft discovered in his house. He always feared for something, and now he fears his neighbors. It is as though a people suddenly turned savage. He expects to be turned out, and believes the people would be justified, since in his own eyes he is already tainted with the Devil.

The superstitions of the townspeople breed greater terror, and Abigail, quick to take advantage, warns her friends: "Let either of you breathe a word, or the edge of a word . . . and I will come to you in the black of some terrible night and I will bring a pointy reckoning that will shudder you. And you know I can do it; I saw the Indians smash my dear parents' heads on the pillow next to mine, and I have seen some reddish work done at night, and I can make you wish you had never seen the sun go down!" Abigail has been drinking blood, a charm to kill John Proctor's wife.

Abigail was a servant in the Proctors' house and loved John, until Elizabeth found them out and dismissed her. Now Abigail admits to him that Betty's sickness has nothing to do with witchcraft. Proctor is one of Miller's ten-feet-tall individualists, a farmer of unshakable integrity and dangerous directness. "I may speak my heart, I think." Putnam accuses him at once of being against Parris and against all authority. Proctor has no patience with Parris and complains that he preaches only hell-fire and forgets to mention God. He sees the man's weakness—a vacillation based on fear that makes it impossible for him to tell his parishioners they are wrong about witchcraft. Instead, he goes along with the mounting superstition and sends for Reverend Hale to discover whether or not there are witches in Salem. This opens the way for demonology to replace law.

For Hale, diabolism is a precise science that has nothing to do with superstition. But by the nature of his belief he could not be immune to the cry of "Spirits!" The shock of Abigail's attack on Tituba releases the hysteria and convinces Hale. Tituba is accused of conspiring with the Devil and a desperate bewilderment breaks upon her. She knows nothing but the terror, and understands nothing but that she will hang. Panic prompts a confession she does not know how to make. She gropes for a placating answer and out of this recounts promises made to her by the Devil: "You work for me, Tituba, and I make you free! I give you pretty dress to wear, and put you way high up in the air, and you gone fly back to Barbados!" It will not serve. Almost hypnotized, she gives names suggested by Putnam. Startlingly, Abigail joins Tituba's confession with her own and in an orgy of relief Betty feverishly joins in the random calling out of names. Blasted with ecstasy, the children cry out as if possessed and the climate is created that makes witch-hunting possible.

Against this background Miller etches the Proctors' bleak relationship. Proctor describes Elizabeth as having an everlasting funeral marching round her heart. They live in isolation, while above them both tower the tremendous values by which they live.

In Salem a court has been set up to try and hang those accused of witchcraft, if they will not confess. Abigail has been elevated to sainthood. "Where she walks the crowd will part like the sea for Israel. And folks are brought before them, and if they scream and howl and fall to the floor—the person's clapped in jail for bewitchin' them." Proctor's servant, Mary Warren, returns with the news that the fourteen arrested have grown to thirty-nine, and that Goody Osburn will hang. Mary, a frightened, lonely girl, danced with the others and preens herself on being an official of the Court. Alarmed herself at its wonders, and alarming them, she explains how witchcraft is proved. "But then—then she sit there, denying and denying, and I feel a misty coldness climbin' up my back, and the skin on my skull begin to creep, and I feel a clamp around my neck and I cannot breathe air; and then—I hear a voice, a screamin' voice, and it were my voice—and all at once I remembered everything she done to me!"

Proctor is about to whip her when she yells that she saved Elizabeth's life that day. While Mary strives precariously for self-respect, Elizabeth realizes that Abigail wants her dead, and will cry out her name until she is taken.

The Reverend Hale interrupts this conflict. He has come to test the Proctors' Christianity. Elizabeth cannot wait to convince him, but Proctor's guilt over Abigail makes him falter. Instead, he tells Hale of Abigail's confession that the children's sickness has nothing to do with witchcraft. Hale reminds him of confessions made to the Court. "And why not, if they must hang for denyin' it?" Those confessions prove nothing.

Intimations of Elizabeth's arrest that began with Mary Warren's outburst are taken further when Proctor's neighbors, Corey and Nurse, come with the news that Martha and Rebecca have been taken. Rebecca is charged with the supernatural murder of Goody Putnam's babies. If she is guilty, Hale insists, "then nothing is left to stop the whole green world from burning."

They come for Elizabeth. When, in spite of her proved innocence, she still leaves Hale questioning, Proctor can bear it no longer. "Why do you never wonder if Parris be innocent, or Abigail? Is the accuser always holy now? Were they born this morning as clean as God's fingers? I'll tell you what's walking Salem—vengeance is walking Salem . . . now the little crazy children are jangling the keys of the kingdom, and common vengeance writes the law!" But Elizabeth is taken and chained, while they watch, helpless.

Proctor insists that Mary testify in court and as her fear mounts so does his conviction. "Make your peace with it! Now Hell and Heaven grapple on our backs, and all our old pretense is ripped away—make your peace! Peace. It is a providence, and no great change; we are only what we always were, but naked now. Aye, naked! And the wind, God's icy wind, will blow!"

On this surge of feeling, attention turns back to the Court. Here other charges are brought. Giles Corey insists that Putnam is killing his neighbors for their land. A man whose pigs die swears that Martha Corey is bewitching them. But primarily, Mary Warren tremblingly admits that she never saw spirits. Judge Danforth cannot believe it. "I have seen marvels in this Court. I have seen people choked before my eyes by spirits; I have seen them stuck by pins and slashed by daggers." He refuses to believe that people fear this Court; if they do there is only one explanation: "There is fear in the country because there is a moving plot to topple Christ in the country!"

Proctor insists that he has not come to overthrow the Court, but to save his wife. In that case, Danforth urges him to drop the charge; Elizabeth will not be hanged because she is pregnant. Proctor finds he cannot; Corey and Nurse are his friends, and their wives are also accused. Danforth agrees to hear Mary Warren. Falteringly she insists that she is with God now and is confronted with the other children and with Abigail's denial. To prove her story, Mary is ordered to faint at will, but lacking the hysteria she cannot. Doubt rises, and out of it the children create terror. They are about to cry out Mary Warren as a witch when Proctor checks them with the truth about Abigail: "A man will not cast away his good name. You surely know that . . . I have made a bell of my honor! I have rung the doom of my good name." Elizabeth is called to confirm his accusation; she lies to save his name.

Danforth believes her. Abigail cries out Mary Warren as a witch: Mary has assumed the shape of a bird and high on a beam she stretches her claws, about to swoop down on the children and tear their faces. Only Proctor and Hale do not share in this horror. The girls scream and Mary finds herself screaming with them. She goes wild and accuses Proctor of being the Devil's man. Danforth clamors for confession.

In the midst of these wild and whirling words that seem to presage a reeling universe, Proctor warns the Judge: "For them that quail to bring men out of ignorance, as I have quailed, and as you quail now when you know in all your black hearts that this be fraud—God damns our kind especially, and we will burn, we will burn together!" Reverend Hale quits the Court.

It is the morning of Proctor's execution. Meanwhile in Salem: "There are orphans wandering from house to house; abandoned cattle bellow on the high-roads, the stink of rotting crops hangs everywhere, and no man knows when the harlots' cry will end his life." Abigail has stolen all Parris' savings and disappeared. Mr. Hale has come to urge those accused to confess, as if they die he counts himself their murderer. And still Danforth refuses to postpone the hangings. "While I speak God's law, I will not crack its voice with whimpering."

Elizabeth is fetched in the hope that she will persuade Proctor to confess. Hale tries to warn her by his own example. "The very crowns of holy law I brought, and what I touched with my bright confidence, it died; and where I turned the eye of my great faith, blood flowed up. Beware, Goody Proctor—cleave to no faith when faith brings blood." To her, this remains the Devil's argument.

Now this whole issue turns on the integrity of John Proctor, on his judgment or Danforth's. Elizabeth tells him how Giles Corey died. "Great stones they lay upon his chest until he plead Aye or Nay. They say he gave them but two words. 'More weight,' he says. And died." Proctor's guilt prompts him to confess, almost as a kind of expiation. He believes that it would be fraud for him to die like a saint and besmirch the honor of those that hang. It is as though his death has to be earned.

He looks to Elizabeth for absolution but she reminds him that her forgiveness means nothing if he cannot forgive himself. All she can do is take her share of the guilt. "Do what you will. But let none be your judge. There be no higher judge under Heaven than Proctor is!" And there is no shedding of this particular responsibility. He decides to confess, but refuses to implicate others. "Then it is proved. Why must I say it? . . . I speak my own sins; I cannot judge another. I have no tongue for it."

But Proctor cannot turn so against himself. Painfully he recants because—"I have three children—how may I teach them to walk like men in the world, and I sold my friends? . . . Because it is my name! Because I cannot have another in my life! Because I lie and sign myself to lies! Because I am not worth the dust on the feet of them that hang! How may I live without my name? I have given you my soul; leave me my name!" In Miller, a man's name is his conscience, his immortal soul, and without it there is no person left.

Proctor recants, and in the wonder that he is capable of letting himself be hanged finds self-respect. Hale begs Elizabeth: "Be his helper!—What profit him to bleed? Shall the dust praise him? Shall the worms declare his truth? Go to him, take his shame away!" Indeed it is a longed-for absolution. But the fact remains that only Proctor can absolve Proctor. "And the drums rattle like bones in the morning air."

Given the plot of the Salem witch hunt, and knowing nothing of the history books, I suspect that one would try to trace it in *The Collected Works of Edgar Allan Poe*. But where Poe would have been content with the dramatic story of a witch-hunt—sanguinary forest orgies, charms of chicken blood, the marvelous murder of babies, a destructive yellow bird, crying out and confession, torture and hangings—for Arthur Miller, it is necessary to explain why these things take place and how, in fact, people come to believe in witches.

In a commentary written for the text Miller explores the background of his play and relates it to the present. He writes that no one can know what the people's lives were like, adding definitively: "They had no novelists—and would not have permitted anyone to read a novel if one were handy." Their hard life rather than their faith protected their morals, and their passion for minding each other's business created suspicions. Their lives were rigid, and with reason because—"To the best of their knowledge the American forest was the last place on earth that was not paying homage to God. . . . They believed, in short, that they held in their steady hands the candle that would light the world. We have inherited this belief, and it has helped and hurt us."

Since they believed they were living according to God's law, they saw in change a total disruption. The theocracy had been developed to keep the people together for their better protection materially and ideologically; but the time came when the imposed order outweighed the dangers. Miller sees the witch-hunt as "a perverse manifestation of the panic which set in among all classes when the balance began to turn toward greater individual freedom." The rest of the cause is in the temperament of the people: tightly reined, fear-driven, and deeply sin-conscious. But they had no means of absolution. The witch-hunt was an opportunity for mammoth public confession, by way of accusation. Miller points out: "Social disorder in any age breeds such mystical suspicions, and when, as in Salem, wonders are brought forth from below the social surface, it is too much to expect people to hold back very long from laying on the victims with all the force of their frustrations."

The scope of *The Crucible* is wide; a general illustration of a witch-hunt and an explanation of how and why they break out. To limit it to one particular twentieth-century witch-hunt is to wear blinkers. Miller's comment is for yesterday as well as for the day after tomorrow, and not merely the here-and-now of American politics. It is surely a kind of vanity to corner-off a section of a large work, identify with it, and claim that as the subject of the whole. It cannot be overlooked that *The Crucible* is applicable to any situation that allows the accuser to be always holy, as it also is to any conflict between the individual and authority. Timeless as *An Enemy of the People*, it symbolizes all forms of heresy-hunting, religious and political.

Miller himself covers the whole field by discussing contemporary diabolism alongside Hale's belief in the Devil. He writes of the necessity of the Devil: "A weapon designed and used time and time again in every age to whip men into a surrender to a particular church or church-state." He traces the Devil's progress, from Lucifer of the Spanish Inquisition to current politics. "A political policy is equated with moral right, and opposition to it with diabolical malevolence. Once such an equation is effectively made, society becomes a congerie of plots and counterplots, and the main role of government changes from that of the arbiter to that of the scourge of God."

In answer to the criticism, and much has been made of it, that witches are an impossibility whereas Communists are a fact, Miller writes that he has no doubt people were communing with the devil in Salem. He cites as evidence Tituba's confession and the behavior of the children who were known to have indulged in sorceries. It was, incidentally, a cardinal fault in Sartre's film of the play, *Les Sorciers de Salem*, that, not believing in witches himself, he allowed none of his characters to believe in them. This uncompromising twentieth-century attitude not only robbed the film of conviction, but of an important seventeenth-century viewpoint that should have been its concern.

It may be that I have a simple mind. But if a dramatist says his play deals with the Salem witch-hunt and goes to the length of writing about it, I am inclined to believe him. By implication the play would be about general witch-hunting and by inference about McCarthyism, which happened to be the current witch-hunt. I believe the play has been distorted by trying to link the two too closely. But some American critics found the link not close enough, and charged Miller with evasion. To ignore their objections would be evasive. I admit that their greater involvement would make them more sensitive to this aspect of the play; it might also lead them to a greater prejudice.

Legendary Arthur Millers range from Lincoln figure to Left-Wing Idol. He is the distinguished American dramatist of theatrical textbooks—from Aeschylus to Arthur Miller. He is the tough American dramatist of the gossip columnist in search of a caption. He is the man whom everybody knows—until you actually want to know something about him. Then suddenly nobody knows him very well. Ken Tynan once defined him as "someone you'd expect to find as a stonemason instead of a playwright." Alongside these, set some American critics' view of evader and fellow traveler. Conflicts surge around him and controversy crowds in.

Having read Eric Bentley, and been directed by him to Robert Warshow's article, "The Liberal Conscience in *The Crucible*," in *Commentary* (March, 1953)—"the best analysis of Mr. Miller yet written"—I assumed, over-hastily, that American criticism of *The Crucible* had been political rather than dramatic. I was wrong. Of seven New York papers, three saw contemporary parallels, three did not, and one found the play just a melodrama. It is significant, perhaps, that all these critics but one mentioned parallels, whether they found them or not. At worst, this was a line on how Miller was regarded, what was expected of him, and what was uppermost in the critics' minds. By way of comparison, A. V. Cookman, critic of *The Times* (London) saw Miller's anger as being directed against human stupidity in general, and thought the play was provoked by contemporary happenings in the States.

To return to the *Commentary* article, couched in the vein of "Brutus is an honorable man," Robert Warshow found in Miller a steadfast, almost selfless refusal of complexity and an assured, simple view of human behavior. This, he believed, was Miller's trump card in captivating an educated audience. An audience which demanded of its artists—and in that case presumably found in Miller—"an intelligent narrowness of mind and vision and a generalized tone of affirmation, offering not any particular insights or any particular truths, but simply the assurance that insight and truth as qualities . . . reside somehow in the various signals by which the artist and the audience have learned to recognize each other." At this point I looked back at the title to check that we were, in fact, discussing the same playwright. Warshow admitted that Mr. Miller speaks out. He did not know what Mr. Miller is speaking out about, but he is speaking out!

In short, he was being evasive, and on this point political criticism of *The Crucible* turned. Arthur Miller said that he doubted whether he should ever have tempted agony by writing a play on the subject of the Salem witch-hunt, which he knew about for many years before McCarthyism. In his own terms, could he have walked away from it? If you believe he is evasive—yes. I think this view of the play as evasive could only be taken by those who expected Miller to hold to the party line. The fellow-traveler, or at best fellow-sympathizer, angle was taken further by Eric Bentley in *The Dramatic Event* and *What Is Theatre?*; in both books he is concerned with Miller's "evasion."

In *The Dramatic Event* (1954) there is a chapter provocatively entitled, "The Innocence of Arthur Miller." It begins with lavish praise; then, while applause still sounds, Bentley conjures Kafkaesque images and reminds us that Miller's mentality is that of the "unreconstructed liberal." *The Crucible* is interpreted politically; Bentley points out that "communism" is a word used to cover the politics of Marx, the politics of the Soviet Union, and, finally, "the activities of all liberals as they seem to illiberal illiterates." The scope of Miller's argument was limited because it was concerned only with the third use. It was Bentley's argument that the analogy between red-baiting and witch-hunting was complete only to communists. "For only to them is the menace of communism as fictitious as the menace of witches. The non-communist will look for certain reservations and provisos. In *The Crucible* there are none."

It must not be thought that Bentley was actually accusing Miller of being a Communist. Perish the thought. "Arthur Miller is the playwright of American liberal folklore." But he was accusing him of assuming a general innocence and there was no doubt that this bothered him. What he seemed to want from Miller was a sense of guilt. He took up the theme again in *What Is Theatre?*, where he found that Miller stacked the cards; that his progressivism was too close to Communism, that *A View From the Bridge* should have been written by a poet, and wasn't, and that he did not recognize any synthesis in Miller. He claims that he could never know what a Miller play is about, and in this suspects a sinister device to mislead the audience. "Mr. Miller stands accused of no disingenuousness—except when he denies the possibility of his plays meaning what at the moment he wishes them not to mean. If *The Crucible* was set in the seventeenth century so that, on convenient occasions its twentieth-century reference could be denied, then its author *was* disingenuous." Would it be ingenuous of me to say that I cannot imagine Arthur Miller doing such a thing?

Some explanation of Bentley's opinion was necessary, and he gave it in the chapter (again provocatively titled) "The Missing Communist." Lenin said: "We must be able to . . . resort to various stratagems, artifices, illegal methods, to evasion and subterfuges. . . ." Bentley takes it up—"Or was Lenin really in favor of evasion, and did certain evasions multiply in geometric progression, until for millions of men, *Communist or not*, they became standard practice. I italicize *Communist or not* because the ultimate triumph of Leninism lies in the mystification of non-communists." The chapter was not about Miller, but he was mentioned in it.

I kept returning to the fact that Bentley never directly accused Miller of being a communist. Instead, I found a cat's cradle of words that never seemed to chime exactly with the implication behind them. I was uncertain at this point who exactly was being evasive. It seemed a reflex with Bentley that whenever he wrote about Communism Miller's name happened to occur. Bentley's view of Miller seemed to be of someone who appeared to be innocent and was not. He suggested a dualism that I would take to be outside Miller's range: that while Miller was being dishonest, he had no doubt of his own integrity. There was nothing wrong with this—except its probability. Integrity is fundamental to Miller; all his plays turn on it, and he is too aware to fool himself in this fashion. This particular view of Bentley's is incredible; it is based on a kind of double negative reasoning— nothing is as it appears, and the only thing that is, is what is not. I was reminded of the dragon Proctor said he might have in his house but nobody had ever seen it.

Howard Fast, writing in the *Daily Worker*, found that *The Crucible* was about the Rosenbergs. I suspect that critics, as well as individuals, find what they seek and tend to line up a play's meaning with their particular problem or preoccupation. The fault looms large beside the ideal of an impartial critic, who is supposed to shed his prejudices with his coat. The difficulty of living up to the old ideal has called the ideal itself into question. It has been argued, and with truth, that dynamic critics were always thoroughly prejudiced—set Hazlitt beside Lamb, or Shaw beside Max Beerbohm. The argument runs that without opinion, prejudice, and preoccupation there is no person left watching the play. Just as the play was not created in a vacuum, it cannot be judged in one. The admission follows that a criticism of a play is a personal statement from a particular individual. For this reason, then, it is likely that the best judge of a play's meaning is the man who wrote it. He is the only person in the world who can know what he started with and what his intentions were.

The Crucible's reception was as contrary and two-headed as its criticism. On its first night, January 22, 1953, it took nineteen curtain calls, and was lightly picketed during its run.

In the general controversy roused by the play, audiences stopped short at the witch-hunt and McCarthyism and overlooked Miller's point. He explains in his Preface how the audience came to misunderstand him. Strong right-wing opinion on the first night inspired the initial confusion by making some people uneasy, afraid, and partisan. They were deflected from the play's inner theme—the handing over of conscience. Miller was concerned with the creation of terror in people, with fear cut off from reason. "The sin of public terror is that it divests man of conscience, of himself. . . . I saw accepted the notion that conscience was no longer a private matter but one of state administration. I saw men handing conscience to other men and thanking other men for the opportunity of doing so." Miller was seeing the witch-hunt from the inside and trying to increase awareness of why it had happened; what exactly prompted that terror that made the rest possible? The audience was looking at it from the outside, more eager to apply it generally to their lives than to understand the questions it raised.

"It was not only the rise of 'McCarthyism' that moved me," he wrote in his Preface, "but something which seemed much more weird and mysterious. It was the fact that a political, objective, knowledgeable campaign from the far Right was capable of creating not only a terror, but a new subjective reality, a veritable mystique which was gradually assuming even a holy resonance. . . . The terror in these people was being knowingly planned and consciously engineered, and yet . . . all they knew was terror. That so interior and subjective an emotion could have been so manifestly created from without was a marvel to me. It underlines every word in *The Crucible.*"

It seemed to Miller that, apart from self-preservation and fear of being exiled by society, social compliance is the result of a sense of guilt that people conceal by conforming. Believing guilt to be the mainspring of terror, *The Crucible* goes further than *All My Sons* and *Death of a Salesman*, which stop at its discovery. In *The Crucible* Miller suggests that it is possible to be aware beyond the point at which guilt begins. Proctor's guilt over Abigail did not blind him to the play-acting of the children and his own innocence of witchcraft. For Miller, guilt has changed from something impenetrable to "a betrayer, possibly the most real of our illusions, but nevertheless a quality of mind capable of being overthrown."

The Salem witch-hunt was a subject ready-made for Miller's preoccupations in the early fifties. The handing over of conscience seemed to be the central fact of the time in Salem. In addition, the individual's abdication in favor of a higher authority was prompted by guilt rampant.

Miller discovered from the Court records that Abigail Williams, a child of eleven, sometime a servant in Proctor's house, cried out Elizabeth as a witch. Uncharacteristically, the child refused to incriminate John Proctor. He was a liberal-minded farmer, ahead of his time in that he insisted the trials were a fake. Miller writes in his Preface: "The central impulse for writing . . . was not the social but the interior psychological question, which was the question of that guilt residing in Salem which the hysteria merely unleashed, but did not create. . . ." Therefore, Miller says, "the structure reflects that understanding, and it centers on John, Elizabeth, and Abigail."

Encouraged by the overpowering feeling of the time, part of the confusion over *The Crucible* arose through a general love of categories that opposed Miller's love of synthesis. Once again it proves that plays should not be categorized any more than people. Through the controversy his plays spark off the fact remains that Miller is a straightforward, factual, and direct dramatist. If I have made him seem tortuous, the fault is mine and not his. A playwright lives by the amount of thought and feeling he can inspire, and traceless plays are like faceless people.

Taking up the running battle of *The Crucible*, it seems as though nothing about it escaped conflict. In spite of the play's success, its every aspect brings Miller squarely up against his critics and his audience. The play was to center on John, Elizabeth, and Abigail. Critics found the character-drawing abstract and accused Miller of replacing people by types, the easier to prove his thesis. Walter Kerr protested unassailably: "It is better to make a man than to make a point." This was cited as the play's main dramatic fault. But Miller was drawn to the people of Salem by their moral size and overwhelming values. Theirs was a society that believed it had found the right way to live and to die. Both prosecution and defense could speak in the name of colossal life values which "often served to raise this swirling and ludicrous mysticism to a level of high moral debate; and it did this despite the fact that most of the participants were unlettered, simple folk." These values are something our society has lost, and a search for them is inherent in all Miller's work.

But the reasons for the disappointment of critics and audience alike is altogether more personal, based on habit and conditioned expectation. Miller says: "The society of Salem was 'morally' vocal. People then avowed principles, sought to live by them and die by them. . . . I believe that the very moral awareness of the play and its characters—which are historically correct—was repulsive to the audience." Because of Miller's driving need to know *why*—his first and last question—the way people think is as important to him as the way they feel. It is this that dictates his move away from subjectivism to greater self-awareness in *The Crucible*. The flaw complained of in Willy Loman was corrected in John Proctor, and, for many reasons, prompted greater dissatisfaction. As Miller points out, audiences and critics alike are conditioned to subjectivism and for this reason found more common ground with Willy, regardless of the period of the play. The character was altogether more graspable to them. An audience will more readily accept a character governed by feeling, like Willy Loman, than one who cannot help thinking aloud, attracted to analysis, like John Proctor or Quentin. Their awareness seems to make them at once remote and detached. Audiences, for the present, tend to walk away from it, primarily because they are less interested in knowing *why* than is Arthur Miller.

Where Miller is interested in causes, the audience cares only for results. Rightly, Miller presupposes: "But certainly the passion of knowing is as powerful as the passion of feeling alone." Only to find that there is nothing certain about it. His passion for awareness is not new. Shaw had it, so did Brecht. What *is* new is Miller's insistence that subjectivism's higher stage is not self-awareness, but a synthesis of feeling and awareness.

In *The Crucible* the synthesis Miller has in mind lies more in the play as a whole than in his characters. It is not achieved in a single character until Quentin in *After the Fall*. *The Crucible* counteracts etched characters with a text full to overflowing with passion. The play is written in a powerful, mounting prose, and the height and pitch of the dramatic scenes are found nowhere else in Miller's work. This particular balance held between play and character is necessary. Without it and with more subjective character-drawing the play could easily collapse into chaos. The second problem solved by this balance is that of "remoteness" in an aware character who, from the audience's point of view, thinks too much. Spare character-drawing is not new for Miller; with his minor characters he has always told you precisely what you need to know of them and nothing more. Here the technique extends from Giles and Rebecca to John and Elizabeth. But this leanness does not make the agony of John Proctor's outbursts any less real. A character does not become unreal because he speaks only those lines that will define him. To assume that he does is to confuse realism with naturalism. The width between the two is no more than a razor's edge, but the difference is basic.

Fortunately, this argument does not stop at theory. We do not need to guess at what *The Crucible* would become with more subjective characters. Sartre's film, a very free version of the play, proves Miller's argument. John Proctor did not become more "real" by being played as a guilt-torn neurotic. He did not have more feeling, but simply the wrong kind. I watched unmoved while Yves Montand twitched in time to his tormented soul, and came out murmuring that Miller would never have created such a character. Miller's John Proctor would fight the final holocaust. The earth could split and rocks could fall like hail, and still he would be there. When Proctor finds he can face hanging, he is discovering again, as have Miller's other heroes before him, what a man can do and how much he can support to keep his own integrity.

Basically the same idea drives both Proctor and Willy Loman, in that neither can break away from the unspoken demand behind the play. And again the belief is Miller's refusal to understand or accept passivity or placidity. When he was in London at a symposium arranged by *Encore*, he protested: "I don't understand why anything has to be accepted. I don't get it." The easygoing English found this laughable. They seemed a little embarrassed by all this high earnestness when everybody else had been playing at debate. Nothing half as serious had been thought on that panel, far less said. This rejection of compliance is fundamental in Miller; that once grasped, laughter changes to alarm. It is the attitude of a man who would smilingly send you out to change the world.

At a performance of the play in Bristol the atmosphere was so faithfully created that the audience reacted as if somebody had thrown a firecracker into the auditorium. If they could, they would have pushed back their chairs. One fragile old lady looked around the delicate eighteenth-century theatre as if in fear for its survival. The production, by Warren Jenkins, included an extra scene for John and Abigail that is not usually staged. Apt as the scene is, with the dark night almost tangible, I think the play stronger, of firmer line and more dramatic impact without it. After Elizabeth's arrest, John follows her request to see Abigail. He warns her that he will denounce her in Court next day unless she frees his wife and promises never to cry witch again. As Miller intended, the scene draws attention to John, Elizabeth, and Abigail, but primarily it explores Abigail's delusion.

Eerie, set in a wood and haunted by Abigail's strangeness, the scene still haunts the mind in Patrick Robertson's miraculous set. Abigail, to herself, has undergone great spiritual change, almost believing in her own martyrdom. How can others be blind to it? A miniature Saint Joan is come to Salem. "And God gave me strength to call them liars, and God made men to listen to me, and by God I will scrub the world clean for love of Him!" Suddenly the religious ecstasy breaks, to reveal the reason behind it. "Oh, John, I will make you such a wife when the world is white again! You will be amazed to see me every day, a light of heaven in your house."

In a London production at the Royal Court Theatre no attempt was made to create the atmosphere of a witch-hunt, and for this, as well as other reasons, the production failed. The mood of the play left unestablished made the soaring language seem out of place. Instead of dear old ladies thoroughly alarmed, there were tough gallery-goers complaining of melodrama and careful stall-holders uncertain what to praise.

Two hurdles in the play's production seem to be the child-Iago in Abigail, who must persuade the audience of her "holiness" while they know of her deviltry, and the evil of Danforth. The text insists that Danforth is evil, and Miller (in his Preface) deplores our inability to face this fact. He protests that if he had the play to write again he would stress this evil and make it an open issue. "I should say that my own—and the critics'—unbelief in this depth of evil is concomitant with our unbelief in good, too."

He wrote to me: "Danforth was indeed dedicated to securing the status quo against such as Proctor. But I am equally interested in his *function* in the drama, which is that of the rule-bearer, the man who always guards the boundaries which, if you insist on breaking through them, have the power to destroy you. His 'evil' is more than personal, it is nearly mythical. He does more evil than he knows how to do; while merely following his nose he guards ignorance, he is man's limit. Sartre reduced him to an almost economic policeman. He is thus unrecognizable to us because he lacks his real ideology, i.e., the ideology which believes that evil is good, that man must be preserved from knowledge. Sartre's Danforth does not see beyond the deception, ever. He too, like Proctor, should come to a realization. He must see that he has in fact practiced deception, and then proceed to incorporate it in his 'good' ideology. When I say I did not make him evil enough, it is that I did not clearly demarcate the point at which he knows what he has done, and profoundly accepts it as a good thing. This alone is evil. It is a counterpart to Proctor's ultimate realization that he cannot sell himself for his life. Hale goes the other way: on seeing the deception he rejects it as evil. One of the actual Salem judges drank himself to death after the hysteria was over. But only one. The others insisted they had done well. In a word, Sartre's conception lacks moral dimension. It precludes a certain aspect of will. Also it is dramatically useless because his Danforth from beginning to end is the same. This serves only to reduce the importance of the whole story, for if it is not horrible enough to force Danforth to know that he must decide how to strengthen himself against what he has done, then he has done very little."

Danforth is "man's limit"; even if he had not been a Salem judge, this would be sufficient for Miller to find him evil; it is a cardinal crime to keep man from knowledge. What, then, is to be said of the rule-bearer who makes this his function? Miller's complaint over Danforth is that he is incomplete. The knowledge of what he has done is vital in any Miller character, and this conclusion has not been forced upon Danforth. Hale is altogether more placid. He does not have the conflicts of Proctor, nor the conflicts Miller regrets not having brought out in Danforth. Hale is the balance between the two.

Sartre's film begins wishfully: "This is a true story." From this point onward it is truer to Sartre's opinion than it is to historical fact and Miller's intention. All Marx, no Miller. It crossed my mind that the film was roughly what the critics who accused Miller of evasion expected from the play. Here was the ideological conflict they, not Miller, had in mind. Crudely blocked, as if in a child's coloring book, we see the evil rich who have no need to fear, who describe the farmers as "rabble," and who deliberately use the witch-hunt to dominate the people, knowing it to be fraud. The farmers are all poor, all noble, and all political martyrs. Danforth warns Parris that unrest through the country is caused by "witches and men of the lower classes." Proctor grows from a guilty neurotic into a workers' hero first class. Instead of reminding Danforth that God damns those who refuse to bring men out of their ignorance, he is led away savagely to the shout of "Defend yourself! They mean to murder you!" I thought John Proctor died to achieve self-respect and in protest against a town run wild. Sartre has him die to save the workers. Throughout the film, contemporary politics cymbal-clashed with the authentic seventeenth-century atmosphere Miller has created.

Sartre could have made an unforgettable film of *The Crucible* with those actors had he been making a film of *The Crucible* in the first place, not merely using it as a basis for something else. Mylene Demongeot is the best Abigail I have seen. She has a face that can change instantly and alarmingly from angelic to apoplectic. Even if she cannot quite stand up and see visions, she is the only Abigail I have yet seen who cannot be older than seventeen. Her fits and her tantrums are those of a child who has been crossed, and so is her vengeance. In her, the original Abigail, the child of eleven, keeps breaking through. Savagely she stabs the poppet with a needle, banging at it relentlessly until the head falls off. The people accused will hang—but—

"I want the light of God, I want the sweet love of Jesus! I danced for the Devil! I saw him; I wrote in his book; I go back to Jesus; I kiss His hand. I saw Sarah Good with the Devil! I saw Goody Osburn with the Devil! I saw Bridget Bishop with the Devil!"

STEPHEN FENDER

Precision and Pseudo Precision in The Crucible

Writing almost four years after *The Crucible* was first performed, Arthur Miller seemed uncertain how to describe the ethics of the society he had tried to reproduce in the play. He notes, for example, that the Puritans 'religious belief did nothing to temper [their] cruelty' but instead 'served to raise this swirling and ludicrous mysticism to a level of high moral debate'. 'It is no mean irony', Miller continues, 'that the theocratic persecution should seek out the most religious people for its victims'.

On the other hand—and in the same essay—Miller claims that he chose Salem for the play's setting precisely because it provided people 'of higher self-awareness than the contemporary scene affords', so that by opposing the articulate John Proctor to an equally articulate society he could, dramatize his theme of the danger of 'handing over of conscience to another' (pp. 44–5).

But Miller's audience did not always appear to understand the theme, and the play's reception was mixed. The author has his own idea of what went wrong:

> I believe that the very moral awareness of the play and its characters—which are historically correct—was repulsive to the audience. For a variety of reasons I think that the Anglo-Saxon audience cannot believe the reality of characters who live by

From *Journal of American Studies* 1:1 (April 1967). © 1967 by Cambridge University Press.

principles and know very much about their own characters and
situations, and who say what they know [pp. 44–5].

Most Miller scholars have more or less accepted his account of the play
as the story of John Proctor at odds with a monolithic society. Arthur Hunt,
for example, writes that the play 'comments on modern fragmentation by
withdrawing to the vantage point of a community which is whole and self
aware'. In an extremely interesting article on Miller, John Prudhoe interprets
Proctor's stance against Salem as the 'most "modern" moment in *The
Crucible*' because in it the hero works out his own solution 'unaided by
comfortable slogans, the weight of opinion of those around him or a coherently worked-out philosophy'. Proctor's thought is free of the traditional
beliefs of Salem and of the 'surprisingly articulate' speech in which the town
expresses its values. Proctor's plea for his 'name' at the end of the play 'is the
cry of a man who has rejected the world in which he lives and hence can no
longer use the language of that world'.

This essay attempts to support Prudhoe's reading of *The Crucible* as a
dramatic contest of language, but to question the assumption that he shares
with Miller himself and with other critics of Miller that the Puritans in the
play have a consistent moral outlook. Indeed, if one examines the language,
both of real Puritans and of the characters in *The Crucible*, it becomes clear
that it is the speech of a society totally without moral referents. Salem
confronts Proctor not with a monolithic ethic (however misguided) but with
the total absence of any ethic. The townspeople are certain of their moral
standards only on the level of abstraction; on the level of the facts of human
behaviour they share no criteria for judgement, and it is this lack which
makes them victims—as well as protagonists—of the witch hunt. Their
language reflects this complete disjunction between their theory and the facts
of human action. Proctor finally demolishes their phoney language and
painfully reconstructs a halting, but integral way of speaking in which words
are once again related to their lexis. But the effect of this achievement is not
to break away from the ethic of Salem; rather it is to construct the first
consistent moral system in the play, a system in which fact and theory can at
last coalesce. Proctor serves himself by recovering his 'name'; he serves
Salem by giving it a viable language.

II

In the Introduction to the *Collected Plays* Miller writes that what struck
him most forcefully when he examined the records of the Salem trials was the

'absolute dedication to evil displayed by the judges' (p. 43). What is more obvious to the audience of *The Crucible* is the extent to which Miller—always sensitive to the spoken word—has picked up and transmitted the language of these verbatim reports, and not only the language but the entire Puritan 'system' of ethics which that language embodies.

The ethics of a society as nearly theocratic as that of the American Puritans owed much to the society's doctrine of salvation. American Puritans called themselves 'Covenanters' and thought of themselves as having achieved a compromise between the Calvinist theory of predestination and the Arminian stress on works as efficacious for salvation. Calvinism taught that before the Creation a certain, immutable number of men were elected to salvation, and the rest left to eternal damnation. Because nothing in the subsequent lives of men could affect their predetermined fate, good works were inefficacious to salvation. The obvious practical application was that no one need bother about his conduct; though behaviour might or might not be an indication of one's predetermined state, it had no formal effect on it.

Covenantal theology tried to soften this demoralizing theory by developing the doctrine of the two Covenants. God was said to have offered man two Covenants: the first, the Covenant of Works, made with Adam, offered everlasting life in return for obedience to the Laws; after Adam had broken this agreement and his sin had been imputed to all mankind, God in his mercy offered another Covenant, first to Abraham, then through Moses to the Israelites, finally through Christ to Christians. This Covenant of Grace offered life in return for a more passive obedience: faith in, and imitation of God. Man must still keep the law to the best of his ability, but, by the new Covenant of Grace, he will be judged by the spirit, not by the letter, of the law. It is doubtful, however, whether the doctrine of the covenants really altered much the basic tenets—and the practical effects—of the notion of predestination. Works might be interpreted as efficacious for salvation, but still only if they proceeded from a state of grace. Man's role was passive; once he had been involved in the Covenant of Grace, he could perform works fruitful to his salvation, but God withheld or extended the initial, 'triggering' grace at his pleasure. There could be no question of a man 'earning' grace by his works.

This, then, was predestination all over again. The Puritan theologian, John Preston, writes: '*All men are divided into these two rankes, either they are good or bad, either they are polluted or cleane, either they are such as sacrifice or such as sacrifice not:* There is no middle sort of men in the world; . . .

How can one tell if he is among the elect?

First; *the tree must be good*, as you have it in *Math*. 7. 16. 17. that is, a man then is said to be a good man, when there is good sap in him . . . when there are some supernatural graces wrought in him. . . . Secondly; consider whether thou *bring forth good fruit*, that is, not onely whether thou doest good actions, but whether they flow from thee, whether they grow in thine heart as naturally, as fruit growes on the tree, that flowes from the sap within . . . and the meaning of the *holy Ghost* is therefore to show, that then a man is good, when his heart is fitted to good workes, when he knowes how to go about them, whereas another bungles them, and knowes not how to doe them . . .

Preston's stress on man's passivity is unmistakable. Man is capable of efficacious works only after he has been touched by God's grace; they must flow 'naturally' from him; he cannot begin the process himself. But how is a man to know if his works—by any objective test 'good'—really and essentially proceed from a state of grace? The Westminster Confession, the articles of faith for the American Covenanters as well as for the Scottish Presbyterians, is even more uncompromising in refusing to answer the question:

Good works are only such as God hath commanded in his holy word, and not such as, without the warrant thereof, are devised by men out of blind zeal, and upon any pretence of good intention [ch. xvi, i]. Works done by unregenerate men, although, for the matter of them, they may be things which God commands, and of good use both to themselves and others; yet, because they proceed not from an heart purified by faith; nor are done in a right manner, according to the word; nor to a right end, the glory of God; they are therefore sinful, and cannot please God, or make a man meet to receive grace from God [ch. xvi, vii].

It is possible to make too little of the Covenantal theologians' attempt to compromise with Calvinism; after all, though they confused Calvinism's brutal logic, they also made it more human and (dare one say it?) more Christian. Nevertheless, the central doctrine of predestination was left intact. Works are no longer exclusively inefficacious; now some good works are more equal than others. But we are still denied objective criteria for determining which is which. This fact, combined with the notion that, as Preston says, all men are 'good or bad' and 'there is no middle sort of men in the world' is the theory behind perhaps the biggest single effect of the Reformation on practical morality. For better or worse, as two American critics have noted, Puritan predestination breaks down the whole structure of Aristotelian-Scholastic ethics, sweeping away any idea of *degrees* of good and evil. H. W. Schneider makes this point in *The Puritan Mind*:

> No one can live long in a Holy Commonwealth without becoming sensitive, irritable, losing his sense of values and ultimately his balance. All acts are either acts of God or of the Devil; all issues are matters of religious faith; all conflicts are holy wars . . . no matter how harmless a fool might be, he was intolerable if he did not fit into the Covenant of Grace; no matter how slight an offence might be, it was a sin against Almighty God and hence infinite.

And Yvor Winters applies this point to *The Scarlet Letter*, another literary re-creation of American Puritan society:

> Objective evidence . . . took the place of inner assurance, and the behaviour of the individual took on symbolic value. That is, any sin was evidence of damnation; or, in other words, any sin represented all sin. When Hester Prynne committed adultery, she committed an act as purely representative of complete corruption as the act of Faustus in signing a contract with Satan. This view of the matter is certainly not Catholic and is little short of appalling.

The Roman Catholic doctrine of salvation was and is a rational system, depending on man's free will to do good and evil—actively and consciously. Sins are either venial or mortal. Everywhere the idea of degree prevails; the sinner can neutralize his transgressions by greater or smaller acts of penance, depending on the degree of sin committed. One spends a greater or lesser time in purgatory, according to one's degree of perfection. The practical psychological effect of this system is that by it man is taught to deal with his acts severally, to analyse the details of his behaviour and experience one by one and to weigh one against the other. On the other hand, the Calvinists, and even the Covenantal Puritans, were taught to think of their behaviour (and the behaviour of their neighbours) as evidence only, not as conscious acts causing salvation or damnation. As evidence of total salvation or total damnation, their several acts were unimportant in themselves; there was less stress on evaluating each act and more on merely identifying it as evidence of grace or damnation.

In the light of these ideas, it is interesting to read, for example, through 'Concerning an History of some *Criminals* executed in *New England* for Capital Crimes . . . ', originally written by 'one of the *New English Ministers* . . . in hopes that the horrible sight would cause that worst

Enemy to fly before it', and reprinted in Cotton Mather's history of New England. Mather includes the accounts of the trials and the confessions of the convicted in an appendix to his chapter '. . . Discoveries and Demonstrations of the Divine Providence in Remarkable Mercies and Judgements on Many Particular Persons . . . of *New England* . . .', remarking that, in the account of executed criminals, 'the *remarkable judgements of God* were wonderfully Exemplify'd' (book iv, p. 37). This statement itself is important. The sins of the criminals (in these cases, their crimes, though the distinction between sin and crime is rather vague in Puritan New England) are not acts leading to their damnation; they are evidence of divine judgement already determined.

The various accounts are written in such a way as to support the construction Mather puts on them. What is particularly interesting is the nature of the criminals' confessions, the way in which they deal with their experience, and the writer's remarks on their behaviour. For instance, James Morgan was a 'passionate fellow' who 'swore he would run a Spit into a man's Bowels' and ' . . . was as good as his word' (book vi, p. 40). He was hanged in Boston in 1686. His confession recounts a number of his sins:

> I have been a great Sinner, guilty of Sabbath-breaking, of Lying, and of uncleanness; but there are especially two Sins whereby I have offended the Great God; one is that Sin of Drunkenness, which has caused me to commit many other Sins; for when in Drink, I have been often guilty of Cursing and Swearing, and Quarrelling, and striking others. But the Sin which lies most heavy upon my Conscience, is that I have despised the word of God, and many a time refused to hear it preached [book vi, p. 40].

It is too harsh, perhaps, to expect a man about to be hanged to analyse his behaviour with any great precision, but one cannot help noticing the curious confusion of values by which drunkenness and refusing to hear the word of God become major sins and murder is not mentioned. Later in his confession, when he does deal with the act that brought him to the gallows, Morgan treats it not as a sin, but as a crime, of civil importance only:

> *I own the Sentence which the Honour'd Court has pass'd upon me*, to be Exceeding Just; inasmuch as (though I had no former Grudge and Malice against the man whom I have kill'd, yet) my Passion at the time of the Fact, was so outragious, as that it hurried me on to the doing of that which makes me now justly proceeded

against as a Murderer [Ibid].

And even here he (or whoever is helping him formulate his confession) speaks as though he were the passive agent in the act of murder. What counts is not the act itself (even the name of 'murder' is carefully circumvented by the periphrastic 'that which makes me now justly proceeded against as a Murderer'), but some ' cause proportionate' which the murderer is powerless to resist: drunkenness and 'Passion'. One recalls Preston insisting that good works must flow from within 'as the fruit growes on the tree'. Presumably this applies also to 'bad' works; either way the need for human responsibility seems to be diminished.

It is worth looking at one more excerpt from this grisly catalogue, a sermon preached at the hanging in 1698 of a 'miserable Young Woman' who had murdered her illegitimate child. The minister makes only a passing reference to her 'crime' and, surprisingly, to her adultery: 'Thus the *God*, whose Eyes are like a Flame of Fire, is now casting her into a Bed of burning Tribulation: and, ah, Lord, where wilt thou cast those that have committed Adultery with her, except they repent!' (book vi, p. 48). The minister is really interested, for the most part, in her other sins:

> Since her Imprisonment, she hath declared, that she believes, God hath left her unto this undoing Wickedness, partly for her staying so prophanely at home, sometimes on *Lords Days*, when she should have been hearing the Word of Christ, and much more for her not minding that Word, when she heard it.
>
> And she has confessed, That she was much given to Rash Wishes, in her mad passions, particularly using often that ill Form of speaking, *I'll be hang'd*, if a thing be not thus or so; and, *I'll be hang'd*, if I do not this or that: Which Evil now, to see it, coming upon her, it amazes her! But this *Chief Sin* of which this *Chief of Sinners* now cries out, is, her undutiful Carriage towards her Parents. Her Language and her Carriage towards her Parents, was indeed such that they hardly durst speak to her; but when they durst, they often told her, It would come to this [book vi, p. 49].

Every aspect of this nasty document is important—the gallows humour, the language, the preacher's total confusion of values. In this strange system ignoring the Sabbath and insulting one's parents become as serious as adultery and murder. The girl's parents could see—where we cannot—that she was unregenerate and thus capable of *anything*. They knew it would come to this because she had been 'undutiful' at home. They knew that unless she finally showed evidence of being among the saved (through confessing and repenting) she was surely among the damned. One piece of evidence was as good as another.

III

Orwell said that if a politician wished to control a democratic country he had to begin by controlling its language that, to put it simply, a man who wanted to persuade people to do things they didn't want to do might profitably begin by calling those things by different names. Advertising, too, depends on distorting the conventional meanings of words, or even on coining deliberately imprecise phrases. Patent medicines are said to cure 'tired blood' or 'night starvation' because these terms are imprecise enough to include a wide spectrum of ailments and thus promote a wide sale. Jonson anticipated this trick when he made Volpone, as mountebank, advertise his elixir as a specific for *tremor-cordia* and retired nerves.

But, as any literary critic knows, language can be distorted less consciously and less maliciously by people who are merely uncertain of their attitude towards whatever they are using words to describe. It seems likely that the vague and ultimately meaningless language which the preacher brings to bear on the 'miserable young woman's' sin ('Tribulation', 'Wickedness', 'prophanely', 'Rash Wishes') results from his own uncertainty about the comparative value of various human acts. This uncertainty may also account for the dubious taste of the passage since what we call 'bad taste' is nothing more than a dislocation between a fact and the level of language used to describe that fact.

So, far from having a 'higher self-awareness', as Miller thought, the American Puritans were undecided about how much importance to give to specific human acts: good works may or may not proceed from a state of grace; all that was certain was that nothing was what it seemed; the concrete fact had no assured validity. But what Miller has caught so successfully, despite his theory, is the peculiar way in which the Puritans spoke whenever they talked about sin. One can say even more than that: Miller has, in fact, made the fullest dramatic use of the language, using its peculiarities to limit the characters speaking it and even making it part of the play's subject.

The language plays its part, for example, in establishing the rather complex ironic structure in the scene in which the Reverend Hale first appears. Betty is lying ill, and Parris, secretly fearing that she might be affected by witchcraft, has called in an expert in detecting witchcraft. The situation itself is ironic; it is a measure of his own confusion about Betty that Parris must call in an expert with weighty volumes under his arm to tell him what to think about his daughter's exhaustion and shock. The audience also suspects that Parris depends on Hale's authority as a compensation for being unable to deal with Abigail. Another aspect of the irony is that the audience knows the expert's opinion will change nothing; the Putnams and the other townspeople—even Parris himself—have now convinced themselves that witchcraft is to blame. Finally, of course, the audience has already been given enough evidence—in the hasty conference between Abigail, Betty and Mary Warren and in Abigail's plea to Proctor—that Hale's knowledge of witchcraft is irrelevant to the situation.

In the light of all this confusion, it is interesting to examine in some detail Hale's first extended speech:

> *Putnam:* She cannot bear to hear the Lord's name, Mr. Hale; that's a sure sign of witchcraft afloat.
>
> *Hale, holding up his hands:* No, no. Now let me instruct you. We cannot look to superstition in this. The Devil is precise; the marks of his presence are definite as stone, and I must tell you all that I shall not proceed unless you are prepared to believe me if I should find no bruise of hell upon her.

We miss the point if we see this scene as the opposition of the frightened, confused townspeople on the one hand, and the sane, certain, rational expert on the other. Hale's precision is pseudo precision: the speech is ironic because the audience knows that Hale's distinction between 'superstition' and real witchcraft is less clear than he supposes. His simile to illustrate the Devil's precision supports this reading: 'definite as stone'; it looks precise, possibly because it is a 'hard' image, but stone is actually an imprecise image for 'definite' because stone seldom appears clearly differentiated from other material, either in nature or in artifact.

Hale's pseudo precision is established beyond doubt a few lines further on in the scene:

> *Hale, with a tasty love of intellectual pursuit:* Here is all the invisible world, caught, defined, and calculated. In these books the Devil stands stripped of all his brute disguises. Here are all your familiar spirits—your incubi and succubi; your witches that go by land, by air, and by sea; your wizards of the night and of the day. Have no fear now—we shall find him out if he

has come among us, and I mean to crush him utterly if he has shown his face!

At first sight this list—with its division of material into various categories—has all the exactness of the encyclopaedia, but at second sight we are not convinced that the categories are well chosen. (Why, for example, should witches be arranged according to how they travel?) A modern audience is uncertain about what all the terms mean (just what is the difference between incubi and succubi?).

The audience familiar with Jonson may experience a tinge of *deja vu* at this point. What we are hearing is a kind of conflation of *Volpone* and *The Alchemist*, Tribulation Wholesome acting the mountebank. In fact, the speech is a wild flight of jargon, quite unrelated to the situation with which Hale has been asked to deal, and if the audience has held out any hope for Hale's ability to recall the community to sanity, they must abandon that hope at this point. It is quite obvious that Hale, in his own unique way, is divorced from reality. The others see evidence of witchcraft in the illness of a hysterical girl, and the witch hunt will express their repressed envy, libido and land lust. Hale, too, sees witchcraft behind the events in Salem. He will use the witch hunt to express his manic expertise.

What makes Hale so vulnerable to the witch hunt is not—as with the other townspeople—his repressed emotions, but his love of abstraction. Hale, like any other educated Puritan, discounts the obvious. The concrete fact is not to be trusted. Thus at his first entrance, he recognizes Rebecca Nurse without having been introduced to her because she looks 'as such a good soul should'. But later, when he begins to apply his theories to the problem of Salem, he tells the Proctors 'it is possible' that Rebecca is a witch. Proctor answers: 'But it's hard to think so pious a woman be secretly a Devil's bitch after seventy year of such good prayer.' 'Aye,' replies Hale, 'but the Devil is a wily one, you cannot deny it.' His search for the form behind the shadow finally leads him to an almost comical reversal of cause and effect:

> I cannot think God be provoked so grandly by such a petty cause. The jails are packed—our greatest judges sit in Salem now—and hangin's promised. Man, we must look to cause proportionate. Was there murder done, perhaps, and never brought to light? Abomination? Some secret blasphemy that stinks to heaven? Think on cause, man, and let you help me to discover it.

When the facts become unimportant (and in this case the fact is Hale's 'petty cause'—Abigail's alleged jealousy of Elizabeth Proctor), the choice of words becomes unimportant also: 'abomination' and 'secret blasphemy' mean little to us because Hale himself is unsure of what he means by them.

Danforth, too, has his pseudo precision:

> . . . you must understand, sir, that a person is either with this court or he must be counted against it, there be no road between. This is a sharp time, now, a precise time—we no longer live in the dusky afternoon when evil mixed itself with good and befuddled the world. Now, by God's grace, the shining sun is up, and them that fear not light will surely praise it. I hope you will be one of those.

This reminds us of Hale's catalogue of witches, of John Preston's statement that ' . . . *all men are divided into these two rankes, either they are good or bad*'; Miller has made good ironic use of the Puritan habit of constructing false disjunctions. Danforth's formulation looks precise, but misses the point because it establishes a false criterion of guilt (whether the accused approves of the court). So not only is it untrue to say that one is either with the court or 'must be counted against it'; it is irrelevant. The trial has now reached its final stage in its retreat from the realities of the situation: it began unrealistically enough by examining the causes for the presence of something which had yet to be proved: then it began to take account of the wrong evidence, to listen to the wrong people; finally it becomes completely self-enclosed, and self-justifying, asking not whether the accused is guilty of being a witch but whether he or she supports the court.

In its withdrawal from reality the court takes advantage of the semantic uncertainty of the Salem townspeople, and, in so doing, makes them even more uncertain. Act Three opens with the sounds of Hathorne examining Martha Corey off-stage:

> *Hathorne's Voice:* Now, Martha Corey, there is abundant evidence in our hands to show that you have given yourself to the reading of fortunes. Do you deny it?
>
> *Martha Corey's Voice:* I an innocent to a witch. I know not what a witch is.
>
> *Hathorne's Voice:* How do you know, then, that you are not a witch?

Later, when even Hale begins to doubt the wisdom of the court, he tells Danforth 'We cannot blink it more. There is a prodigious fear of this court in the country—' And Danforth answers: 'Then there is a prodigious guilt in the country.' Terms are now quite rootless; the parallelism of the syntax suggests that 'fear' and 'guilt' are interchangeable.

How can the honest man combat this utter confusion of language and of the values which language transmits? One solution is simply to reject the slippery terminology and revert to a more primitive way of speaking:

> *Danforth, turning to Giles:* Mr Putnam states your charge is a lie. What say you to that?
> *Giles, furious, his fists clenched:* A fart on Thomas Putnam, that is what I say to that!

This is one of the funniest moments in the play because it is true *discordia concors*. The audience senses the discrepancy (to say the least) between Giles's level of speech and the rhetoric of the court, but it also appreciates the desperate need to break away from the court's dubious terminology.

John Proctor's attack on the court's language is more serious, and more complex. He first meets it straightforwardly, trying to reverse the distorted meanings of the words it uses, or at least to restore the proper words to their proper places. When Cheever visits his house to tell him Elizabeth has been accused, Proctor says: 'Is the accuser always holy now? Were they born this morning as clean as God's fingers? I'll tell you what's walking Salem—vengeance is walking Salem. We are what we always were in Salem but now the little crazy children are jangling the keys of the kingdom, and common vengeance writes the law!' Although Proctor is talking here to Cheever, he is also trying to put right a false formulation that Hale has made earlier in the scene, a characteristically imprecise use of a concrete image as an abstraction: 'the Devil is alive in Salem'. Proctor is trying to reassert the authority of the proper word. 'We are what we always were'; only the words to describe us have changed.

But Proctor, of course, has his own guilt. Already he has been unable to say the word 'adultery' when asked to recite the commandments. Finally when he faces his guilt—and tries to make the community accept it—in court, his formulation is painfully inarticulate: 'It is a whore!' The statement contrasts powerfully with the smooth, meaningless language of his wife's accusers. At the end of the scene, when even his painful confession has failed to move them, he indicts them in *their* language, as though as a last resort he is trying to turn their own weapons upon them: 'A fire, a fire is burning! I hear the boot of Lucifer, I see his filthy face! And it is my face, and yours, Danforth!'

Even if Miller's stage direction didn't call for Proctor to 'laugh insanely' at this point, we could not accept this as the right solution; turnabout may be fair play, but in choosing to use their language even against them, Proctor cannot escape its imprecision. There is, after all some distinction between him and Danforth, and, in the terms of this play, this difference can only be asserted by a total rejection of Danforth's language. This rejection comes— by implication, at least—when Proctor makes his genuine sacrifice at the end of the play, when he reclaims his 'name': 'Because it is my name! Because I cannot have another in my life! Because I am not worth the dust on the feet of them that hang! How may I live without my name? I have given you my soul; leave me my name.' It is as though in regaining his name he finally ends the confusion about names which has been the town's sickness.

Proctor must indeed cast off the terminology of Salem. But what he is rejecting is not a monolithic system, not a 'coherently worked-out philosophy'. Salem speech is 'articulate' in only a very limited sense of the word; 'voluble' or 'smooth' would apply more aptly. One needs to make this point because our response to the play is more complex than it would be if Proctor were a modern existential hero working out his own solution in opposition to the conventions of society. Salem has no conventions. Its evil is not positive. Its ethics are not wrong; they are non-existent. What makes the progress of the witch-hunt so terrifying for the audience is the realization that the trial has no programme. If Proctor and the others were being tested—and found wanting—according to a wrong-headed but consistent set of values, our reaction to the play would be quite different. What terrifies us is that we never know from what direction the next attack will come, and we are struck more by what Miller, in his introduction to the *Collected Plays*, calls 'the swirling and ludicrous mysticism [elevated] to a level of high moral debate' of the characters than we are by their 'moral awareness'. John Proctor acts not as a rebel but as the restorer of what the audience take to be normal human values. What Miller actually achieved in *The Crucible* is far more important than what he apparently feels guilty for not having achieved.

THOMAS E. PORTER

The Long Shadow of the Law: The Crucible

Among popular forms perennially in favor on Broadway and in the television ratings, the courtroom drama ranks with the leaders. Numerous television series have used the format, from simple whodunits like *Perry Mason*, in which the trial is a device for discovering the criminal, to *The Defenders*, which used the courtroom drama to present controversial issues in legal principle and in practice. Recent Broadway seasons have featured a wide spectrum: *Billy Budd, The Caine Mutiny Court Martial, Witness for the Prosecution, The Andersonville Trial, Twelve Angry Men*. This format has inherent qualities that attract the playwright of any age: a clear division between protagonist and antagonist, gradual revelation of the facts, application of facts to principles, suspense leading to the climax of verdict. Though the formula has never been neglected (*Oresteia, Measure for Measure, Volpone, St. Joan*), it is most favored in democracies, where the Law is venerated and the Court the principle instrument of justice. Beneath the trial formula and the trappings of the Law, there is a complex of attitudes that includes veneration for these institutions. The courtroom has become the sanctuary of modern secularized society and the trial the only true ritual it has left.

The development of these attitudes toward the Law and its ritual began early in American history. Our society from its beginnings had a respect for, and confidence in, the Law. Tom Paine, in *Common Sense*, voiced an ideal

From *Myth and Modern American Drama*. © 1969 by Wayne State University Press.

which, though it has been variously interpreted, has retained its fascination for the American mind:

> But where say some is the King of America? I'll tell you Friend he reigns above; and doth not make havoc of mankind like the Royal Brute of Great Britain. Yet that we may not appear to be defective even in earthly honors, let a day be solemnly set apart for the proclaiming of the Charter; let it be brought forth placed on the Devine Law, the Word of God; let a crown be placed thereon, by which the World may know, that so far as we approve of monarchy, that in America THE LAW IS KING.

For the contemporary bureaucrat as for the revolutionary patriot, "government under the Law" expresses the democratic ideal: equal rights for all, protection both for the individual in his legitimate endeavors and for society from the depredations of unprincipled individuals, justice meted out with an impersonal, unprejudiced hand according to ordinance. In the Law, so the democrat holds, all opposites are reconciled; the individual and the community, freedom and regimentation, the rule of principle and the rule of men. As the King is the principle of order in a monarchy, so the Law is considered the source of order in a democracy.

In America more obviously than elsewhere, there has been a tendency to regard the Law as the embodiment of "moral law" and "natural law," as well as a *corpus juris* inherited from legal tradition. The nineteenth-century concept of "fundamental law" was made up of these two and was looked on as absolute and immutable. This attitude, foreshadowed in Paine's juxtaposition of Bible and Charter, received concrete expression in the dominance of church and courthouse in the nineteenth-century village and town. When the influence of the church declined, the Law necessarily exerted a greater influence than ever. The corpus of the common law and the system by which it is administered has acquired an aura of permanence and infallibility. On these elements, according to the American creed, rests the security of the citizen and the stability of his way of life.

Belief in this idea has engendered a veneration also for the courts and the lawyers who practice in them. Every culture has some sort of spiritual government that is entrusted with the ideals of that culture. In America the Courts are at once the receptacle and the guardian of those ideals. "Our spiritual government today centers in the judicial system. Here is the bulwark of all the older symbols and theories both legal and economic. Here is the stage on which the ideals of society are given concrete reality." This attitude is most manifest when the courts come under attack.

Americans alone of Western people made constitutionalism a religion and the judiciary a religious order and surrounded both with an aura of piety. They made the Constitution supreme law, and placed responsibility for the functioning of the federal system on the courts. The Supreme Court, in time, became the most nearly sacrosanct of American institutions.

The dignity and inviolability accorded the Supreme Court is shared by the whole judicial system. The judge, *ex officio*, holds a position of influence and respect, and in his own courtroom, he is absolute master. The legal profession, while not so exalted, shares some of this distinction with the judiciary. Reverence for the Court and respect for the lawyer is a reflection of an abiding belief in justice and equality administered under the Law.

One of the most persistent attitudes embodied in the myth of the Law is the notion of a "fair trial." "The notion that every man however lowly is entitled to a fair trial and an impartial hearing is regarded as the cornerstone of civilized government." The Law is seen as watching over legal procedures and guaranteeing impartiality by "due process." The general outlines of the procedure are: a preliminary hearing; an indictment which discloses to the accused the nature of the offense; a trial in which evidence is presented fully and an opportunity given to the accused to introduce and respond to all relevant issues an appellate review of both the law and the evidence; a permanent written record of the entire proceedings. The "fair trial" aspect of our view of the Law provides for the protection of the individual from "mob rule" and tyranny.

Another attitude, generally and vaguely opposed to the ideal of fair trial, is the sacredness of law enforcement. As the Law protects the individual from injustice, it also secures the rights of society against the criminal. This aspect of the myth emphasizes the absolute nature of the principles involved and demands that principles be applied to the facts impersonally, beyond purely personal discretion. If laws are not enforced, and disrespect for the law allowed to flourish, then chaos results.

If we look at the two attitudes expressed by the myth, in theory they seem to involve a number of contradictions: the individual in the democracy must be free, yet the rules laid down by society constrain him; a permanent unyielding code must be enforced without respect to persons, yet justice can never ignore persons; the majority must rule, yet minorities are entitled to their rights. When these theories are applied to criminal law, the same type of contradiction appears:

An attorney should not take cases the winning of which imperils the forces of law and order; every criminal, however, is entitled to a defense; criminal lawyers, however, should not resort to mere technicalities; nevertheless, they should do everything legally possible for their clients.

These contradictions, if spelled out and adverted to, would paralyze the legal system; they can subsist together only because they are resolved in practice. In the American system, the trial reconciles these attitudes in a ritual action. It is a genuine ritual—a communal, sacrosanct ceremony that expresses the beliefs of the community and, within the limits of the myth, provides for the purgation of the individual and order in the society.

The trial ritual—the structure of the action and the actors involved—dramatizes both the fair-trial and the law-enforcement aspects of the myth. It is an investigation of innocence and guilt in terms of an application of facts and motives to principles. There is a clear declaration of the issues, a marshalling of forces into opposing camps, a verdict in which justice is done. The opposing camps—prosecution and defense—represent, broadly speaking, the two extremes; the prosecution maintaining the rights of society and the defense the rights of the individual. The judge represents the absolute nature of the law and arbitrates the application of facts to principles. In its verdict, the jury resolves the opposition between these two forces under the direction of the judge. As peers who can evaluate the motives and actions of the accused and as citizens who respect the law, the members of this body represent both the individual and society. Thus they can weigh the case and make an objective judgment. Ideally, the verdict has the status of absolute truth that encompasses all the attitudes of society. Dramatically, it is the epiphany that resolves the agon.

The ceremonial nature of this action is underscored by the circumstances that surround it and by the formalized treatment it is given. Even the criminal taken red-handed is not considered guilty until the jury is in and the verdict rendered. The protocol of the courtroom—the bailiff's cry, the judge's robes, the formal language—are all part of the ritual atmosphere. The set procedure, with its rubrical consistency, also emphasizes the ceremonial structure. These details declare that the trial is a ritual in which (ideally) justice is done and in which the contradictions in the democratic system are reconciled.

One of the most instructive attempts by a contemporary playwright to make use of the trial ritual and the attitudes that surround it is Arthur Miller's *The Crucible*. Plays like *The Caine Mutiny Court Martial* use the formula in a straight-forward way to vindicate the hero's actions or, at least, his motives; in such plays the trial is a convenient dramatic device for presenting the action. The probity of the court is taken for granted; due process is the means by which the defense can insure justice for the individual. Miller's play not only uses the formula as a dramatic framing device, but also raises the question about the value of the trial itself as an instrument of justice. At the heart of *The Crucible* is the relation of the individual to the Law, and the author's probing into this area makes the play a significant work. Miller has described the playwright's art in terms of the Law: "In one sense a play is a species of jurisprudence, and some part of it must take the advocate's role, something else must act in defense, and the entirety must engage the Law." Whether or not this analogy holds true for his other efforts is a moot point; in *The Crucible* he consciously uses history and the trial formula to investigate the American attitude toward the Law.

Miller's play is based on actual records of a seventeenth-century incident in colonial Salem, but it has clear parallels with contemporary events. Attempts to write historical drama for the modern theatre have not been notably successful; perhaps they have never been except when the past is dealt with in terms of the present. Maxwell Anderson failed in spite of his Shakespearean style, and his *Elizabeth the Queen* and *Mary of Scotland*, while they tap a remote sense of Anglo-Saxon pride, today seem almost as dated as Boker's *Francesca da Rimini*. Conversely, currently popular history plays— *Man for All Seasons, Luther, Becket*—make the story a vehicle for modern themes: the folly of depending on the common man or the purity of the law, religion as a psychophysical phenomenon, the inevitability of a cultural clash even when individuals are personally engaged. For the dramatist, history serves as a glass in which the audience sees its own image.

The Crucible opened on Broadway January 22, 1953, at the height of the furor stirred up by the accusations of Senator Joe McCarthy. In February of 1950 McCarthy had addressed the Ohio County Women's Republican Club in Wheeling, West Virginia. In his speech, as the Wheeling *Intelligencer* reported it, he claimed to have "in his hand" a list of two-hundred-and-five known Communists in the State Department. With this broadside the panic was on. The "threat of Communism from within" became a serious consideration in national politics and in the attitudes of Americans; McCarthy became a rallying point for conservatives the country over. By 1953 investigations of this charge (and the variants which McCarthy later added) were being undertaken on a nation-wide scale. The Senator used his Congressional privilege to investigate people in public life, and everyone who had had any connection with the Party felt the pressure of public opinion and a sense of insecurity about their position and their public image. Miller's own record in this regard was not unblemished and the matter became a personal threat.

> It was the fact that a political, objective, knowledgeable campaign from the far Right was capable of creating not only a

terror but a new subjective reality, a veritable mystique which was gradually assuming even a holy resonance. The wonder of it all struck me that so practical and picayune a cause, carried forward by such manifestly ridiculous men, should be capable of paralyzing thought itself, and worse, causing to billow up such persuasive clouds of "mysterious" feelings within people.

He was deeply disturbed as he watched men who had known him well for years pass him by "without a word" because of this terror "knowingly planned and consciously engineered." McCarthyism was in the air and it had all the qualities—for those personally affected—of the witch-hunt. Miller consciously draws the parallel; his plays are efforts to deal with what was "in the air." "They are one man's way of saying to his fellow men, 'This is what you see every day, or think or feel; now I will show you what you really know but have not had the time or the disinterestedness, or the insight, or the information to understand consciously.'" Once the Communist issue settled into the background, the playwright could protest that the real inner meaning of the play is not simply an attack on McCarthyism, but a treatment of the perennial conflict between individual conscience and civil society—"the handing over of conscience to another and the realization that with conscience goes the person, the soul immortal, and the 'Name.'" In any event, there is a parallel between what happened in Salem under the Puritan theocracy and what happened in Washington under the aegis of anti-Communism, and this parallel has its impact on Miller's treatment of the historical record. In a broader perspective, the myth of the Law and the ritual of the trial shape the structure of the play and help determine its ultimate dramatic meaning.

If the reign of Law is central to the American democratic ideal and if the "fair trial" is the ritual which insures its inviolability, the worst of all perversions in this area is a "bad" law enforced by a "corrupt" court. It is quite clear that, in the real order of things, any particular law is judged not by an absolute standard, but by one relative to a public consensus, and that this consensus can change. Thus, for instance, the trial of Joan of Arc seems a blatant miscarriage of justice, not because the judges failed to adhere to due process or to apply the letter of the law, but because a heresy law itself no longer compels any agreement from society at large. Prosecutions for heresy no longer fit into popular notions about the area of legal inquiry. Therefore, Joan's trial, by standards of due process "so eminently fair," has long appeared to be a travesty of justice! Because the last appeal in a democratic system is to the courts and because the Law is the bulwark of social order, any vision of corruption in the judiciary, any use of the law against the tenor of the popular mind, becomes the occasion for a general outcry. So, after the fact, the Sacco-Vanzetti case and the McCarthy investigations can be dubbed witch-hunts, whether due process was observed or not. This corruption is always laid at the door of particular individuals or a particular community because it cannot be attributed to the idea of the Law itself. Miller, in *The Crucible*, deals with the perversion of the Law in the township of Salem and, by extension, with a persistent threat to any democratic system.

In the light of this belief—that corruption is of the individual—it is worth noting that Miller found inspiration for the play in a bit of personal information embedded in the trial records:

> I had known of the Salem witch-hunt for many years before "McCarthyism" had arrived. . . . I doubt I should even have tempted agony by actually writing a play upon the subject had I not come upon a single fact. It was that Abigail Williams, the prime mover of the Salem hysteria, so far as the hysterical children were concerned, had a short time earlier been the house servant of the Proctors, and now was crying out Elizabeth Proctor as a witch, but more—it was clear from the record that with entirely uncharacteristic fastidiousness she was refusing to include John Proctor, Elizabeth's husband, in her accusations, despite the urging of the prosecutors.

Though the major issue in the play deals with the individual and society and with judicial corruption, Miller found his dramatic motivation in a domestic triangle. There is no question of the law as such being at fault; it is the motivations of individuals that are to provide an understanding of the hysteria that created and prolonged the witch-hunt. Within the structure of the trial formula Miller investigates these motivations and the actions which flow from them in relation to the guilt or innocence of individuals and of the community.

The trial formula, when it is not simply a framing device for a detective-story plot, is an investigation of innocence and guilt in terms of an application of facts and motives to principles. In order that guilt or innocence be proven, the individual declared responsible for evil or exonerated of it, the ritual provides for a clear definition of the issues, and a marshalling of forces into opposing camps. The resulting agon is presided over by judge and/or jury representing the impartiality of the principles (which are not always included in any particular law or set of laws) from which justice emanates.

The dramatic uses of this formula can be various. In the melodramatic treatment, the hero is falsely accused and vindicated by the verdict with the onus falling on a clearly defined group of villians or on a single vicious individual. More complex versions of the pattern depend on a less definite division of responsibility. For instance, the hero can be declared legally guilty according to a "bad" law or by a corrupt court, thus throwing the real guilt on the community that supports the law or fails to impeach the court. The implied result is the purgation of society for whose renewed sense of justice the hero is responsible. A third version declares the hero really guilty under a good law, thus revealing a hitherto unacknowledged guilt to him (and to the audience). When the protagonist as individual or type stands convicted in the light of genuine principles, the trial is essentially a purification ritual, its dramatic effect varies according to the distribution of guilt and innocence. *The Crucible*, even though it does indict the community, includes a complicating variant because the protagonist, besides answering a formal charge, must satisfy his own conscience about his innocence.

The structure of events, then, involves two investigations, two indictments, and two verdicts. Proctor is arraigned by the court for witchcraft; Proctor weighs the guilt of his infidelity to his wife. These two issues are carefully interwoven by the playwright, for Proctor's guilty relationship with Abigail Williams provides him with the evidence to prove the official testimony of Abby and the girls fraudulent. Thus the investigation of the witchcraft charge involves his confessing to adultery. These two issues, both of which involve Proctor's guilt, interrelate to determine the meaning of the play. What is ultimately at stake is the relation of the individual to a society governed by men under the Law. Whatever Miller intended to do in his play, *The Crucible* makes a statement about this relationship.

In one of his headnotes Miller makes a claim for his historical accuracy in depicting the events of the witch trials. The play is situated in the appropriate historical context of time and place. Salem of 1692 is depicted as an isolated community, self-contained by the surrounding forest; its spiritual government and the secular arm are in the hands of Puritan divines and the law is the law of the covenantor; the dialogue has a suitable seventeenth-century flavor. The action runs chronologically within the setting so that the realistic progression fits with the logic of the trial formula and the historical event. But the playwright adds to this perspective another dimension—a consciousness of the significance of these events to a present-day democracy. The "good people" in the cast of characters have attitudes which reflect contemporary ideals rather than the historical Puritan outlook. Thus the playwright does not mechanically reproduce the 1692 situation and exploit it for its inherent dramatic values; rather through the attitudes of the protagonist, his allies among the villagers and one of the inquisitors, he includes a perspective relevant to the audience. Miller himself was aware of this broader dimension. He explains that his realism does not imply an attempt at slice-of-life drama; he felt that the expressionism of *Death of a Salesman* would be unnecessary:

> I had found a kind of self-awareness in the bloody book of Salem and had thought that since the natural realistic surface of that society was one already immersed in the questions of meaning and the relations of men to God, to write a realistic play of that world was already to write in a style beyond contemporary realism.

Perhaps this self-awareness is better attributed to the playwright than to the trial records; in any event, there is a dimension in the play which anticipates the modern attitude toward the Salem incident, whether history includes it or not.

As a defendant in the courtroom and protagonist in the drama John Proctor is very recognizable. He is a farmer, a man of substance in the community without being a land-grabber like the malicious Thomas Putnam. Though he lives outside the ambit of the village, he acts as a respected member of the community. In his dealings with others, neighbors and servants, he is straightforward, honest and somewhat unpolished. When he comes looking for his delinquent servant girl, there will be no nonsense: "I'll show you a great doin' on your arse one of these days. Now get you home; my wife is waitin' with your work!" This rugged individualism also informs his attitude toward religion—positive, undogmatic with more than a touch of scepticism on the witchcraft issue.

> *Putnam.* I do not think I saw you at Sabbath meeting since the snow flew.
>
> *Proctor.* I have trouble enough without I come five miles to hear him preach only hellfire and bloody damnation. Take it to heart, Mr. Parris. There are many others who stay away from church these days because you hardly ever mention God any more. (CRUCIBLE, p. 245.)

He cannot brook the idea of the minister who should be a servant to the parish making himself the authority: "I do not like the smell of this 'authority.'" Neither is he a sombre or a solemn man; he has that quality which distinguishes a line of American heroes, a love of nature and the outdoors. His first scene with Elizabeth dwells on fertility and the beauties of nature.

> *Proctor.* This farm's a continent when you go foot by foot droppin' seeds in it.
>
> *Elizabeth.* (coming with the cider) It must be.
>
> *Proctor.* (drinks a long draught; then, putting the glass down) You ought to bring some flowers in the house.
>
> *Elizabeth.* Oh, I forgot! I will tomorrow.
>
> *Proctor.* It's winter in here yet. On Sunday let you come with me, and we'll walk the farm together; I never see such a load of flowers on the earth.... Lilacs has a purple smell. Lilac is a smell of nightfall, I think. Massachusetts is a beauty in the spring. (CRUCIBLE, p. 262.)

This quality—the touch of the poet, the appreciation of nature—relates to Proctor's predicament with Abby. The girl has gauged his temper, he is no "cold man." She tempted him and, being a man of strong passions, he fell. By the time the play opens, the nagging of conscience has produced a resolve not to touch her again. The affair, as far as Proctor is concerned, is over and done with; he has confessed to his wife and honestly is trying to make it up to her. In short, Miller's protagonist is no Puritan, no hypocrite; he has the democratic virtues (and vices) that render him recognizable to the audience.

With Proctor are associated the "good people" of the village. Giles Corey, the homespun old curmudgeon who battles for his rights in court, Rebecca Nurse, the sainted lady of the village with a wide reputation for charity, are also caught in the web of the law, the one because he injudiciously wanted to know what his wife was reading in her books, the other because she could not save Goody Putnam's children. Corey manifests the same kind of individualism as Proctor; he will not accept the tyranny of his neighbors or the injustice of the court. Rebecca Nurse also shows a blessed scepticism by suggesting perhaps the malice of the villagers, rather than the practice of witchcraft, is responsible for the evil that is abroad. During the course of the action one of the prosecutors, Mr. Hale, is converted in a dramatic acknowledgement of Proctor's position. These personae reflect the protagonist's qualities and so are related to him in the course of the action.

The opposition is concentrated in Abigail Williams who bridges the official investigation and Proctor's personal struggle. The "evil" in the play focuses on Abigail as fountainhead, even though she is not its most chilling expression. It is not her actions that condemn her: dancing in the woods by modern standards is no crime, her desire for John Proctor is rendered quite understandable, her uncle's superciliousness is riding for a fall. Rather, it is the means she uses to pursue her ends She is willing to sacrifice the community and everyone in it, to subvert the function of the Law, in order to gain her objectives. Her wickedness, then, amounts to a shrewd use of the hypocrisy, greed and spite that thrive in her neighbors under the pretext of seeing justice done. Her power arises from her ability to convert her psychic energies and the willful pursuit of her own objectives into a genuine visionary hysteria. At bottom Abby knows that her prophetic fit is self-induced, that the witchcraft she denounces is non-existent; but once the fit is on her, she can produce a convincing performance and induce the same kind of hysteria in the children. Her real diabolism is her misuse of the sacrosanct office of witness to gain her own ends.

With her are associated the "bad people" of Salem, those who are shown to be greedy and spiteful like the Putnams, those who are envious of power and status like Parris and Cheever. When witchcraft is murmured in the streets, the concealed feelings and grudges come to the surface. Thus the sterile Putnams cry out on Giles Corey for his land and Rebecca Nurse for her good name and her large brood. Parris sees an opportunity to put down the rebellious "faction" (Proctor and Corey) in the parish which refuses him ownership of his house and golden candlesticks for his altar. They can invoke the letter of the law, the witchcraft ordinance, for their own purposes. Conventional belief supports the mischief they do in the name of tradition. Their evil, like Abigail's, is a misuse of law and the court, institutions which everyone must respect as the source of order in the community. This evil, if execrable, is intelligible, for it looks to personal gain and satisfaction of the ego.

Between the Proctor faction and the bad people is the official judiciary, the judges and members of the court. The court represents the force of the Law, impersonal and impartial, which reconciles letter and spirit, law enforcement and individual rights. An attitude of reverence for the Law permeates the play. Mr. Hale comes armed with its authority, "allied to the best minds of Europe—kings, philosophers, scientists, and ecclesiasts of all churches." His armful of tomes, he pompously declares, are weighted with authority. Here are principles with the certainty of law to test by:

> *Hale.* Now let me instruct you. We cannot look to superstition in this. The Devil is precise; the marks of his presence are definite as stone, and I must tell you all that I shall not proceed unless you are prepared to believe me if I should find no bruise of hell upon her. (CRUCIBLE, p. 252.)

Hale proceeds with his investigation calmly, impersonally, sounding his warning about going beyond the facts, and relying on his authoritative books. When the official inquiry opens, the court possesses the same sense of solemnity and definitiveness. Elizabeth calls it "a proper court, four judges

sent out of Boston, weighty magistrates of the General Court." When
Proctor threatens to rip the Governor's warrant, Cheever, the clerk of the
court, warns him not to touch it. Constable Herrick's nine men must arrest
Elizabeth—it is so ordered by the court. (CRUCIBLE, p. 281.) When, in the
third act, Judge Danforth is introduced, he is wrapped in the dignity of his
office and knowledge of the law; After a disturbance in the courtroom and an
outcry by Giles Corey, he interrogates the old man:

> *Danforth.* Who is this man? . . .
> *Giles.* My name is Corey, sir, Giles Corey. I have six hundred
> acres, and timber in addition. It is my wife you be condemning
> now.
> *Danforth.* And how do you imagine to help her cause with such
> contemptuous riot? Now be gone. Your old age alone keeps you
> out of jail for this.
> *Giles.* They be tellin' lies about my wife, sir, I—
> *Danforth.* Do you take it upon yourself to determine what this
> court shall believe and what it shall set aside?
> *Giles.* Your Excellency, we mean no disrespect for—
> *Danforth.* Disrespect, indeed! This is disruption, Mister. This
> is the highest court of the supreme government of this division.
> (CRUCIBLE, p. 287.)

Even the rough old yeoman is impressed with Danforth and has no doubts
about his being a good judge. On this point the record shows, and Miller
acknowledges, that due process is Danforth's middle name. Even in the face
of Proctor who ripped his warrant and damned the court, the judge is
prepared to "hear the evidence." Whatever motives they might have, the
men-at-law conduct their cases with a fine show of impartiality. In the end
Danforth and Hale are shown to have been on different sides of the fence;
Danforth is joined to Abigail and the forces of evil and Hale becomes an
advocate of the individual with Proctor. But this fourth-act epiphany
derives its full significance only in contrast to the image of dignity and
impartiality that the judges and the lawyers demonstrate in the first three
acts.

　　Though she is one of the accused and John Proctor's wife, Elizabeth,
in the early scenes, shares this dramatic function of the judiciary because she
rules on Proctor's personal guilt with regard to his infidelity. Proctor makes
this function clear:

> *Proctor.* I cannot speak but I am doubted, every moment

judged for lies, as though I come into a court when I come into this house!

Elizabeth. John, you are not open with me. You saw her in a crowd, you said. Now you—

Proctor. No more! I should have roared you down when first you told me your suspicion. But I wilted, and, like a Christian, I confessed. Confessed! Some dream I had must have mistaken you for God that day. But you're not, you're not, and let you remember it! Let you look sometimes for the goodness in me, and judge me not.

Elizabeth. I do not judge you. The magistrate sits in your heart that judges you. I never thought you but a good man, John—(with a smile)—only somewhat bewildered.

Proctor. (laughing bitterly) Oh, Elizabeth, your justice would freeze beer! (CRUCIBLE, p. 265.)

The wife is a mirror of the magistrate; she is unemotional, impersonal about the relationship. She stands in much the same position with regard to John and Abigail as Danforth does to the witches and the community. This is another link between the two plot-lines. The "cold wife" cannot arrive at a fair decision about her husband because she relies on the "evidence" and the letter of the law.

The opposing camps are finally drawn up according to their attitude toward the Law. The protagonist and his allies, whether or not they believe in the existence of witchcraft, do not believe in the rigid enforcement of this law in Salem. They see that, literally, the letter killeth. The antagonists, whether believers or not, stand by the rigid enforcement of the letter for their own purposes. The judiciary, bound by the Law to do justice, is charged with deciding between these two camps.

By choosing the witchcraft law and by giving his protagonist modern attitudes, Miller puts audience judgment and sympathy beyond all doubt. Today's audience cannot take the possibility of witchcraft seriously; the implication for us is that no enlightened citizen of any age would be able to take it seriously. When some of the citizens of a community see a law as outmoded, that is, when a significant minority take a contrary stance, any rigid enforcement of such a law must be considered unjust and undemocratic. (Consider the civil rights issues of the recent past.) The audience can reasonably anticipate that the trial, as a ritual that reconciles differences and vindicates the right, will justify the position of Proctor and his allies.

The events that precede the trial dramatize at once a fear that reason may not prevail and a confidence that the Court will acknowledge the right.

In spite of the hysteria of the children, the malevolence of townsfolk like the Putnams and the self-interest of Pastor Parris, Hale is convinced that the innocent have nothing to fear. The orderly course of official inquiry by an impartial investigator should guarantee the outcome, but it is clear that Hale cannot control the forces at work. Though we want to share his confidence in the legal process, the indictments, based on Abby's evidence, raise serious doubts about the outcome of the trial.

In the trial itself Miller carefully compounds faith in the ritual as the instrument of justice with the fear that it cannot cope with the irrational forces at work in Salem. The solemnity of the Court and Danforth's attention to due process accords with the sense of confidence in the ritual. The Judge follows its prescriptions faithfully, he works calmly and impersonally with the government at his side. "This is the highest court of the supreme government of this province," he thunders at Giles Corey, "do you know it?" (CRUCIBLE, p. 287.) When Giles wishes to present evidence in his wife's defense, Danforth insists on form: "Let him submit his evidence in proper affidavit. certainly are aware of our procedure here, Mr. Hale." (CRUCIBLE, p. 287). When John Proctor protests that the children have been lying and that the Putnams are guilty of collusion, Danforth replies that he has found their evidence convincing:

> You know, Mr. Proctor, that the entire contention of the state in these trials is that the voice of Heaven is speaking through the children? . . . I tell you straight, Mister, I have seen marvels in this court. I have seen people choked before my eyes by spirits; I have seen them stuck with pins and slashed by daggers. I have until this moment not the slightest reason to suspect that the children may be deceiving me. (CRUCIBLE, pp. 289, 291.)

With this warning Danforth hears Proctor's evidence. He is too good a lawyer to act arbitrarily. When Cheever cries out that Proctor plows on Sunday and Hale breaks in to protest that a man cannot be judged on such evidence, Danforth replies: "I judge nothing." Hale then pleads for a lawyer to plead Proctor's case, and Danforth replies, logically enough, that since witchcraft is an invisible crime, only the witch and the victim know the facts and that there is nothing left for a lawyer to bring out. Proctor's case is built on Mary Warren's confession, and Danforth properly charges the children to consider the seriousness of their position:

> Now, children, this is a court of law. The law, based upon the Bible, writ by Almighty God, forbid the practice of witchcraft,

and describe death as the penalty thereof. But likewise, children, the law and the Bible damn all bearers of false witness. (Slight pause.) Now then. It does not escape me that this deposition may well be devised to blind us; it may well be that Mary Warren has been conquered by Satan, who send her here to distract our sacred purpose. If so, her neck will break for it. But if she speak true, I bid you now drop your guile and confess your pretense, for a quick confession will go easier with you. (CRUCIBLE, p. 299.)

The rhetoric of this charge to the witnesses may lean toward raising doubts about the advisability of retraction, but its burden is fair enough. Danforth applies the rules of procedure scrupulously, yet the tide is running against Proctor and the good people. The ritual is seen to be no guarantee that justice will be done as it becomes painfully clear that the Court, with the blessing of the Law, is going—as Giles Corey cried out earlier—*to hang all these people.*

There is a factor missing from Danforth's administration of the law; Miller dramatizes one aspect of this missing ingredient in the actions and attitudes of Mr. Hale. When he first appears on the scene to conduct his inquiry, Hale uses the conventional tests that he finds in his books. John Proctor is suspect when he is able to recite only nine of the Commandments; his wife has to prompt the tenth "Adultery, John." From his experience in Salem the minister learns to see beyond logic and authority and assess the human motives necessary to balance the scales of justice. In the courtroom John Proctor finally has to play his trump card and accuse Abby of lechery; his wife Elizabeth alone can support his allegation. Though Proctor testifies that he has never known his wife to lie, rather than expose her husband to infamy she speaks "nothing of lechery." (CRUCIBLE, p. 307.) Danforth has his answer; Proctor has perjured himself. But Hale speaks out for intuition against the legal process:

Hale. Excellency, it is a natural lie to tell; I beg you, stop now before another is condemned! I may shut my conscience no more—private vengeance is working through this testimony! From the beginning this man Proctor has struck me as true. . . . (Pointing at Abigail) This girl has always struck me false. (CRUCIBLE, p. 307.)

Though the minister has no law to back up his intuition, he is willing to make it a conscience matter. As Proctor has used "common sense" to object to the witchcraft investigation, Hale invokes his feelings to support Proctor's accusations against Abigail. But the Law as due process has no room for intuition. Danforth refuses to add this in; Hale's intuition and Proctor's common sense are not evidence. Because the Judge refuses to admit this human factor, the good people have no recourse.

The other aspect of the human factor for which the Law makes no provision is emotion. Due process provides no tool for coping with the kind of hysteria that the children's shrieking generates. Emotional reactions have a real impact on the Court (and the audience), yet this impact cannot be included in the record. "The witness cried out" or "(confusion in the courtroom)" is no substitute for the atmosphere of mystery and/or conviction that results from the emotional outburst. From the beginning of the investigations Abigail has been able to turn this weapon against logic and common sense. Whenever her probity is called into question, she transmutes the dry, question-and-answer proceedings into enthusiastic pulsings. In his preliminary investigation, Hale is searching for the truth about the dancing in the forest and begins to close in:

> *Abigail.* I want to open myself! (They turn to her, startled. She is enraptured, as though in a pearly light.) I want the light of God, I want the sweet love of Jesus! I danced for the Devil; I saw him; I wrote in his book; I want to go back to Jesus; I kiss his hand. I saw Sarah Good with the Devil! I saw Goody Osburn with the Devil! I saw Bridget Bishop with the Devil! (CRUCIBLE, p. 259.)

Neither Hale's authoritative books nor his fledgling intuition are proof against this kind of outburst. Here Abby discovers a power that can be summoned up at will against her enemies.

The source of this emotional power, as is evident from the imagery, lies in Abby's sexual experience. Her outbursts are orgiastic, full of latent sexuality. It is this energy that cannot be weighed in the balance, that initially paralyzes Hale and terrifies the onlookers. Abby's experience with Proctor, hidden from the town, is channeled into her vision, producing a real hysteria in herself and the rest of the children. She introduced them to this mystery in the forest—the naked dancing—and so established a covenant of secret guilt and desire that supports their conspiracy in court. At this point John Proctor's "private sin" has implications for the community.

This emotional outburst has as much to do with Proctor's downfall as Elizabeth's lie. At the crisis of the trial, when Mary Warren's testimony threatens her, Abby calls up this hysteria. Danforth has turned his questioning on her: "Is it possible, child, that the spirits you have seen are illusion only, some deception that may cross your mind when—" (CRUCIBLE, p. 303.) Abby calls up a "cold wind" and all the girls shiver. She sees a yellow bird on the rafters—Mary Warren's spirit tempted from her by John Proctor's diabolism. Threatened by the same fate she has helped thrust on others, Mary Warren breaks and cries out against Proctor. Again this hysteria has a complement of sexual overtones. The yellow bird with claws and spreading wings recalls Tituba's flying to Barbados and the sexual freedom of the forest; the serving girl responds by describing Proctor's tempting in sexual images: "He wake me every night, his eyes were like coals, and his fingers claw my neck, and I sign, I sign . . ." (CRUCIBLE, p. 310.) Though Abby is shamming and the children recognize it, the emotions that fly about the courtroom are very real, the more so because they tap that forbidden well-spring, sexuality, which the Puritan community cannot (or will not) recognize for what it is.

This emotional factor in the case is not accounted for by the rules. It is irrational, a-logical, but very real. Once the witchcraft scare has spread through town, it becomes the channel by which fear, greed, sexual repressions, irresponsibility can be sublimated into "evidence." The Law can help create a scapegoat on which the secret sins of the community can be visited. Judge and jury must ferret out the secret source of such emotion and expose it to view. This is asking a great deal of the judiciary; yet if the trial is to work at all, it works because judge and jury manage to have proper intuitions about human values in a case. So the conditions by which the Law is an effective tool of justice include an ability to perceive, through a maze of technicalities, the whole issue and to deal with it in a humane fashion. The "evil" in Danforth and in Abigail is their lack of this humanity.

Because the Law cannot cope with emotion and its irrational springs and because the ritual cannot substitute for a lack of intuition (willful or not), the verdict goes against John Proctor and his allies, the order of things is reversed, justice is not done and the Law itself becomes the instrument of perversion.

In the trial, Miller has dramatized the deficiencies of the Law in the hands of an evil court interpreting a bad law. In the fourth act he attempts to frame a solution to this problem. He reintroduces Danforth and Hale, representatives, respectively, of the letter and of the humane view of the Law. Danforth visits the jail to find Parris overwrought because of Abby's treachery and Hale defiantly working to persuade the prisoners to confess. It becomes perfectly clear to the Judge that the girls' testimony was fraudulent, if he had not known this all along. But the hanging verdicts are now on record; twelve have been hanged for the crime of witchcraft, and pardon for the rest would necessarily be a confession of error on the part of the court.

Rebellion is stirring in a neighboring town and chaos threatens the theocracy that Danforth represents. So the decision must be upheld and the law enforced.

> *Danforth*. Now hear me, and beguile yourselves no more. I will not receive a single plea for pardon or postponement. Them that will not confess will hang. . . . Postponement now speaks a floundering on my part; reprieve or pardon must cast doubt upon the guilt of them that died till now. While I speak God's law, I will not crack its voice with whimpering. If retaliation is your fear, know this—I should hang ten thousand that dared to rise against the law. (CRUCIBLE, p. 318.)

Danforth makes explicit here an attitude which underlies his role during the trial sequence. Though misapplied, the principle of law enforcement is recognized as valid by the audience.

As we have seen above, law enforcement is part of the American attitude toward the Law; it must be upheld or anarchy follows. It is just as important to the American ideal as the fair trial. When the individual takes upon himself the prerogative of deciding which law may be obeyed and which disregarded, the community feels that the bulwark of order has been breached. Thus the icy wind that blows when Danforth speaks is not the chill of his malevolence and inhumanity only, as some critics claim and as Miller himself seems to think. Danforth appeals to a principle that the audience recognizes as plausible. Otherwise, he would pose no real threat. In spite of the fact that his own personal motives include the preservation of his own position in power, and thus are evil, he is defending an attitude that Americans recognize as necessary. Thus the tension in the position between respect for the Law as such—even a bad law—and a respect for the right of the individual to dissent.

Miller finally tries to reconcile these polarities by turning attention to John Proctor. Proctor is no Puritan and no hypocrite; he has, as pointed out above, all those qualities that make a man acceptable to modern society, including a sense of isolation in his guilt. His private sin which, through Abby, contributed to the conviction of the innocent remains unabsolved. His wife, in their final confrontation before the execution, confesses that his guilt is also hers: "It needs a cold wife to prompt lechery." (CRUCIBLE, p. 323.) But Proctor, who has set himself outside the law, cannot accept martyrdom; he is not fit to die with Rebecca Nurse in the odor of sanctity. There is no final assurance that he is worthy, either in his sacrificial defense of the innocent before the court or in Elizabeth's assumption of responsibility for his sin.

> *Elizabeth.* You take my sins upon you, John—
> *Proctor.* (in agony) No, I take my own, my own! . . .
>
> *Elizabeth.* Do what you will. But let none be your judge.
> There be no higher judge under Heaven than Proctor is!
> (CRUCIBLE, p. 323.)

The ultimate verdict of the play, then, is to be Proctor's decision about his own state of soul.

To clarify this situation dramatically, Miller has his hero hesitate before the prospect of dying for his beliefs. Mr. Hale, who has failed to move Danforth from his purpose, has been urging the condemned to confess because "Life is God's most precious gift; no principle, however glorious, may justify the taking of it." (CRUCIBLE, p. 320.) Though Proctor confesses in Hale's terms: "I want to live," a natural fear of death is not his only motive, it is rather a continuing sense of guilt and unworthiness. Elizabeth has to remind him that he is his own judge now; he cannot find justification or condemnation except in his own conscience.

John Proctor does find justification within; his "motive" lies in the discovery that Danforth intends to publish his confession. He will neither implicate others in his "crime" of witchcraft, nor allow Danforth to use his name to justify their deaths. When he discovers that he cannot concur in their legal lie, he is able to absolve himself and so die for his convictions:

> *Hale.* Man, you will hang. You cannot!
> *Proctor.* I can. Now there's your first marvel, that I can. You have your magic now, for now I think I see some shred of goodness in John Proctor. Not enough to weave a banner with, but white enough to keep it from the dogs. (CRUCIBLE, p. 328.)

When Proctor goes to execution, personal honor triumphs over the deficiencies of the Law and the conspiracy of malicious clique and corrupt court.

This epiphany satisfies the exigencies of the structure; Proctor goes to his death purged of guilt and seeing meaning in his sacrifice. But his triumph is an individual victory only; it does not touch the radical oppositions dramatized in the play. In fact, it only adds another dimension to them. The legal system in America, because it is the font of order and justice, has acquired a sacral aura. Progressively it has been dealing, not only with crime, but also with moral guilt. Because, in the popular mind, the verdict of the court is also

a moral judgment, we tend to operate on the assumption that the Law, insti-
tution and ritual, can one day become a *perfect* instrument of justice, that is,
it can become an instrument of absolution as well as acquittal. So in contemporary criminal law, the issue is not confined to the fact of commission, but
is equally engaged with the motive. Psychiatric observation is increasingly
admissible as evidence. Thus the law reaches out toward those hitherto
private areas, dealt with in the past by pastor or priest, to create a strategy
that will deal with the communitarian forgiveness of guilt. (Whether or not
we can ever hope to achieve this objective is not at issue here.) Miller, in *The
Crucible*, dramatizes the tensions that make the trial a questionable instrument of justice and the contradiction that lurks at the center of our myth of
the Law. He tries to resolve these polarities by insisting that only the individual can be an adequate judge of his own private actions. The hero, all his
sins upon him, must cope with the spectre of guilt alone. The audience is left
with the suspicion that self-absolution begs the question; the old adage
applies: no man is a good judge in his own case.

In stereotype, dramatic use of the trial pattern depends on the public's
faith that this ritual infallibly reconciles contraries, *solvuntur ambulando*.
When it is used as a framework in conventional drama, for instance, the
verdict of the court resolves all differences between individual and society
and makes evident the innocence or guilt of the individual and his society.
The logical progression of the ritual gives the verdict the appearance of
absolute truth (or as close an approximation as man can reasonably expect).
In plays like *The Caine Mutiny Court Martial* or *Saint Joan*, the trial reveals
the truth even when the verdict is one-sided. The audience, whose posture is
that of the jury, can detect prejudice in the judge, or a vicious prosecutor, or
an inept defense counsel. The dramatist can see to it that they do. So this
ritual, at least on the stage, ordinarily does what a ritual should do, that is,
guarantee the desired result.

The Crucible, however, uses the trial pattern, not as a framework, but to
explore the attitudes that underlie the ritual itself. The formal symmetry of
orderly investigation, indictment, presentation of evidence and verdict is
broken by hysterical outbursts; the support that due process, in the hands of
an humane and unbiased judiciary, provides the truth is undermined by the
inhumanity of Danforth. The man who is caught between the grinding
stones of a corrupt court and an evil law may save himself in the end by
becoming his own judge and jury, but the dramatic fact in *The Crucible* is the
grinding. The ritual fails, and the hero is isolated with his guilt.

In his epilogue, Miller tries to insist that sacrifices like Proctor's eventually do have a relationship to the whole community.

In solemn meeting, the congregation rescinded the excommunications—this in March 1712. But they did so upon orders of the government. The jury, however, wrote a statement praying forgiveness for all who had suffered. . . . To all intents and purposes, the power of the theocracy in Massachusetts was broken. (CRUCIBLE, p. 330.)

This comment may allay the playwright's scruples, but it is not part of the dramatic experience. The play makes its own statement by conveying, with a sense of urgency, the opposition between two American ideals: the need for Law and law enforcement and the right of the minority to dissent. In dramatizing this tension, it also calls attention to the need for a ritual that can deal with communal and individual guilt. In the absence of such a ritual John Proctor's triumph is finally a mystery, unaccommodated man holding, for personal reasons, to a personal vision. The black-gowned shadow of Danforth is not blotted out by the rising sun and Proctor's sacrifice.

ROBERT A. MARTIN

Arthur Miller's The Crucible:
Background and Sources

When *The Crucible* opened on January 22, 1953, the term "witchhunt" was nearly synonymous in the public mind with the Congressional investigations then being conducted into allegedly subversive activities. Arthur Miller's plays have always been closely identified with contemporary issues, and to many observers the parallel between the witchcraft trials at Salem, Massachusetts in 1692 and the current Congressional hearings was the central issue of the play.

Miller has said that he could not have written *The Crucible* at any other time, a statement which reflects both his reaction to the McCarthy era and the creative process by which he finds his way to the thematic center of a play. If it is true, however, that a play cannot be successful in its own time unless it speaks to its own time, it is also true that a play cannot endure unless it speaks to new audiences in new times. The latter truism may apply particularly to *The Crucible*, which is presently being approached more and more frequently as a cultural and historical study rather than as a political allegory.

Although *The Crucible* was written in response to its own time, popular interest in the Salem witchcraft trials had actually begun to surface long before the emergence of McCarthyism. There were at least two other plays based on the witchcraft trials that were produced shortly before *The Crucible* opened: *Child's Play* by Florence Stevenson was produced in November, 1952

From *Modern Drama* 20 (1977). © 1977 by the University of Toronto.

at the Oklahoma Civic Playhouse; and *The Witchfinders* by Louis O. Coxe appeared at about the same time in a studio production at the University of Minnesota. Among numerous other works dealing with Salem witchcraft, a novel, *Peace, My Daughter* by Shirley Barker, had appeared as recently as 1949, and in the same year Marion L. Starkey had combined an interest in history and psychology to produce *The Devil in Massachusetts*, which was based on her extensive research of the original documents and records. Starkey's announced purpose was "to review the records in the light of the findings of modern psychology," and to supplement the work of earlier investigators by calling attention to "a number of vital primary sources of which they seem to have been ignorant."

The events that eventually found their way into *The Crucible* are largely contained in the massive two volume record of the trials located in the Essex County Archives at Salem, Massachusetts, where Miller went to do his research. Although he has been careful to point out in a prefatory note that *The Crucible* is not history in the academic sense, a study of the play and its sources indicates that Miller did his research carefully and well. He found in the records of the trials at Salem that between June 10 and September 22, 1692, nineteen men and women and two dogs were hanged for witchcraft, and one man was pressed to death for standing mute. Before the affair ended, fifty-five people had confessed to being witches, and another hundred and fifty were in jail awaiting trial.

Focusing primarily upon the story of John Proctor, one of the nineteen who were hanged, Miller almost literally retells the story of a panic-stricken society that held a doctrinal belief in the existence of the Devil and the reality of witchcraft. The people of Salem did not, of course, invent a belief in witchcraft; they were, however, the inheritors of a witchcraft tradition that had a long and bloody history in their native England and throughout most of Europe. To the Puritans of Massachusetts, witchcraft was as real a manifestation of the Devil's efforts to overthrow "God's kingdom" as the periodic raids of his Indian disciples against the frontier settlements.

There were, surprisingly, few executions for witchcraft in Massachusetts before 1692. According to George Lyman Kittredge in his *Witchcraft in Old and New England*, "not more than half-a-dozen executions can be shown to have occurred." But the people of Salem village in 1692 had recent and—to them—reliable evidence that the Devil was at work in the Massachusetts Bay Colony. In 1688 in Boston, four children of John Goodwin had been seriously afflicted by a "witch" named Glover, who was also an Irish washwoman. In spite of her hasty execution and the prayers of four of the most devout Boston ministers, the Goodwin children were possessed by spirits of the "invisible world" for some months afterward. One of the leading Puritan ministers of the time was Cotton Mather, who in 1689 published his observations on the incident in "Memorable Providences, Relating to Witchcrafts and Possession." Although the work was intended to warn against witchcraft, Mather's account can also be read as a handbook of instructions for feigning possession by demonic spirits. Among numerous other manifestations and torments, Mather reported that the Goodwin children were most often afflicted by "fits":

> Sometimes they would be Deaf, sometimes Dumb, and sometimes Blind, and often, all this at once. One while their Tongues would be drawn down their Throats; another-while they would be pull'd out upon their Chins, to a prodigious length. They would have their Mouths opened unto such a Wideness, that their Jaws went out of pint; and anon they would clap together again with a Force like that of a strong Spring Lock.

Four years later, in February, 1692, the daughter and niece of the Reverend Samuel Parris of Salem village began to have "fits" very similar to those experienced by the Goodwin children as reported and described by Mather. According to Marion Starkey, Parris had a copy of Mather's book, and, in addition, "the Parrises had probably had first-hand experience of the case, since they appear to have been living in Boston at the time. The little girls might even have been taken to see the hanging."

In spite of an apparent abundance of historical material, the play did not become dramatically conceivable for Miller until he came upon "a single fact" concerning Abigail Williams, the niece of Reverend Parris:

> It was that Abigail Williams, the prime mover of the Salem hysteria, so far as the hysterical children were concerned, had a short time earlier been the house servant of the Proctors and now was crying out Elizabeth Proctor as a witch; but more—it was clear from the record that with entirely uncharacteristic fastidiousness she was refusing to include John Proctor, Elizabeth's husband, in her accusations despite the urgings of the prosecutors. Why? I searched the records of the trials in the courthouse at Salem but in no other instance could I find such a careful avoidance of the implicating stutter, the murderous, ambivalent answer to the sharp questions of the prosecutors. Only here, in Proctor's case, was there so clear an attempt to differentiate between a wife's culpability and a husband's.

As in history, the play begins when the Reverend Samuel Parris begins to suspect that his daughter Betty has become ill because she and his niece Abigail Williams have "trafficked with spirits in the forest." The real danger Parris fears, however, is less from diabolical spirits than from the ruin that may fall upon him when his enemies learn that his daughter is suffering from the effects of witchcraft:

> *Parris.* There is a faction that is sworn to drive me from my pulpit. Do you understand that?
> *Abigail.* I think so, sir.
> *Parris.* Now then, in the midst of such disruption, my own household is discovered to be the very center of some obscene practice. Abominations are done in the forest—
> *Abigail.* It were sport, uncle!

As Miller relates at a later point in the play, Parris was a petty man who was historically in a state of continual bickering with his congregation over such matters as his salary, housing, and firewood. The irony of the above conversation in the play, however, is that while Parris is attempting to discover the "truth" to prevent it from damaging his already precarious reputation as Salem's minister, Abigail actually is telling him the historical truth when she says "it were sport." Whatever perverse motives may have subsequently prompted the adult citizens of Salem to cry "witch" upon their neighbors, the initiators of the Salem misfortune were young girls like Abigail Williams who began playing with spirits simply for the "sport" of it, as a release from an emotionally oppressive society. A portion of the actual trial testimony given in favor of Elizabeth Proctor (John Proctor's wife) by one Daniel Elliott suggests that initially, at least, not everyone accepted the girls' spectral visions without question:

> The testimony of Daniel Elliott, aged 27 years or thereabouts, who testifieth and saith that I being at the house of lieutenant Ingersoll on the 28 of March, in the year 1692, there being present one of the afflicted persons which cried out and said, there's Goody Proctor. William Raiment being there present, told the girl he believed she lied, for he saw nothing: then Goody Ingersoll told the girl she told a lie, for there was nothing; then the girl said that she did it for sport, they must have some sport. [punctuation added]

Miller's addition in *The Crucible* of an adulterous relationship between

Abigail Williams and Proctor serves primarily as a dramatically imperative motive for Abigail's later charges of witchcraft against Elizabeth Proctor. Although it might appear that Miller is rewriting history for his own dramatic purposes by introducing a sexual relationship between Abigail and Proctor, his invention of the affair is psychologically and historically appropriate. As he makes clear in the prefatory note preceding the play, "dramatic purposes have sometimes required many characters to be fused into one; the number of girls . . . has been reduced; Abigail's age has been raised; . . ." Although Miller found that Abigail's refusal to testify against Proctor was the single historical dramatic "fact" he was looking for, there are two additional considerations that make adultery and Abigail's altered age plausible within the historical context of the events.

The first is that Mary Warren, in the play and in history, was simultaneously an accuser in court and a servant in Proctor's household. If an adulterous affair was probable, it would more likely have occurred between Mary Warren and Proctor than between Abigail Williams and Proctor; but it could easily have occurred. At the time, Mary Warren was a fairly mature young woman who would have had the features Miller has represented in Abigail: every emotional and sexual impulse, as well as the opportunity to be involved with Proctor. Historically, it was Mary Warren who attempted to stop the proceedings as early as April 19 by stating during her examination in court that the afflected girls "did but dissemble": "Afterwards she started up, and said I will speak and cried out, Oh! I am sorry for it, I am sorry for it, and wringed her hands, and fell a little while into a fit again and then came to speak, but immediately her teeth were set, and then she fell into a violent fit and cried out, oh Lord help me! Oh Good Lord save me!" As in the play, the rest of the girls prevailed by immediately falling into fits and spontaneously accusing her of witchcraft. As her testimony of April 21 and later indicates, however, she soon returned to the side of her fellow accusers. On June 30, she testified:

> The deposition of Mary Warren aged 20 years here testifieth. I have seen the apparition of John Proctor senior among the witches and he hath often tortured me by pinching me and biting me and choking me, and pressing me on my Stomach till the blood came out of my mouth and also I saw him torture Mis Pope and Mercy Lewis and John Indian upon the day of his examination and he hath also tempted me to write in his book, and to eat bread which he brought to me, which I refusing to do, John Proctor did most grievously torture me with a variety of tortures, almost Ready to kill me.

Miller has reduced Mary Warren's lengthy and ambiguous trial testimony to four pages in the play by focusing on her difficulty in attempting to tell the truth after the proceedings were under way. The truth that Mary has to tell—"It were only sport in the beginning, sir"—is the same that Abigail tried to tell Parris earlier; but the telling has become compounded by the courtroom presence of Proctor, Parris, Hathorne and Danforth (two of the judges), the rest of the afflected girls, and the spectators. In a scene taken directly from the trial records, Mary confesses that she and the other girls have been only pretending and that they have deceived the court. She has never seen the spirits or apparitions of the witches:

> *Hathorne*. How could you think you saw them unless you saw them?
> *Mary Warren*. I—I cannot tell how, but I did. I—I heard the other girls screaming, and you, Your Honor, you seemed to believe them, and I—It were only sport in the beginning, sir, but then the whole world cried spirits, and I—I promise you, Mr. Danforth, I only thought I saw them but I did not.

The second, additional consideration is that although Miller has raised Abigail's age from her actual eleven to seventeen, and has reduced the number of girls in the play to five only, such alterations for purposes of dramatic motivation and compression do not significantly affect the psychological or historical validity of the play. As the trial records clearly establish, individual and family hostilities played a large role in much of the damaging testimony given against those accused of witchcraft. Of the ten girls who were most directly involved in crying out against the witches, only three— Betty Parris (nine years old), Abigail Williams (eleven years), and Ann Putnam (twelve years) were below the age of sexual maturity. The rest were considerably older: Mary Walcott and Elizabeth Booth were both sixteen; Elizabeth Hubbard was seventeen; Susanna Sheldon was eighteen; Mercy Lewis was nineteen; Sara Churchill and Mary Warren (Proctor's servant) were twenty. In a time when marriage and motherhood were not uncommon at the age of fourteen, the hypothesis of repressed sexuality emerging disguised into the emotionally charged atmosphere of witchcraft and Calvinism does not seem unlikely; it seems, on the contrary, an inevitable supposition. And it may be worth pointing out in this context that Abigail Williams was not the only one of the girls who refused to include John Proctor in her accusations against his wife, Elizabeth. In her examination of April 21, Mary Warren testified that her mistress was a witch and that "her master had told her that he had been about sometimes to make away with himself because of his wife's quarreling with him. . . . "A few lines later the entry reads "but she would not own that she knew her master to be a witch or wizzard."

With the exception of Abigail and Proctor's adultery, the events and characters of *The Crucible* are not so much "invented" data in a fictional sense as highly compressed representations of the underlying forces of hatred, hysteria, and fear that paralyzed Salem during the spring and summer of 1692. And even in this context Abigail Williams's characterization in the play may be more restrained in the light of the records than Miller's dramatization suggests. For example, one of the major witnesses against John Proctor was twelve year old Ann Putnam, who testified on June 30 that "on the day of his examination I saw the apparition of John: Proctor senior go and afflict and most grievously torture the bodies of Mistress Pope, Mary Walcott, Mercy Lewis, Abigail Williams. . . ." In projecting several of the girls into Abigail, Miller has used the surface of the trial records to suggest that her hatred for Proctor's wife is a dramatic equivalent for the much wider spread hatred and tension that existed within the Salem community. Abigail, although morally corrupt, ironically insists upon her "good" name, and reveals at an early point in the play that she hates Elizabeth Proctor for ruining her reputation:

> *Parris.* [*to the point*] Abigail, is there any other cause than you have told me, for your being discharged from Goody Proctor's service? I have heard it said, and I tell you as I heard it, that she comes so rarely to the church this year for she will not sit so close to something soiled. What signified that remark?
> *Abigail.* She hates me uncle, she must, for I would not be her slave. It's a bitter woman, a lying, cold, sniveling woman, and I will not work for such a woman!

On a larger scale, Miller brings together the forces of personal and social malfunction through the arrival of the Reverend John Hale, who appears, appropriately, in the midst of a bitter quarrel among Proctor, Parris, and Thomas Putnam over deeds and land boundaries. Hale, in life as in the play, had encountered witchcraft previously and was called to Salem to determine if the Devil was in fact responsible for the illness of the afflicted children. In the play, he conceives of himself, Miller says, "much as a young doctor on his first call":

> [*He appears loaded down with half a dozen heavy books.*]
> *Hale.* Pray you, someone take these!

> *Parris.* [*delighted*] Mr. Hale! Oh! it's good to see you again! [*Taking some books*] My, they're heavy!
>
> *Hale.* [*setting down his books*] They must be; they are weighted with authority.

Hale's entrance at this particular point in the play is significant in that he interrupts an argument based on private and secular interests to bring "authority" to the question of witchcraft. His confidence in himself and his subsequent examination of the girls and Tituba (Parris's slave who inadvertently started the entire affair) represent and foreshadow the arrival of outside religious authority in the community. As an outsider who has come to weigh the evidence, Hale also helps to elevate the issue from a local to a regional level, and from an unofficial to an official theological inquiry. His heavy books of authority also symbolically anticipate the heavy authority of the judges who, as he will realize too late, are as susceptible to misinterpreting testimony based on spectral evidence as he is:

> *Hale.* [*with a tasty love of intellectual pursuit*] Here is all the invisible world, caught, defined, and calculated. In these books the Devil stands stripped of all his brute disguises. Here are all your familiar spirits—your incubi and succubi; your witches that go by land, by air, and by sea; your wizards of the night and of the day. Have no fear now—we shall find him out if he has come among us, and I mean to crush him utterly if he has shown his face!

The Reverend Hale is an extremely interesting figure historically, and following the trials he set down an account of his repentance entitled "A Modest Inquiry into the Nature of Witchcraft" (Boston, 1702). Although he was at first as overly zealous in his pursuit of witches as everyone else, very much as Miller has portrayed him in *The Crucible*, Hale began to be tormented by doubts early in the proceedings. His uncertainty concerning the reliability of the witnesses and their testimony was considerably heightened when his own wife was also accused of being a witch. Hale appears to have been as tortured spiritually and as dedicated to the "middle way" in his later life as Miller has portrayed him in *The Crucible*. Five years after Salem, he wrote in his "Inquiry":

> The middle way is commonly the way of truth. And if any can show me a better middle way than I have here laid down, I shall be ready to embrace it: But the conviction must not be by vinegar or drollery, but by strength of argument. . . . I have had a deep

sence of the sad consequence of mistakes in matters Capital; and their impossibility of recovering when compleated. And what grief of heart it brings to a tender conscience, to have been unwittingly encouraging of the Sufferings of the innocent.

Hale further commented that although he presently believed the executions to be the unfortunate result of human error, the integrity of the court officials was unquestionable: "I observed in the prosecution of these affairs, that there was in the Justices, Judges and others concerned, a conscientious endeavour to do the thing that was right. And to that end they consulted the Presidents [Precedents] of former times and precepts laid down by Learned Writers about Witchcraft."

In *The Crucible*, Hale's examination of Tituba is very nearly an edited transcription of her testimony at the trial of Sarah Good, who is the first person Abigail accuses of consorting with the Devil. At the time of the trials, Sarah Good had long been an outcast member of the Salem community, "unpopular because of her slothfulness, her sullen temper, and her poverty; she had recently taken to begging, an occupation the Puritans detested." When she was about to be hanged, her minister, the Reverend Nicholas Noyes, made a last appeal to her for a confession and said he knew she was a witch. Her prophetic reply was probably seen later as proof of her guilt when she said to Noyes "you are a lyer; I am no more a Witch than you are a Wizard, and if you take away my Life, God will give you Blood to drink." A few years after she was hanged, Reverend Noyes died as a result of a sudden and severe hemorrhage.

Largely through the Reverend Hale, Miller reflects the change that took place in Salem from an initial belief in the justice of the court to a suspicion that testimony based on spectral evidence was insufficient for execution. This transformation begins to reveal itself in Act Two, as Hale tells Francis Nurse that the court will clear his wife of the charges against her: "Believe me, Mr. Nurse, if Rebecca Nurse be tainted, then nothing's left to stop the whole green world from burning. Let you rest upon the justice of the court; the court will send her home, I know it." By Act Three, however, Hale's confidence in the justice of the court has been badly shaken by the arrest and conviction of people like Rebecca Nurse who were highly respected members of the church and community. Hale, like his historical model, has discovered that "the whole green world" is burning indeed, and fears that he has helped to set the fire.

Partially as a result of Hale's preliminary investigation into the reality of Salem witchcraft, the Court of Oyer and Terminer was appointed to hear testimony and conduct the examinations. The members of the court immediately encountered a serious obstacle: namely, that although the Bible does not define witchcraft, it states unequivocally that "Thou shalt not suffer a witch to live" (Exodus 22:18). As Proctor attempts to save his wife from hanging, Hale attempts to save his conscience by demanding visible proof of the guilt of those who have been convicted on the basis of spectral testimony:

> *Hale*. Excellency, I have signed seventy-two death warrants; I am a minister of the Lord, and I dare not take a life without there be a proof so immaculate no slightest qualm of conscience may doubt it.
> *Danforth*. Mr. Hale, you surely do not doubt my justice.
> *Hale*. I have this morning signed away the soul of Rebecca Nurse, Your Honor. I'll not conceal it, my hand shakes yet as with a wound!

At first, the witches who were brought to trial and convicted were generally old and eccentric women like Sarah Good who were of questionable character long before the trials began. But people like Rebecca Nurse and John Proctor were not. As Miller has Parris say to Judge Hathorne in Act Four "it were another sort that hanged till now. Rebecca Nurse is no Bridget that lived three year with Bishop before she married him. John Proctor is not Isaac Ward that drank his family to ruin." In late June, Rebecca Nurse was found guilty and sentenced to hang after an earlier verdict of "not guilty" was curiously reversed. Her minister, the Reverend Nicholas Noyes again, decided along with his congregation that she should be excommunicated for the good of the church. Miller seems to have been especially moved by her character and her almost unbelievable trial and conviction, as he indicates by his comments in the "Introduction" and his interpolated remarks in Act One. On Tuesday, July 19, 1692, she was hanged on Gallows Hill along with four others, all women. She was seventy-one years old. After the hanging, according to Starkey:

> The bodies of the witches were thrust into a shallow grave in a crevice of Gallows Hill's outcropping of felsite. But the body of Rebecca did not remain there. Her children bided their time . . . and at night when the crowds and the executioners had gone home again, they gathered up the body of their mother and took it home. Just where they laid it none can know, for this was a secret thing and not even Parris, whose parsonage was not a quarter of a mile up the road past the grove where the Nurses buried their dead, must see that a new grave had been opened

and prayers said. This was the hour and the power of darkness when a son could not say where he had buried his mother.

Historically, Proctor was even more of a victim of the laws of his time than Miller details in *The Crucible.* Although the real John Proctor fought against his arrest and conviction as fervently as anyone could under the circumstances, he, like Miller's Proctor, was adamant in his refusal to confess to witchcraft because he did not believe it existed. And although fifty-two of his friends and neighbors risked their own safety to sign a petition in his behalf, nothing was done to reexamine the evidence against him. Ironically, Proctor's wife—in whose interest he had originally become involved in the affair—had become pregnant and, although sentenced, would never hang. She was eventually released after enduring her husband's public execution, the birth of her child in prison, and the seizure and loss of all her possessions.

Under the law, the goods and property of witches could be confiscated after their trial and conviction. In Proctor's case, however, the sheriff did not wait for the trial or the conviction. A contemporary account of the seizure indicates that neither Proctor nor his wife were ever expected to return from prison:

> John Proctor and his Wife being in Prison, the Sheriff came to his House and seized all the Goods, Provisions, and Cattle that he could come at, and sold some of the Cattle at half-price, and killed others, and put them up for the West-Indies; threw out the Beer out of a Barrel, and carried away the Barrel; emptied a Pot of Broath, and took away the Pot, and left nothing in the House for the support of the Children: No part of the said Goods are known to be returned.

(The Proctors had five children, the youngest of whom were three and seven.) Along with three other men and one woman, John Proctor was hanged on August 19. On September 22, seven more witches and one wizard were hanged, and then the executions suddenly ended.

Miller has symbolized all the judges of the witchcraft trials in the figures of Danforth and Hathorne (Nathaniel Hawthorne's ancestor), and presented them as being more "official" in a legal sense than their historical models actually were. None of the judges in the trials had any legal training, and, apparently, neither had anyone else who was administering the law in the Massachusetts Bay Colony. According to Starkey, the curious nature of the trials was in part due to the Puritans' limited understanding of the law, their contempt for lawyers, and their nearly total reliance on the Bible as a guide for all matters of legal and moral authority:

The Puritans had a low opinion of lawyers and did not permit the professional practice of law in the colony. In effect the administration of the law was in the hands of laymen, most of them second-generation colonists who had an incomplete grasp of current principles of English jurisdiction. For that matter, this chosen people, this community which submitted itself to the direct rule of God, looked less to England for its precepts than to God's ancient and holy word. So far as was practicable the Puritans were living by a legal system that antedated the Magna Carta by at least two millennia, the Decalogue and the tribal laws codified in the Pentateuch.

As historians occasionally have pointed out, the executions did not stop because the people in Massachusetts suddenly ceased to believe in either the Devil or witchcraft; they stopped, simply and ironically, because of a legal question. There never was any doubt for most people living in New England in 1692 whether or not witchcraft was real or whether witches should be executed; the question centered around the reliability of spectral evidence coming from the testimony of the afflicted. It was largely through the determinations of Increase Mather and fourteen other Boston ministers that such testimony was declared to be insufficient for conviction and therefore became inadmissable as evidence. It was better, they concluded, to allow ten witches to escape than to hang one innocent person. In late October, Governor Phips officially dismissed the Court of Oyer and Terminer, and—although the trials continued through the following April—in May, 1693 he issued a proclamation discharging all the remaining "witches" and pardoning those who had fled the colony rather than face arrest, trial, and certain conviction.

Miller has said that if he were to rewrite *The Crucible*, he would make an open thematic issue of the evil he now believes to be represented by the Salem judges. His altered viewpoint toward the play may be accounted for partially as a reconsideration of his intensive examination of the trial records which, he has said, do not "reveal any mitigation of the unrelieved, straightforward, and absolute dedication to evil displayed by the judges of these trials and the prosecutors. After days of study it became quite incredible how perfect they were in this respect."

Miller's subsequent view of evil, however, did not come entirely from his study of the trial records. Between writing *The Crucible* in 1952 and producing the "Introduction" to the *Collected Plays* in 1957, he underwent a personal crucible when he appeared before the House Un-American Activities Committee in 1956. Although the experience was understandably not without its effect, on his later attitude toward Congressional "witchhunters," it should, nevertheless, be considered in relation to his comments on the judges and evil quoted above. A more accurate reflection of Miller's attitude while writing *The Crucible* appears perhaps most clearly in the account published in February, 1953 of his thoughts while standing on the rock at Gallows Hill:

> Here hung Rebecca, John Proctor, George Jacobs—people more real to me than the living can ever be. The sense of a terrible marvel again; that people could have such a belief in themselves and in the rightness of their consciences as to give their lives rather than say what they thought was false. Or, perhaps, they only feared Hell so much? Yet, Rebecca said, and it is written in the record, "I cannot belie myself." And she knew it would kill her. . . . The rock stands forever in Salem. They knew who they were. Nineteen.

Like the rock at Salem, *The Crucible* has endured beyond the immediate events of its own time. If it was originally seen as a political allegory, it is presently seen by contemporary audiences almost entirely as a distinguished American play by an equally distinguished American playwright. As one of the most frequently produced plays in the American theater, *The Crucible* has attained a life of its own; one that both interprets and defines the cultural and historical background of American society. Given the general lack of plays in the American theater that have seriously undertaken to explore the meaning and significance of the American past in relation to the present, *The Crucible* stands virtually alone as a dramatically coherent rendition of one of the most terrifying chapters in American history.

WILLIAM T. LISTON

John Proctor's Playing in The Crucible

ACT II of Arthur Miller's *The Crucible* begins with John Proctor entering the common room of his house. As we hear his wife Elizabeth offstage singing softly to the children, we see Proctor swing a pot out of the fire, taste its contents, and then season the brew to his liking. A moment later Elizabeth enters, and as they talk of the day's doings, Elizabeth ladles a plate of the stew out to John for his supper. Tasting it, John says, "It's well seasoned." Elizabeth, taking the statement for a compliment to her cooking, replies, "*blushing with pleasure*: 'I took great care'" (pp. 261–62).

This little incident seems almost irrelevant to the main action of the play, and yet it isn't; it establishes something about John Proctor that complements everything else in his character, and no other incident in the play exactly duplicates the point of this incident, at least not so economically. In reading and teaching the play I have wondered what Miller intended by the incident, and in the defaced library copy in front of me I see that someone has penciled in "busy work." I have seen the play three times, all good productions, and in the last production, a college production, the director cut John's seasoning of the stew, though he retained John's complimenting of Elizabeth; the cut suddenly made obvious the point of the little episode. What the incident dramatizes is that John Proctor is a liar (by implication), is playful, is imaginative, is a poet, and, in sum, is a dangerous man

---

From *The Midwest Quarterly* 20:4 (Summer 1979). © 1979 by Pittsburg State University.

in a community such as Salem. In calling Proctor a liar, I do not intend the term pejoratively. I merely wish to point out that when he says that the stew is well seasoned he induces Elizabeth to take the statement as a compliment, though he is not literally complimenting her. He causes, or allows, Elizabeth to believe something that is not literally true. He lies by implication, as he does in the much more serious matter of representing himself as a proper citizen of Salem when he is in reality guilty of lechery.

What is most important about the incident is that it demonstrates Proctor's playfulness and his imagination. Miller, despite his very full stage directions, gives no indication of how this little incident is to be played, but I think that playfulness is its essence, though Elizabeth will not be aware of the playfulness. There is no malice or anything of the sort intended. When, a moment later, John says of another matter "I mean to please you, Elizabeth," we are to understand this statement as applying to all of John's behavior with respect to Elizabeth, including the seasoning incident. From this point on in the play there develops a characteristic in Proctor's speech which sets him off from everyone else in the play—from most of the characters absolutely, from a couple of them only in degree, but in large degree. This characteristic is the ability to think and speak in metaphor: *i.e.*, the ability to think and speak poetically, playfully, imaginatively, non-literally.

For instance, a few minutes after the seasoning incident, Elizabeth suggests that Proctor has not fully forgotten Abigail Williams, and in his anger at the suggestion Proctor retorts: "I have gone tiptoe in this house all seven month since she is gone. I have not moved from there to there without I think to please you, and still an everlasting funeral marches round your heart" (p. 265). No further metaphors appear for some time, but a cluster of them come at the end of the act, and almost all from Proctor. When Elizabeth is summoned to court and Hale assures the Proctors that nothing will happen to her if she is innocent, Proctor retorts with "If *she* is innocent! Why do you never wonder if Parris be innocent, or Abigail? Is the accuser always holy now? Were they born this morning as clean as God's fingers?" (p. 281), and a moment later as Elizabeth is led off, John assures her that "I will fall like an ocean on that court! Fear nothing, Elizabeth" (p. 282). As Reverend Hale leaves, Proctor says, "Though you be ordained in God's own tears, you are a coward now!" (p. 282).

The act closes with Proctor and Mary Warren alone as Proctor plans to save his wife, and his last three speeches are metaphorical. Finding out that Mary Warren knows of his affair with Abigail, Proctor says "Good. Then her saintliness is done with. . . . We will slide together into our pit; you will tell the court what you know." As the fearful Mary protests that she cannot, Proctor continues: "My wife will never die for me! I will bring your guts into your mouth but that goodness will not die for me!" (p. 293). Finally he says "Now Hell and Heaven grapple on our backs, and all our old pretense is ripped away—make your peace! ... . Peace. It is a providence, and no great change; we are only what we always were, but naked now. . . . Aye, naked! And the wind, God's icy wind, will blow!" (p. 284). The only metaphorical word uttered in the scene by anyone other than Proctor is by Elizabeth, who had said earlier that Abigail "must be ripped out of the world!" (p. 281) when she learned that Abigail had charged her with witchcraft. Under severe emotion, people resort to metaphor, but John Proctor more than anyone else.

Act III introduces Deputy Governor Danforth, who turns out to be another user of metaphor. If we are reading carefully we will not be surprised by this ability in Danforth, for Miller tells us as Danforth enters that he is "*of some humor and sophistication*" (p. 286). Nevertheless, we are likely to miss some of his metaphors, because they are frequently conventional. For example, when Proctor asks Danforth to accept Mary Warren's deposition which alleges that the girls of Salem are only pretending to having trafficked in witchcraft, Danforth warns him that "We burn a hot fire here; it melts down all concealment" (p. 289). And a few minutes later Danforth characterizes the times in which the Salemites live:

> But you must understand, sir, that a person is either with this court or he must be counted against it, there be no road between. This is a sharp time, now, a precise time—we live no longer in the dusky afternoon when evil mixed itself with good and befuddled the world. Now, by God's grace, the shining sun is up, and them that fear not light will surely praise it. (p. 293)

Danforth goes on to warn the girls as he is about to begin his investigation: "Children, a very augur bit will now be turned into your souls until your honesty is proved" (p. 299).

Proctor himself resorts to a conventional religious metaphor during the scene when he tries to reassure Mary Warren that she has nothing to fear if she tells the truth. He reminds her of what the angel Raphael said to Tobias, which he had quoted to her earlier—"Do that which is good, and no harm shall come to thee" (p. 293)—and assures her that "there is your rock" (p. 296).

Shortly later, at one of the most emotionally intense moments in the play, the metaphors come in thickly again, almost all from Proctor. As Abigail, to divert the investigation from herself, begins to create hysteria by pretending to be bewitched by Mary Warren, Proctor breaks the tension (and substitutes another one) by crying "Whore! Whore!" and goes on to say,

"Now she'll suck a scream to stab me with" (p. 304). Required to specify the time and place of his adultery with Abigail, Proctor replies "In the proper place—where my beasts are bedded. On the last night of my joy, some eight months past" (p. 304). Now there is nothing really metaphorical about the phrase "on the last night of my joy," and in a sense there is everything metaphorical and poetic about it. No one else in the play could think of such a way to specify a particular date, nor could the average citizen of any age or community. W. H. Auden might think in such phrases, but not a common farmer steeped in the ways of thought of a plain community. The phrase implies the terrible joylessness and emptiness that has come over the Proctors' marriage since that night, due not entirely to Elizabeth's having elicited a confession from John but as much to John Proctor's own realization of his dishonesty and his failure to live up to his own, and the community's, ideals.

Continuing, he calls Abby "a lump of vanity," and charges that "She thinks to dance with me on my wife's grave! And well she might, for I thought of her softly" (p. 305). As Danforth is staggered by the turn events have taken, Proctor tries to convince him of his earnestness by asserting, "I have made a bell of my honor! I have rung the doom of my good name" (p. 305). Believing that this charge against Abigail can best be tested by questioning Elizabeth, Danforth sends for her, declaring, "Now we shall touch the bottom of this swamp" (p. 305). Elizabeth lies to protect her husband, and Abby re-starts the hysteria, eventually breaking the will of Mary Warren until she turns against Proctor and allies herself with Abby and the girls. As the scene closes, Proctor, in despair, cries out that "God is dead!" and then declares:

A fire, a fire is burning! I hear the boot of Lucifer, I see his filthy face! And it is my face, and yours, Danforth! For them that quail to bring men out of ignorance, as I have quailed, and as you quail now when you know in all your black hearts that this be fraud—God damns our kind especially, and we will burn, we will burn together! (p. 311)

This speech has little metaphor in it. What is noteworthy about it is Proctor's insistence that Danforth and he are of the same kind, are despite their opposition similar in the sight of God. They share a face with Lucifer, and are guilty of failing to lead men out of ignorance. Clearly he means that those of superior intellectual abilities have the responsibility to lead others. One method by which Miller has made evident the intellectual and imaginative superiority of Proctor and Danforth is by restricting the use of metaphor almost exclusively to them.

Metaphor is almost absent from Act IV, but it appears in the other major educated character in the play, Reverend Hale. When Danforth challenges Hale, who had quit the court at the end of the preceding act, as to his presence in the prison, Hale answers, "I came to counsel Christians they should belie themselves. . . . There is blood on my head!" (p. 319). This speech hardly seems striking until we consider it in the context of Salem. Hale has answered non-literally, or imaginatively, in two ways, first with irony, and second with metaphor, though it is true that the metaphor is so conventional as to be almost unnoticeable. Turning to Goody Proctor a moment later, he begs her to convince her husband to lie to save his life, and he gives her a short history of his experience in Salem, all in metaphor:

> I came into this village like a bridegroom to his beloved, bearing gifts of high religion; the very crowns of holy law I brought, and what I touched with my bright confidence, it died; and where I turned the eye of my great faith, blood flowed up. (p. 320)

The imagery is conventional Biblical imagery, probably owing something to the Song of Solomon, but despite its conventionality, effective nevertheless.

Proctor has one more metaphorical speech at the end of the play. Tearing up his false confession he declares, "now I do think I see some shred of goodness in John Proctor. Not enough to weave a banner with, but white enough to keep it from such dogs" (p. 328). He then goes off to his death as the play ends.

John Proctor differs from all other characters in *The Crucible* in his linguistic habits, which are, as they are for everyone, a revelation of the real nature of the person. He uses metaphor to a much greater extent than anyone else in the play, and only he of those few people goes outside conventional Biblical metaphor to any great degree, though of course he derives some of his metaphors from that stock also. What this habit reveals is that he has a playful and imaginative mind, the same sort of thing dramatized in the seasoning incident which opens Act II. This playful and imaginative bent is not greatly obvious, but it is there nevertheless, and it is the streak in his character which makes him a revolutionary, a threat to the community. It is worth noting that the word "imagination" never appears in the play (if it did, it would have a pejorative connotation, as it always has in the Bible), and that play, and images, are inherently sinful, as is dramatized in the poppet incident in Act II.

To put all this another way, John Proctor has the essential characteristics of a literary mind. He is capable of imagination and playfulness, and such people are always dangerous and disruptive. Plato would banish the poet from his republic because of his imaginative power to arouse our passions.

The church forced Galileo to retract his revolutionary theory of the revolution of the heavens by merely exploiting his own imagination, as Jacob Bronowski points out: "He was to be shown the instruments of torture as if they were to be used." With Galileo's medical background, "His imagination could do the rest. That was the object of the trial, to show men of imagination that they were not immune from the process of primitive, animal fear that was irreversible" (pp. 214, 216).

Recently, Richard Ohmann has reminded us of the paradoxical nature of the literary profession:

> The literature we are to preserve includes works by Milton, Voltaire, Rousseau, Swift, Goethe, Byron, Blake, Shelley, Carlyle, Shaw, and others of that rebellious ilk. Beyond that, I think it is accurate to say that every good poem, play, or novel, properly read, is revolutionary, in that it strikes through well-grooved habits of seeing and understanding, thus modifying some part of consciousness. Though one force of literature is to affirm the value of tradition and the continuity of culture, another, equally powerful, is to criticize that which is customary and so attack complacency. That second side of literary culture is extremely valuable . . . since it ensures a difficult time for barbarism posing as humanity, for debasement of values, for vapid or devious rhetoric, for hypocrisy in all forms. (pp. 48, 49)

The passage does not seem immediately and exactly relevant to John Proctor and *The Crucible*, but it states in another way what John Proctor is talking about at the end of Act III when he asserts that he and Danforth are similar: himself the apparent revolutionary on the one hand, but with a great awareness of and adherence to the conservative tradition of which he is a part, and Danforth the reactionary on the other hand, who is gifted with intelligence and humor and imagination, but who refuses to give them the freedom necessary for their proper operation.

A glance at *The Republic* suggests one further point to be made. Among the bad effects of poetry is that it encourages us to indulge our feelings at the expense of our reason. Focusing specifically on the dramatic representation of grief, Socrates says:

> Yet in our private griefs we pride ourselves on just the opposite, that is, on our ability to bear them in silence like men, and we regard the behaviour we admired on the stage as womanish. (p. 436)

The fact that Plato uses "womanish" as a pejorative term by which to describe indulgence of the passions recalls an excellent performance of the play in the late summer of 1975 by the Stratford Festival Theatre in which there seemed to be a thread of a women's liberation theme running through the performance. I do not think that either Arthur Miller or John Wood, the director, intended such a theme, but the fact that our consciousness has been alerted to such a theme made it stand out at times in the performance. The play frequently seemed to be concerned with the oppression by males of females and of those males who defend them. John Proctor begins by defending his wife and some other women, for example; and no where does the theme seem more explicit than in Danforth's condemnation of Elizabeth as unnatural because of her refusal to weep for her husband (p. 320).

Broadly speaking, imagination, poetic and creative ability, and other such artistic characteristics are frequently thought to be essentially feminine rather than masculine, and largely because of their passionate and emotional nature, despite great historical evidence that these abilities exist also in men. And Abby, though never granted a metaphor, has great imaginative power, demonstrated by her ability to mesmerize the reasonable men of Massachusetts and break the will of Mary Warren when she claims to see the soul of Mary in a yellow bird up on the rafters. The physical attractiveness of Abby for John Proctor is obvious in the play, but, I think, so is the passionate imagination which finds its outlet in one way in her and in another in Proctor.

The distrust of the imagination and of imaginative literature, and of the people who write it and of those who are its protagonists, is a timeless problem. This distrust eventually closed the theaters in England in 1642, and in the recent past did the same in Greece; it prevented the establishment of a theater in colonial America.

WLLLIAM J. MCGILL JR.

The Crucible of History: Arthur Miller's John Proctor

Commenting on the historical accuracy of his play *The Crucible*, Arthur Miller wrote: "The play is not history in the sense in which the word is used by the academic historian. . . . However, I believe that the reader will discover here the essential nature of one of the strangest and most awful chapters in human history." While admitting that American society in the early 1950s directly affected the shaping of the drama, the playwright, whether from conviction or discretion, has never been specific about *The Crucible's* contemporary relevance. Yet Miller's most vigorous critics, calling his disclaimers about the political purposes of the play cowardly at best, have stressed the play's failure as a political analogy and chided him for fuzzy-minded liberalism. Some critics have regarded his treatment of John Proctor as a serious weakness, but they have not approached this treatment as a historical problem. Miller may have prevented such criticism with his assertion that the characters are historically accurate "except for Proctor and his wife." Contrarily, critics have made much of Miller's alteration of one historical fact (the only one he specifically admits to): the raising of Abigail Williams's age from eleven to seventeen. Nevertheless, his claim to have captured the "essential nature" of the events depends more on his treatment of Proctor than on Abigail's age.

From *The New England Quarterly* 54:2 (June 1981). © 1981 by The New England Quarterly.

Miller maintains that the change in Abigail's age merely intensifies a possibility implicit in the circumstances. To Miller the circumstances which gave dramatic form to the events in Salem Village (modern Danvers) were that "Abigail Williams, the prime mover of the Salem hysteria . . . had . . . been the house servant of the Proctors" and that the court records indicate she was reluctant to implicate John. From these facts he developed the adulterous relationship which has so perturbed the critics. Henry Popkin suggests that the presumption of adultery enables Miller to avoid the "inartistic danger" of making an entirely innocent character suffer; wrongly condemned for witchcraft, Proctor suffers instead for his adultery and ultimately for his hostility to Salem's obsession with sin. David Levin argues that the adultery changes the dynamic of the situation by obscuring the psychological and sociological conditions which made the witchcraft hysteria possible, while Robert Warshow characterizes the relationship between Proctor and Abigail as a retreat into easy theatricality which does not even explain anything in theatrical terms.

We can say two things for Miller's extrapolation. First, it is consonant with the fact that the events of early 1692 began with experiments in the occult among a group of young girls curious about their romantic futures. The girls reportedly danced and practiced "abominations" in the woods; the witchcraft hysteria resulted from the interpretation which adults in the community attached to these activities. Miller's first scene, though it foreshortens the actual time involved, does not violate the sequence or basic scheme of events. In the giddy, unsupervised circle of nubiles, it is not implausible that an Abigail, even if only eleven, could develop a romantic fixation on her employer. Furthermore, the likelihood that such a fixation might have issued in a sexual relationship cannot be dismissed. Miller had to adjust Abigail's age not to create the possibility of such an affair but to make it more acceptable to and thus more dramatically effective for an audience in the 1950s.

This argument, however, omits another fact which Miller freely altered: he describes John Proctor as being in his middle thirties in 1692 when he was actually sixty years old. In his historical note, Miller remarks, "As for the characters of the persons, little is known about most of them. . . . They may therefore be taken as creations of my own, drawn to the best of my ability in conformity with their known behavior, except as indicated in the commentary I have written for this text" (p. 2). But nowhere does Miller acknowledge this drastic alteration of Proctor's age without which the putative affair with Abigail would seem a patent, and dramatically unattractive, fiction. In addition, because Miller's Proctor is a strong, vital man in the prime of life both his confession of witchcraft and the subsequent passion

hysteria, he recognizes that such dimensions did exist and, more importantly, he recognizes, though he does not fully articulate, the complexity of the causal pattern. Because complex patterns of historical causation do not lend themselves to dramatic art, Miller makes no attempt to develop them. What he attempts is to provide a historical example to demonstrate that "the sin of public terror is that it divests man of conscience, of himself."

For all his tampering with events, Miller has captured one of the fundamental realities of the Salem events: that while typical of their times in many ways, they also represented a loss of balance, a breakdown in the conventions which make communal life possible and human life bearable. That Miller means to speak to his own time is self-evident, but it is a falsehood to declare he "has nothing to say about the Salem trials and makes only the flimsiest pretense that he has." John Proctor is not Alger Hiss, Julius Rosenberg, or Owen Lattimore, but the fates of John Proctor, Giles Corey, and Rebecca Nurse do tell us about the dangers of public terror in any age when it overthrows social conventions. Whatever view one takes of the guilt or innocence of those celebrated figures of the Cold War, one must acknowledge that all hysterias produce injustice because hysteria denies the individual conscience and destroys the standards of rational proof. To assert, as some critics have, that no analogy is possible because communists exist and witches do not begs the question. Perceived reality and not scientific truth determines human behavior. Miller knows that and he knows that the people of Salem Village believed in witches as did virtually all of their contemporaries. He also knows that that belief alone did not kill John Proctor and the others, for nowhere else in seventeenth-century America did that belief have such a horrifying sequel. If in his life Miller's Proctor is more fiction than fact, in his death he is all too real.

MICHAEL J. O'NEAL

History, Myth, and Name Magic in
Arthur Miller's The Crucible

In the climactic "jail scene" at the end of Arthur Miller's *The Crucible*, John Proctor, unwilling yet to suffer martyrdom at the hands of the Salem theocracy, confesses falsely to having "bound himself in the service of the Devil." Almost incredibly, though, Judge Danforth lets his prize catch slip away by demanding that Proctor relinquish his signed confession, which is then to be posted on the church door, "for the instruction of the village." Proctor, however, refuses to give up the document, crying out in anguish: "I have confessed myself! Is there no penitence but it be public? God does not need my name nailed upon the church! God sees my name: God knows how black my sins are! It is enough!" (p. 137). Moments before tearing up the document, he continues:

> Because it is my name! Because I cannot have another in my life! Because I lie and sign myself to lies! Because I am not worth the dust on the feet of them that hang! How may I live without my name? I have given you my soul leave me my name! (p. 138)

While Proctor's recantation of his confession heightens tension in the closing moments of the play, Miller's more fundamental dramatic intentions here are not immediately apparent. Proctor has already confessed before a

From *CLIO* 12:2 (Winter 1983). © 1983 by Robert H. Canary and Henry Kozicki.

stage full of townspeople to sins of which he is not guilty—though he alludes to his private feelings of guilt about his relationship with Abigail. In this light, his refusal to give up a confession which he has already signed seems to be an almost gratuitous act of stubbornness, or at best a final gesture that allows Miller to apotheosize him into a martyr. To resolve this problem, commentators have focused on Proctor's concern for the handling of his name, which, they argue, reflects a theme that underlies much of Miller's work—the need for the individual to "confront his essential self, to discover that self in the void between being and seeming." One critic, for example, writes that "[i]n Miller, a man's name is his conscience, his immortal soul," and without that name, nothing is left. Similarly, another sees in *The Crucible* a theme indigenous to twentieth-century literature, the "loss of self in modern society." The final success of Proctor's search for the truth about himself would be suggested by his refusal to surrender his "name," symbolic of that essential self holding out against an authority that would usurp the functions of individual conscience. But while these views are suggestive, they run the risk of turning *The Crucible* into a theme play; they tell us *what* Miller was thinking, but they leave unexamined *how* Miller conceived these ideas in dramatic and historical terms. I would like to take a broader view of the jail scene, and see Proctor's cry for his name as integral not only to the play's theme, but to its dramatic and historical method as well.

Before we can understand the role of "name" in *The Crucible*, we have to come to an understanding of the historical terms in which Miller has conceived the events he has depicted. Herbert Lindenberger has noted that "Historical drama, insofar as it reflects upon and interprets past events, can be considered a branch of historical thought, though one which projects hypotheses and individual theories about history more than it does fully worked out philosophies." If this observation is correct, then Miller's play, as a historical play, embodies at some level a view of history—it images forth, through plot and character, a way of making coherent the manifold events of our culture's past. The view of history that Miller projects in *The Crucible* is what I will call a "vertical" view. To understand what a vertical view of history is, consider first that ordinarily our view of history is a horizontal one; in a phrase such as "the march of history," for example, we regard history as duration, as movement, as irreversible sequence, as progress from point to point toward a destination. The horizontal view seeks in history the antecedent conditions giving rise to any state of affairs under examination. Often, by the way, the events depicted in the play itself are the "antecedent conditions" to the audience's present, the *real* "state of affairs under examination." Miller, in contrast, is less interested in exploring a diachronic sequence of historical facts, all distributed along an axis which points toward the events of the play, than he is in depicting synchronically, or "vertically," a cross-section of history by exposing a recurrent pattern of human behavior independent of pre-existent conditions.

The distinction I am making has been formulated in a useful way by Claude Lévi-Strauss, and is fundamental to structuralist views of culture and history. Seeking to establish the way historians discover patterns in the facts of history, Lévi-Strauss points out what in his view is the inadequacy of a diachronically conceived history:

> Now, thanks to the temporal dimension, history seems to restore to us, not separate states, but the passage from one state to another in a continuous form. And as we believe that we apprehend the trend of our personal history as a continuous change, historical knowledge appears to confirm the evidence of inner sense. History seems to do more than describe beings to us from the outside . . . it appears to re-establish our connection, outside ourselves, with the very essence of change.

But it must be emphasized that history can only "seem" or "appear" to do these things, for each point along the temporal dimension is "inexhaustibly rich" in the physical and mental events that make up the totality of history. Confronted with this chaos, the historian has to make meaning: "Insofar as history aspires to meaning, it is doomed to select regions, periods, groups of men and individuals in these groups to make them stand out, as discontinuous figures, against a continuity . . ." In other words, for Lévi-Strauss the facts of history are not arranged sequentially, like beads on a string; rather, "history is a discontinuous set composed of domains of history." History seeks the recurrences, the autonomous patterns that cut across the data of linearity, and encodes them vertically by regarding the members of historical subsets as coexistent within the historical imagination.

Viewed in these terms, the historical framework for Miller's play is not the sense of crisis in American politics surrounding its appearance in 1953. Rather, the Salem delusion and post-World War II anti-Communist hysteria are both coordinate elements in the same discontinuous historical subset, a subset that would include other historical "facts" as well. So when critics insisted that *The Crucible* was little more than an elaborate gloss on McCarthyism (a "horizontal" view), Miller countered by inducing us to see the play in a vertical or synchronic dimension. He wrote, for example, that "[Danforth's] *function* in the drama . . . is that of the rulebearer, the man who always guards the boundaries which, if you insist on breaking through them, have the power to destroy you. His 'evil' is more than personal, it is nearly mythical." Further, Miller's remarks on the historical underpinnings of the play in the stage directions, with their discussions of the "political inspiration of the Devil," "Dionysiac forces," or the "two diametrically opposed absolutes" our world is "gripped between," make clear that the real historical framework of the play is not to be found in an irreversible sequence of events causally related in time along a diachronic axis. Rather, it is to be found in the superordinate set its events belong to—the apocalyptic conflict between the forces of light and those of darkness. Later, we will see the role that "name" plays in delineating this conflict.

Yet to suggest that the view of history on which *The Crucible* is built is a synchronous one is not to suggest that Proctor is presented *en tableau*, a transcendent representation of Light. Quite the contrary, the play succeeds because it traces a sequence of discernible stages in Proctor's moral development; that is to say, it sees Proctor as an individual constituted along a horizontal axis, a character whose destiny is in part the product of a sequence of determining events. Early in the play, Proctor remains aloof, washing his hands of Salem and the growing panic. As the play progresses, he is forced by circumstances (the jealousy of Abigail, the arrest of his wife, her pious but untimely lie to Danforth denying knowledge of his "lechery" with Abigail) to involve himself in Salem's affairs. This unwilling involvement leads to confrontations with the authorities, the crucible in which he discovers his essential "goodness." A dramatist rather than a theoretician, Miller recognizes an important distinction: that we understand Proctor's story vertically, as part of a set of timeless recurrencies, but that the story of Proctor's growth can be told only horizontally, as a sequence of determining events.

Now within the tight confines of a play, the growth and development of a protagonist has to be seen not in the gradual unfolding of events—the privilege of novelists—but as the product of a rather quickly moving "dialectical ascent through a hierarchy of stages," as Lindenberger describes the process. To give form and direction to this ascent, the dramatist must call on some structural principle, some high-water marks that will distinguish each of its stages. One structural principle at the writer's disposal is the reiteration of key words and phrases that are assigned different meanings for the characters who use them, or that acquire new meanings at different stages of the drama. This principle governs Proctor's cry for his name during the final scene of *The Crucible*, for in this scene, words such as "name" and "signature" are the culmination of repeated references to "name" that, taken together, begin to give form to the historical conflict Proctor is engaged in. "Name," then, is both a structural device in the play and a vehicle for Miller's historical vision. The remarks that follow will suggest how Miller uses "name" to these ends.

To begin, consider that in the closed society of a theocracy, an individual can violate the strong sense of community essential to its "fortress" mentality in two ways. One is to "go out into the forest" to make contact with Satan, unleashing those Dionysiac forces incompatible with the unwavering discipline necessary to a community that regards itself as under seige. This is the way taken by Tituba and "the girls," so that for Hathorne, Danforth, and others, the line of battle in the play runs between Salem and the unregenerate forest beyond its walls. The other way of violating community—Proctor's way, eventually—is to reject the very assumptions on which the community is built by asserting a more enlightened view of social order, one which values the lone voice of skepticism. For the audience, then, the play's battle is among different visions of the individual's place within the larger community. One significance of "name" is that it reflects the assumptions the characters make about their relationship with their community.

On one level, for example, "name" refers simply to something like "reputation." Early in the first act, for instance, Parris quizzes Abigail about her activities in the forest. He asks her, "Your name in the town—it is entirely white, is it not?" She responds, "Why, I am sure it is, sir. There be no blush about my name." Moments later, she insists, "My name is good in the village! I will not have it said my name is soiled!" (pp. 9-10). Other characters feel the same pressure to maintain a good name. One stage direction states that "Thomas Putnam felt that his own name . . . had been smirched by the village" (p. 12). Parris, too, equates name and reputation. In the third act, he says to Danforth, referring to Proctor, "Excellency, since I come to Salem this man is blackening my name" (p. 100). In these and similar instances, "name" refers not to an "essential self"; rather, it suggests that the Puritan authority maintains its ascendancy by enforcing, through the need of its citizens for evidences of God's grace, a social system that admits no diversity of thought or action.

This restricted view of "name" is a yardstick we use to measure Proctor's spiritual growth, for Proctor himself uses "name" in this way until late in the play. After revealing his past dalliance with Abigail, for instance, he responds to the incredulity of Danforth and others with, "A man will not cast away his good name. You surely know that" (p. 105). Later, he says, "I have rung the doom of my good name" (p. 106). When Elizabeth lies to Danforth about her husband's lechery, foiling Proctor's plan to save her, he exclaims, "She only thought to save my name!" (p. 109). Proctor's willingness to "cast away his good name" is again a gesture of submission to the demands that his community makes on him, for even this late in the play, Proctor sees his place in his community in terms similar to Abigail's: the self is measured by its burden of *public* acceptance, of *public* guilt. Proctor's contrivance to save

Elizabeth fails, Miller seems to say, because Proctor must first outgrow the limited view of the self that his community enforces.

The word "name," then, functions as a synecdoche for the tyranny exercised by the community over its members. Yet the term acquires other meanings equally important to our understanding of the play's climax. A person's name also carries power—power, for example, to crush those that oppose one. Danforth, in particular, is fully aware of the power of his "signature." In Act III he says to Francis Nurse, "And do you know that near to four hundred are in the jails . . . and upon my signature? . . . And seventy-two condemned to hang by that signature?" (p. 85). Similarly, Hale says to Danforth, "Excellency, I have signed seventy-two death warrants. . . . I have this morning signed away the soul of Rebecca Nurse, your Honor" (p. 95). Thomas Putnam, Miller notes, reestablishes the efficacy of his "smirched" name by his enthusiastic participation in the delusion, where "his name is . . . often found as a witness corroborating the supernatural testimony" (p. 13). "Name" and "signature," we conclude, are also synecdoches for power in the hands of authority. Miller's insistence on the figure of speech makes clear that the instrument of law itself is of less consequence than the name affixed to it, suggesting that one's name can be invested with efficacy, with force.

In fact, power in the Salem community is derived not from a reasoned ability to promote the common good, but from a force granted to names. And just as a signature is a locus of power over others, so is possession of their names. Instead of giving proof that someone is consorting with the Devil, members of the court merely have to invoke *names*, and once a person's name is mentioned, his guilt is established and his fate is inevitable. In the first act, Parris and Hale press Tituba for the names of the women she has seen in the company of the Devil: "Their names! their names . . . you must give us all their names" (pp. 44–45). Elizabeth speculates on Abigail's motives for dragging her name through the court: "There be a thousand names; why does she call mine? There be a certain danger in calling such a name" (p. 59). Moments later, Hale says to Proctor, "your wife's name is—mentioned in the court" (p. 61). The "crying-out" itself consists of the mere mentioning of names, suggesting the power that control of a name has in a community that takes a view of the world that can be described only as magical.

What I am finally suggesting is that the Salem Miller depicts functions by a kind of "name magic," characteristic of cultures that take a "magical-mythical" view of the world. Only by first understanding the structure of this world view can we grasp fully the historical function of name in this play. One of the best explorations of the nature of mythical consciousness as it attempts to structure the world it perceives is still Ernst Cassirer's

Mythical Thought. Discussing the relationship between signification (such as a name) and reality, Cassirer notes:

> But if we examine myth itself, . . . we see that [the] separation of the ideal from the real, [the] distinction between a world of immediate reality and a world of mediate signification . . . is alien to it. . . . Where we see mere "representation," myth . . . sees real identity. The "image" does not represent the "thing"; it *is* the thing. . . . Consequently, mythical thinking lacks the category of the ideal, and in order to apprehend pure signification it must transpose it into a material substance or being.

"Lacking the category of the ideal," primitive societies are characterized by such activities as fertility rites, where the boundaries between symbol and reality dissolve and where reality is transposed into magical-mythical action. In the play this mode of consciousness is represented in its most recognizable form by Tituba and "the girls" dancing in the forest. The primitive rites they enact are symbolic of more than the "heathenish" element of the forest feared by Danforth and others: they define, in images that we apprehend immediately, a form of consciousness that permeates the *entire* Salem community and that Proctor is impelled to resist.

The magical-mythical world view is manifested most clearly in the repeated use of the word "name" to suggest that one can control another by possessing his name, a belief we have all encountered as children in the story of Rumplestiltskin. Again, Cassirer is instructive:

> Word and name magic are . . . an integral part of the magical world view. But in all this the basic presupposition is that word and name do not merely have a function of describing or portraying but contain within them the object and its real powers. Word and name do not designate and signify, they are and act. In the mere sensuous matter of language, in the mere sound of the human voice, there resides a peculiar power over things. . . . And it is most of all the proper name that is bound by mysterious ties to the individuality of an essence. (*Mythical Thought*, p. 40)

If Cassirer is correct, and if his observations have any bearing on Miller's depiction of the Salem community, then name magic is at the heart of the belief, depicted so pervasively in *The Crucible*, that one enlists in the service of the Devil by signing his name in the Devil's book. In Act I, for instance, Abigail begins her admission of guilt by saying, "I danced with the Devil; I saw him; I wrote in his book" (p. 45). Mary Warren, describing the proceedings of the Court to Proctor, says of one of the accused women, "she sometimes made a compact with Lucifer, and wrote her name in his black book" (p, 54). This motif culminates at the end of the third act; Proctor has persuaded Mary to admit to the court that she and the other girls have been lying, but Abigail, whose strength enables her to bully the others, sets off further panic, causing Mary to turn on Proctor:

> Danforth, *to Mary*: He [Proctor] bid you do the Devil's work?
> Mary Warren, *hysterically, indicating Proctor*: He come at me by
>   night and every day to sign, to sign, to—
> Danforth: Sign what?
> Parris: The Devil's book? He come with a book?
> Mary Warren, *hysterically, pointing at Proctor, fearful of him*: My
>   name, he want my name. . . . He wake me every night, his
>   eyes were like coals and his fingers claw my neck, and I sign,
>   I sign. . . . (p. 114)

The magical-mythical view of the world I have been referring to, which endows names with force in the physical world, emerges in other ways throughout the play. In Act I, for example, we are reminded that one sign of Betty's affliction is that "She cannot bear to hear the Lord's name!" (p. 22; also p. 35). More noteworthy is the motif of the "poppets." Mary Warren gives Elizabeth a poppet of her own making; later, when Abigail has been found stuck with a needle, the poppet is used as evidence against Elizabeth because it too has a needle stuck into it. The poppet, then, is understood to be an image of Abigail. As Cassirer makes clear, an image, as a form of signi-fication, bears the same relationship to the category of the ideal as a name does, a relationship mythical consciousness is not equipped to see:

> And the *image*, like the name, of a person or thing reveals the
> indifference of mythical thinking towards distinctions in the
> "stage of objectivization." For mythical thinking all contents
> crowd together into a single plane of reality; the image like the
> word is endowed with real forces. It not only represents the thing
> for the subjective reflection of a third party, an observer; it is a
> part of its reality and efficacy. (*Mythical Thought*, p. 42)

A mode of perceiving that fails to distinguish object and signification, cause and effect, ground and essence, conditional relationship and spatial contiguity, will regard Elizabeth's poppet as damning evidence indeed, for it represents in the eyes of Salem an illicit show of power. Yet that power issues from the same world view that sanctions name magic in the courts.

As Miller has envisioned them, the people of Salem are enchained by this world view—enchained because it denies them the power to act responsibly. "Once the Devil has gained control over my name," so the thinking goes, "He absolves me from personal responsibility for my actions." And if the Devil has gained control over my name (or my image) because I have been duped by one of his lieutenants, so much the better. For the people of Salem, "real" and "ideal" are indistinguishable, to use Cassirer's terms, for people manifest their potency in precisely the same way that Satan manifests his in the realm of physical being. In contrast stands Proctor, whose critical intelligence tests perceptions against ideal principles, and whose ability to distinguish real and ideal enables him to trace his share in the world's diabolism to a principle—his own failure to live up to his ideals of personal conduct.

Viewed in these terms, the jail scene in Act IV is the capstone not only to the play's theme, but to Miller's dramaturgy and historiography as well, for all of these motifs intersect in Proctor's final cry for his name. On one level, Proctor is still concerned about his name-as-reputation, for as he had said to Putnam in the first act, a person's "name" not "acreage," is what gives him a place in the community. On another level, Proctor instinctively sees that only by refusing to relinquish his name can he thwart Danforth's attempt to possess him. To do otherwise would be to surrender to a governing consciousness.

But on a higher level, it is in Proctor's cry that the clash between the public and the private values depicted in the play reaches its climax. The public side of the play treats the way a closed social system uses sin and guilt to keep individuals pliable, illustrating Karl Popper's assertion that "history," as the term is most widely understood, is really the history of power and power politics. Within this public sphere, there is contained a private story, which treats Proctor's relationships with his wife and Abigail. In the public sphere, Proctor's "guilt" is the consequence of "public sins," sins which in the eyes of the community have opened a crack in the Salem fortress through which the Devil could enter. But in the private sphere, his sin—the sin that paralyzes him throughout much of the play—lies with having violated personal standards of behavior. Far from being box-office sensationalism, the Abigail-Proctor-Elizabeth triangle provides a vehicle for Proctor, finally, to assert the superiority of private ethical judgment in the face of public norms, for it is worth noting that his seduction of a seventeen-year-old, so regrettable to him privately, barely raises an eyebrow among his accusers, yet his inability to recollect the Sixth Commandment renders him suspect.

By exposing the falsity of Salem's public values, Miller has inverted the traditional procedure of historical drama, at least as that tradition has been analyzed by Lindenberger. Discussing the relationship between public and private in historical drama, Lindenberger argues that "despite the surprises to which we are subjected as we reassess the changing frameworks within the play, the direction of growth within historical drama is fairly predictable, for we are made to grow from an adherence to essentially private values toward an acceptance of public ones. The private realm comes to be associated with the disorder which, as we come to see, results from the desire of an individual . . . to exert his will at all costs" (*Historical Drama*, p. 145). Yet as we have seen, public values are advocated by a "rule-bearer" whose mythical power is challenged by a new dispensation. As the audience undergoes a growth in its own consciousness analogous to Proctor's, it comes to feel the anguish of the self-determined individual who imperils a social, political, or economic order not by challenging its authority, but by challenging the conceptual grounds of its authority, by seeing the world in a new way.

On the highest level, Proctor's cry for his name is the last stage in his struggle to distinguish the human personality from the mythically perceived unity surrounding it. The play establishes Salem's inability to separate the particulars of its world from one another, regarding them instead as a unity, as evidences of a primal force. But from our perspective, Tituba's incantations, the Devil's book, Mary's poppet, the "crying out" of names in court, and finally, Proctor's confession signed under pressure take shape as a synchronously conceived backdrop against which Proctor's diachronically conceived moral struggle is played out. Proctor's real offense against the Salem community is that he challenges its picture of reality, which "crowds" the world's contents, tangible and intangible, onto a single "plane of reality." By affirming his name as he does, Proctor affirms his historical separation as an active, self-contained individual, almost in the manner of the protagonists of Greek tragedy. By assigning the contents of his world to places in hierarchies of conditions and by testing perceptions, including perceptions of self, against ideal categories, he elevates himself to the position of ethical agent, conscious of his personality and raised above the substratum of cult and ritual beneath him.

The Crucible holds our attention because it suggests the heavy price to be paid for challenging a mode of consciousness without turning its tragic hero into an abstract symbol. Miller represents Proctor as a simple man, living close to the soil, unable to understand fully the implications of the events that finally destroy him. No allegorical figure of Progress, or Enlightenment, or Empiricism, he is both a product of his community and a rebel from it, a self-determined agent attempting to rescue himself from the prison of others' minds and to hold to the uniqueness of his own principles. In his final speech he sees, in the concrete terms of a simple man, the nature of the struggle he has won: "And there's your first *marvel*, that I can [i.e., tear the confession]. You have made your *magic* now, for now I do think I see some shred of goodness in John Proctor. Not enough to weave a banner with, but white enough to keep it from such dogs" (p. 138, emphasis mine). For Proctor, the only magic is his dawning self-consciousness, his sense of the determinacy of his own personality.

E. MILLER BUDICK

History and Other Spectres in
Arthur Miller's The Crucible

In his *Defense of Historical Literature*, David Levin has argued that Arthur Miller's *The Crucible* fails to achieve artistic profundity because of Miller's inability to project seventeenth-century sensibilities and thus to sympathize with them. The play, in Levin's view, and in the views of many other critics as well, is not seriously historical and, therefore, not seriously literary or political. "Mr. Miller's pedagogical intention," writes Levin, "leads him into historical and, I believe, aesthetic error. . . . Since Mr. Miller calls the play an attack on black-or-white thinking, it is unfortunate that the play itself aligns a group of heroes against a group of villains." Levin concludes his discussion with the observation that "stupid or vicious men's errors can be appalling; but the lesson would be even more appalling if one realized that intelligent men, who tried to be fair and saw the dangers in some of their methods, reached the same conclusions and enforced the same penalties." Miller's *Crucible*, it would seem, fails to reach the social, historical, and (therefore) moral depth of a great work of art, because it cannot imaginatively conjure the world that it pretends to describe.

And yet, as Cushing Strout has pointed out, "Miller has argued for [the] historical truth [of the play], pointed to its contemporary parallels, and defined its transhistorical subject as a social process that includes, but also transcends, the Salem witchcraft trials and the anticommunist investigations

From *Modern Drama* 27:4 (December 1985). © 1985 by the University of Toronto.

of the 1950s." Furthermore, Miller has declared that the Salem witchcraft trials, which form the central action of the drama, were of interest to him long before he confronted McCarthyism and decided to write a play implicating the country's contemporary hysteria. How historically accurate, then, is Miller's play? And what are we to make of its use of historical materials, both past and present?

Though *The Crucible* is, to be sure, unrelenting in its opposition to the authoritarian systems represented by Puritanism and McCarthyism, its use of historical materials and the position on moral tyranny which it thus projects seem to me far more complex than criticism on the play would suggest. For Miller's play is not interested only in proclaiming a moral verdict, either on historical or on contemporary events. It does not want simply to inculcate a moral by analogizing between past experiences, on which we have already reached a consensus, and contemporary problems, from which we may not have the distance to judge. Indeed, as Miller himself has stated, while "life does provide some sound analogies now and again, . . . I don't think they are any good on the stage. Before a play can be 'about' something else, it has to be about itself." Analogizing, then, is not, I think, either the major subject of the play or its major structural device. Rather, *The Crucible* is concerned, as Miller has claimed it is, with clarifying the "tragic process underlying the political manifestation," and, equally important, with describing the role of historical consciousness and memory in understanding and affecting such a process.

History is not simply a device which Miller employs in order to escape the unmediated closeness of contemporary events. Rather, it is a fully developed subject within the play itself. For history is for Miller precisely what enables us to resist the demon of moral absolutism. As Miller himself puts it:

> It was not only the rise of "McCarthyism" that moved me, but something which seemed much more weird and mysterious. It was the fact that a political, objective, knowledgeable campaign from the far Right was capable of creating not only a terror, but a new subjective reality, a veritable mystique which was gradually assuming even a holy resonance. . . . It was as though the whole country had been born anew, without a memory even of certain elemental decencies which a year or two earlier no one would have imagined could be altered, let alone forgotten.

It is this "subjective reality," and the problem of "memory," that are, I believe, at the heart of Miller's play. And for this reason Miller turns to the Puritan Americans for his subject. For the Salem witch trials raised supremely well the same terror of a "subjective reality" metamorphosing into a "holy resonance" and assuming an objective truth. Indeed, in one sense, this is what the controversy of spectre evidence was all about. Furthermore, the re-creating of this "subjective reality" in the equally "subjective reality" of a drama representing both history and literature—themselves two versions of reality created by the human imagination—directly confronts the relationship of the subjective and the objective, and provides a model for mediating between the two, a model which has at its centre the very issue of memory which is also of paramount importance to Miller. Whether by intuition or by intention, "the playwriting part" of Miller digs down to the essential historical issues of the period as the historians themselves have defined them—issues such as spectral evidence, innate depravity, and its paradoxical corollary, visible sanctity—and relates these issues to the problem of human imagination and will.

Like so much historical fiction and drama, *The Crucible* forces a revolution in our perception and definition of reality. It causes what appears to us to be immediate and real—the present—to become dreamlike and subjective, while it enables what we assume to be the less stable aspects of our knowledge—the ghosts of the past—to assume a solidity they do not normally possess. As Miller says of his own relationship to the Salem of his play, "Rebecca, John Proctor, George Jacobs—[these] people [were] more real to me than the living can ever be"; the "only Salem there ever was for me [was] the 1692 Salem." The past for Miller is "real." Conversely, the subject of his play, the guilt which characterizes both Proctor and, by implication, many of the victims of McCarthyism, is an "illusion" which people only mistake for "real." What could be closer to the spirit of the Salem witch trials, in which people mistook illusions of guilt and sinfulness for "real" witches; in which they assumed a necessary correlation between inner goodness and outward manifestations of that grace? Guilt, writes Miller, is the "betrayer, as possibly the most real of our illusions." "Nevertheless," he continues, it is "a quality of mind capable of being overthrown." If Miller's play intends to be revolutionary, it is in terms of this psychological revolution that it expresses itself.

Miller's play, we would all agree, is an argument in favour of moral flexibility. The fundamental flaw in the natures of the Puritan elders and by extension of the McCarthyites, as Miller sees it, is precisely their extreme tendency toward moral absolutism. "You must understand," says Danforth, "that a person is either with this court or he must be counted against it, there be no road between" (p. 293). But Miller is interested, not only in establishing the fact of such absolutism and condemning it, but also in isolating the factors which cause the rigidity which he finds so dangerous. And he is anxious to propose avenues of escape from the power of an over-active, absolutizing moral conscience. As we have seen, critics have objected to Miller's apparently one-sided moralizing in the play. But this moralizing, we must note, is concentrated almost exclusively in the prologue introductions to characters and scenes, and these narrative intrusions into the action of the play may no more represent Miller, the playwright, than Gulliver represents Jonathan Swift or Huck Finn, Mark Twain. Indeed, as other critics have pointed out, the play proper portrays a remarkably well-balanced community of saints and sinners which deserves our full attention and sympathy. Despite the annoying persistence of such unmitigated villainy as that represented by judges Danforth and Hathorne, there is moral education in the course of the drama (in Hale and Parris), while throughout the play such characters as Goody Nurse and Giles Corey represent unabated moral sanity and good will. Furthermore, John Proctor, the opponent of all that seems evil in the play, is not an uncomplicated hero. If we put aside for a moment Proctor's indiscretion with Abigail Williams, which itself has serious social, not to mention ethical, implications, Proctor, who has not taken his sons to be baptized, who does not appear regularly in church (all because of a personal dislike for the appointed representative of the church), and who does not respect Puritan authority even before the abhorrent abuse of power during the trials (cf. pp. 246ff.), does represent, if not an enemy, then at least a potential threat to a community which, Miller is quick to acknowledge, is involved in a life-death struggle to survive (cf. "Overture to Act I," pp. 225–229).

In fact, it is in the ambiguous nature of the play's hero and his relationship to the rest of the community that Miller begins to confront the complexity of the work's major issue. For if the Salem judges suffer from an unabidable moral arrogance, so does John Proctor, and so, for that matter, do many other of the play's characters. *The Crucible* is a play seething with moral judgements on all sides, on the parts of its goodmen (and goodwomen) as well as of its leaders. The courts condemn the "witches," to be sure, and this act is the most flagrant example of over-zealous righteousness in the play. But the Proctors and their friends are also very free in their moral pronouncements (note the otherwise exemplary Rebecca's much resented "*note of moral superiority*" in Act One [p. 253]), as is Miller's own narrator, who, as we have already observed, is totally unselfconscious in his analyses of his Puritan forbears' ethical deficiencies. The point, I think, is that moral arrogance, the tendency to render unyielding judgements, is not confined within the American power structure. It is at the very heart of the American temperament, and therefore it is at the heart of Miller's play as well. For *The Crucible* attempts to isolate the sources of moral arrogance, to determine the psychological and perceptual distortions which it represents, and thus to point the direction to correcting our moral optics.

Obviously John Proctor does not represent the same threat to freedom posed by Danforth and Hathorne. But this may be the point exactly, that Proctor does not possess the power, the authority, which converts stubbornness, arrogance, guilt, and pride into social dangers. We must remember, however, that neither did the Puritans wield such dangerous authority until after they had ascended to power in the new world. The story of Proctor, therefore, may be in part the story of American Puritanism itself, Puritanism which wrestled with its own sense of original sin and damnation, which overcame enemies like the Anglican Church which would judge and persecute it, and which finally fought to establish the pure church, the church of the individual saints, in America. Proctor fails in his struggle against persecution of conscience. The Puritan church succeeded—but only for a time. Indeed, this apparent difference between Proctor and the Puritans serves only to stress how corrupting power can become in the hands of a certain kind of person, the Puritan American who is obsessed by his own guilt and driven by the desire to determine sanctity in himself and in others, and to make it conform to the visible human being.

As Miller himself states, guilt is a major force behind and throughout his drama. The major action of the play revolves, therefore, not around the courts and their oppression of the community (the natural analogue to the McCarthy trials), but rather around the figure of Miller's goodman, John Proctor. Miller's real interest resides neither in the sin of tyranny (the courts) nor in the crime of subversion (Proctor's rebellion from authority), but in the sources of tyranny and rebellion both, and in the metaphysical (or religious) assumptions and psychological pressures which cause individuals to persecute and be persecuted for arbitrarily defined crimes of conscience. The personal history of Proctor is the very best kind of history of the Puritan theocracy, just as the story of the Puritans is the very best kind of history of America itself, for both stories probe to the roots, not only of a community, but of the very mentality which determined that community. It is a most powerful irony of the play that Proctor is victimized and destroyed by the very forces which, despite his apparent opposition, he himself embodies. The witch trials do, as Miller says in his "Echoes Down the Corridor," break "the power of theocracy in Massachusetts" (p. 330). But the seeds of this destruction were less within the chimerical crime of witchcraft than within the rigours of the Puritan definition of sainthood which identified moral goodness with outward manifestations of salvation, a belief which, as we shall see momentarily, characterized "witches" and judges alike. For, as the Puritans themselves came to recognize, the implications of spectre evidence, the realization that the devil could assume the person of a child of light, essentially undermined the Puritans' conviction in visible sanctity and hence in the possibility of a federal community predicated upon such sanctity. If devils could parade as saints, how could one determine who in fact was saved, who damned? The danger which Miller sees for his contemporary American public is not that it will fail to recognize totalitarianism in the Puritans, or even in McCarthy. Totalitarianism is too easy an enemy, as the McCarthy phenomenon itself demonstrates in its hysterical reaction to Communism. The danger is that the Americans will not be able to acknowledge the extent to which tyranny is an almost inevitable consequence of moral pride, and that moral pride is part and parcel of an American way of seeing the world, an aspect of the tendency to externalize spiritual phenomena and claim them as absolute and objective marks of personal or political grace.

The major historical fabrication of the play is, of course, the adulterous relationship between Proctor and Abigail Williams. Many explanations have been offered for this alteration of the historical facts (Miller himself comments on it), but the chief necessity for inventing this adultery is, I think, that it provides precisely that inclination to perceive oneself as sinful, as innately depraved, which characterizes both Proctor and the Puritans, and which therefore delineates that field of ambiguous moral constitution in which both the individual and his community must define and measure moral "goodness." Proctor's adultery with Abigail establishes the hero a fallen man, fallen even before the action of the play begins. This may not be original sin as the Puritans defined it, but it is a sin which is prior and unrelated to the specific sin which the play explores, the covenanting of oneself to the devil, or, to put the problem in the more secular terminology that Miller would probably prefer, to the pursuing of a course of consummate, antisocial evil.

The question being raised in Miller's play is this: on what basis can an individual exonerate himself of evil, knowing that he is indeed sinful and that according to his own beliefs he is damned? To put the question somewhat differently: how can John Proctor or any man believe in his own possible redemption, knowing what he does about the nature of his sexual, sinful soul? Our distance from Proctor's dilemma may enable us to understand levels of complexity which Proctor cannot begin to acknowledge. But this does not alter in the least the conflict which he must resolve. Nor does it protect us from analogous complexities in our own situations which we do not have the distance to recognize. Indeed, as Miller himself argues, "guilt" of the vague variety associated with Proctor, was directly responsible for the "social compliance" which resulted in McCarthy's reign of terror in the 1950s: "Social compliance . . . is the result of the sense of guilt which individuals strive to conceal by complying. . . . It was a guilt, in this historic sense, resulting from their awareness that they were not as Rightist as people were supposed to be." Substituting "righteous" for Rightist, one has a comment equally valid for the Puritans.

Puritan theology, to be sure, had its own sophisticated answers to the question of the sinner's redemption. According to the Puritan church, the crucifixion of Christ represented the final act of reconciliation between man and God after man's disobedience in the garden of Eden had rent their relationship asunder. God in His infinite mercy chose to bestow upon certain individuals his covenant of grace, and thus to bring them, sinful as they might be, back into the congregation of the elect. God's will, in the process of election, was total, free, and inscrutable. Human beings were passive recipients of a gift substantially better than anything they deserved. This theological position is hinted at in the play when Hale pleads with Elizabeth Proctor to extract a confession from her husband:

> It is a mistaken law that leads you to sacrifice. Life, woman, life is God's most precious gift; no principle, however glorious, may justify the taking of it. . . . Quail not before God's judgment in this, for it may well be God damns a liar less than he that throws his life away for pride. (p. 320)

Miller has secularized and diluted Puritan theology in Hale's speech, but the references to "sacrifice," "judgment," and "pride" suggest the outlines of Christian history from the Puritan perspective, and they point to the central fact that divine charity has made human sacrifice unnecessary, even presumptuous, in the light of the divine sacrifice which has already redeemed humankind.

But, as we shall see in a moment, factors other than the covenant of grace had entered into the Puritans' religious views, forcing a conflict already evident in the first generation of New Englanders, and threatening to tear the community apart by 1660, between a strict Calvinism on the one hand and a federal theology on the other. This conflict was essentially a competition between the covenant of grace, which emphasized the charity implicit in Christ's crucifixion, and the covenants of church and state, which were essential to the Puritans' political objectives and which manifested themselves as legal contracts designed to forge an identity between inner grace and outer saintliness. In other words, in demanding outward obedience to the federal form of government which they had conceived for their "city upon a hill," the organizers of the new community of saints had hedged on their Calvinism; they had muted the doctrine of the absoluteness of the covenant of grace, the ineffectiveness of signs to evidence justification, in order to assert the importance of social conformity, of "preparation," and of an external obedience to the covenant, not of grace, but of church and state.

From one point of view, the tragedy of John Proctor, which culminates in his execution for witchcraft, can be seen as stemming from his and his wife's inability to relent in their own moral verdicts, both of themselves and of each other, and to forgive themselves for being human. It originates, in other words, in their failure to understand the concept of divine charity which has effected their salvation and saved them from damnation. "I am a covenanted Christian woman," Elizabeth says of herself (p. 273), but neither she nor John seems to understand what this covenant of grace means. Like the Puritan community of which they are a part, they seem to feel compelled personally to exact from themselves justice and to punish themselves for the sinfulness for which Christ's crucifixion has already atoned.

Not understanding the model of divine charity which determines their sanctity, they and their fellow Puritans are incapable of understanding the concept of charity at all. True, they plead charity. "We must all love each other now," exclaims Mary Warren in Act II (p. 266). "Excellency," pleads Hale, "if you postpone a week and publish to the town that you are striving for their confessions, that speak mercy on your part, not faltering" (p. 318). "You cannot break charity with your minister," Rebecca cautions John (p. 246); "Learn charity, woman," Proctor begs Elizabeth (p. 265); "Charity Proctor, charity" asks Hale (p. 282); "I have broke charity with the woman, I have broke charity with her," says Giles Corey (p. 287). But even as they beg for mercy and sympathy, charity in the largest, most theologically mean- ingful sense of the word, they act in accordance, not with charity, but with that other component of the divine will—justice—which God has specifically chosen not to express by substituting the covenant of grace for His justifiable wrath. Thus, in the name of justice, Parris forces a confession from Abigail, Hale from Tituba; Abigail threatens Betty and the other girls; Proctor (significantly) does not *ask* Mary Warren to tell the truth but demands it of her, and so on. We know we are in terrible trouble when Hale, upon hearing of Rebecca's arrest, pleads with her husband to "rest upon the justice of the court" (p. 277). Justice alone simply will not do. Indeed, when justice forgets charity, it subverts the whole divine scheme of salvation, as the Puritans' theology had itself defined it.

Miller uses the issues of charity and justice both in order to locate the historical controversy which destroyed Salem, Massachusetts, and to develop an argument concerning the relationship between charity and justice as theo- logical concepts, and charity and justice as the major features of human rela- tionships—public and private. These issues, therefore, not only frame the play, but specifically define the relationship between John and Elizabeth Proctor, and they largely determine the course of their tragedy. In John and

Elizabeth's first extended conversation, set in the "court" which is the Proctors' home, a play in miniature is enacted, a dramatic confrontation which explores the same issues of charity and justice portrayed in the play as a whole:

> PROCTOR Woman . . . I'll not have your suspicion any more
> ELIZABETH . . . *I* have no—
> PROCTOR I'll not have it!
> ELIZABETH Then let you not earn it.
> PROCTOR *with a violent undertone* You doubt me yet?
> ELIZABETH *with a smile, to keep her dignity* John, if it were not Abigail that you must go to hurt, would you falter now? I think not. . . .
> PROCTOR *with solemn warning* You will not judge me more, Elizabeth. I have good reason to think before I charge fraud on Abigail, and I will think on it. Let you look to your own improvement before you go to judge your husband any more. . . . Spare me! You forget nothin' and forgive nothin'. Learn charity, woman. I have gone tiptoe in this house all seven month since she is gone. I have not moved from there to there without I think to please you, and still an everlasting funeral marches round your heart. I cannot speak but I am doubted, every moment judged for lies, as though I come into a court when I come into this house! . . . I'll plead my honesty no more. . . . No more! I should have roared you down when first you told me your suspicion. But I wilted, and, like a Christian, I confessed. Confessed! Some dream I had must have mistaken you for God that day. But you're not, you're not, and let you remember it! Let you look sometimes for the goodness in me, and judge me not.
> ELIZABETH I do not judge you. The magistrate sits in your heart that judges you. I never thought you but a good man, John—*with a smile*—only somewhat bewildered.
> PROCTOR *laughing bitterly* Oh, Elizabeth, your justice would freeze beer! *He turns suddenly toward a sound outside. He starts for the door as Mary Warren enters. As soon as he sees her, he goes directly to her and grabs her by her cloak, furious.* How do you go to Salem when I forbid it? do you mock me? *Shaking her.* I'll whip you if you dare leave this house again! (pp. 264–265)

What is important in this scene is not just that Elizabeth's lack of charity toward John leads directly to Proctor's lack of charity both toward Elizabeth

and toward Mary Warren as she enters the house; or that this cycle of anger
and recrimination causes further hostility on the parts of the two women who
hold each other's and John's fate in their hands. (An analogous kind of
reading could be made for John's confrontation with Abigail earlier in the
play, when John not only fails to respond to Abigail's very real and understandable hurt ["Pity me, pity me!", she pleads], but absolutely refuses even
to acknowledge that the affair ever occurred: "PROCTOR Wipe it out of
mind. We never touched, Abby. ABIGAIL Aye, but we did. PROCTOR Aye,
but we did not." [p. 241].) The point is not simply that anger begets anger,
nor that the characters do not trust each other. Rather, the problem is that
the characters have not admitted humankind's very paltry powers of moral
judgement. They have not accepted in their hearts that God alone can render
judgement on humankind. The characters of the play—*all* the characters,
and not just Danforth and Hathorne—have mistaken themselves for God, to
paraphrase Proctor, and this misunderstanding is precisely the problem.
Elizabeth cannot see the "goodness" in John just as she cannot see the "goodness" in herself (and John, later, cannot see the "goodness" in himself),
because what both John and Elizabeth have forgotten is that according to
their own beliefs, the goodness within them is not a natural goodness but the
goodness implanted there by God's grace, despite the fact that they are, to
apply Elizabeth's own words about herself, "so plain" and "so poorly made"
(p. 323). We can expand the argument by pointing out John and Elizabeth's
unwillingness to recognize that goodness is not contingent upon a single
action or even upon a series of actions. Goodness does not depend upon what
the Puritans would call "works." Rather, goodness is an indwelling poten-
tiality—whether innate, for the secularists, or implanted there by God—
which must be nurtured and allowed to express itself. On a larger theological
scale, the fundamental problem for both John and Elizabeth is a lack of faith
in a true sense, a failure to recall their religion telling them that God has
saved them *despite* the fact that they are sinners, and that the means of their
salvation was divine charity itself.

This playing out of the drama's theological issues as a conflict between
a guilty adulterer and his suspicious wife serves supremely well Miller's ultimate object of "examining . . . the conflict between a man's raw deeds and his
conception of himself; the question of whether conscience is in fact an
organic part of the human being, and what happens when it is handed over
not merely to the state or the mores of the time but to one's friend or wife."
The Puritan Proctor could not have provided a fitter subject for the study of
the organicism of conscience, because for the Puritans inner grace and outer
obedience to the "state" and to the "mores of the time" had become hope-
lessly confused. Goodness had lost its theological meaning and degenerated

into a merely human concept. Hence, to the end of the play neither Elizabeth nor John fully understands the meaning of the word "goodness,"
although Hale, again in an abbreviated and somewhat debased form, gives
a basis for the theological definition when he tells us in the fourth act that
"before the laws of God we are as swine" (p. 320). The point is valid,
despite the somewhat crude and objectionable formulation. Yet, even
though in the final act of the play Elizabeth knows that she "cannot judge"
Proctor (p. 322), especially not his goodness, and even though Proctor has
again and again reiterated that he and his goodness cannot be judged either
by Elizabeth or by the courts, Elizabeth does continue to judge him and,
more seriously, he accepts those judgements. Furthermore, John judges
himself, and both John and Elizabeth pronounce these judgements about
John's goodness, not in terms of divine grace or inherent humanness, but in
terms of the kinds of superficial, worldy actions (in this case, silence and
martyrdom) which have caused Elizabeth to misjudge John in the past. "Yet
you've not confessed till now. That speak goodness in you," Elizabeth says to
John as he is deciding whether or not to give a false confession (p. 323); while
John imagines that he himself is capable of estimating his place within the
kingdom of God: "It is a pretense, Elizabeth," he says of his decision to hang
for a crime which he has not committed:

> I cannot mount the gibbet like a saint. It is a fraud. l am not
> that man. . . . My honesty is broke . . . I am no good man.
> Nothing's spoiled by giving them this lie that were not rotten
> long before. . . . Let them that never lied die now to keep their
> souls. It is a pretense for me, a vanity that will not blind God
> nor keep my children out of the wind. . . . (pp. 322–323)

Elizabeth immediately confirms John in his belief that he is his own judge:
"there be no higher judge under Heaven than Proctor is," she exclaims (p.
323) and she recurs to her martyristic definition of goodness: "I never knew
such goodness in the world" (p. 323).

What is wrong with John's decision to confess, as it is presented in the
play, is not only that it is a lie, though this of course is crucial, but more subtly
that it is based on a definition of "saint"-hood which is a heretical offence
against Proctor's own faith, a definition which depends upon setting oneself
up as one's own judge, judging one's works and outer manifestations as
evidences of sanctification or damnation. John confesses, not to his true sin,
but to a sin he did not commit; not to his God, but to a community of men.
In a sense, however, he does commit the sin of demonry when he thus falsely
confesses, for he veritably signs a pact with the devil the moment he chooses

both to lie and to inaugurate himself as his own judge, his own God as it were. We might even say that he has already begun the process of "devil worship" earlier in the play when he cries out in court that "God is dead" (p. 311), or when he damns the Deputy Governor (p. 281); and he extends that position later when he damns the village (p. 327).

But the crisis of faith is further compounded when John refuses to sign the confession and thus assumes a stance of total silence. For Proctor covenants himself with the devil a second time when he refuses to sign, not because he ought to have signed what is a damning and false document, but because his refusal to sign it has more to do with protecting his "good name" than it does with the more noble virtues which the deed pretends to express (pp. 326ff.). It has more to do, in other words, with precisely that same mistaken sense of his own authority and his own ability to project outwardly as a name the inner components of spirit.

The matter of the "good name" is a tricky issue in the play. On the one hand, the "good name" is as important to the playwright as it is to the protagonist. On the other, as again "the playwriting part" of Miller seems eminently aware, attention to one's good name represents an inability to separate inner goodness from outer goodness. In a phrase, the Puritan Proctor has confused "goodness" with a "good name," and this is a confusion, Miller suggests, which we must avoid at all costs. After all, it is also to protect John's good name that Elizabeth perjures herself in court and, in not confessing her real reasons for firing Abigail Williams, effectively ensures John's death ("She only thought to save my name," says John [p. 307]). And we cannot forget Reverend Parris's and Abigail Williams's concern for their good names in Act I (pp. 231ff.; cf. also Parris: "[Proctor] is blackening my name" [p. 300]). Goodness for John and Elizabeth, and for their community, is identical with one's worldly deeds, with one's good name. "Now I do think I see some shred of goodness in John Proctor," says John of his final refusal to confess to witchcraft to which he has no reason to confess (p. 328). He cannot see that his goodness pre-dates this decision, that it was implanted by his God despite his sinfulness.

Proctor's silence, Miller is suggesting, like his desire to confess, does not represent spiritual velour. Indeed, silence itself, rather than representing a virtue, is associated throughout the play with a lack of human feeling and warmth, with a lack of charity, we might say. It is silence, for example, that causes Elizabeth to indict John of continued unfaithfulness in Act II. It is silence which is directly responsible for Abby's not being seen for the whore that she is; silence which finally seals John's doom when Elizabeth refuses to confess the adultery in court; silence which encourages Proctor on his path to martyrdom: "PROCTOR I cannot mount the gibbet like a saint. . . . [ELIZABETH] *is silent*" (p. 322). Furthermore, silence is connected, throughout the play, by both John and Danforth, with a stony coldness. "[Y]our justice would freeze beer!", John says to Elizabeth in the scene I have already quoted (p. 265); "Are you a stone?" Danforth asks her (p. 320); and John's last rebellious advice to Elizabeth is to "show a stony heart and sink them with it, . . ." (p. 328). Giles Corey is pressed to death between stones because of his silence. Coldness and silence, furthermore, are very likely what prompted John's adultery in the first place. "It needs a cold wife to prompt lechery," Elizabeth confesses; "suspicion kissed you when I did. . . . It were a cold house I kept!" (p. 323; cf. Abigail: "she is a cold, sniveling woman." [p. 241]). And coldness, of course, is also associated with the presence of the devil (see Act III, pp. 303ff.). What Miller seems to be getting at is that silence itself may be a kind of presumption, a kind of pride. It may be a way of asserting one's control over events and their meanings by refusing to respond to the humanness of a human situation (note Elizabeth's silent smiles in Act II which are associated with her preserving her dignity). Hence, silence is associated with the condition of a stone, because it denies the importance of human communication. Silence, ultimately, divorces the individual from true repentance and true charity, either to other human beings or, more seriously, to their God.

Miller has created a true dilemma for Proctor, a literally damned-if-you-do, damned-if-you-don't situation. Both Proctor's confession and his silence represent a misunderstanding of the terms of divine grace, a mistaken worldly pride, and a commitment to external signs and symbols. Hence, Proctor's fate is sealed, not by his deeds, but by a mind-set which does not allow him to view himself or his actions charitably and thus truly. But this dilemma exists only because the Puritans, Proctor included, had identified saintedness with external goodness, a good name. Goodness, Miller implies, is a purely spiritual, inward state. It is not subject to the laws and dictates of men. In Miller's view, Senator McCarthy and judges Danforth and Hathorne were not the major enemies of American liberty. Moral absolutism, pride, contempt, and a marked tendency to see outward signs as evidence of inner being—these McCarthy-like, Puritan-like qualities—were the opponents of liberty, and they characterized victim as well as victimizer. The reason that McCarthy and the Puritan judges were able to hold court in America was that the Americans judged themselves as their dictators would judge them. The dilemma of John Proctor, then, was the dilemma of America itself. As Miller put it in his introduction to Proctor: "these people had no ritual for the washing away of sins. It is another trait we inherited from them, and it has helped to discipline us as well as to breed hypocrisy among us" (p. 239). John and Elizabeth Proctor, like many other Puritans, perhaps like many other Americans, assumed a priori that they were sinful and thus worthless. Therefore they misread and misjudged their lives' experiences. They judged themselves guilty and were willing to accept the verdict of guilty by others. Most frightening for the nation, this self-destructive attitude of guilt had become institutionalized in the American theocracy, and when it was given power, these qualities which defined the victim became the instruments which supported and strengthened the oppressor. Neither the Proctors nor the Puritan elders, neither the American public nor the McCarthyites, were willing to recognize that only the moral authority of God or of some code larger than man (a secular equivalent of God) was absolute and binding. They had allowed a concept of visible sanctity to outweigh their commitment to inner grace; they had preferred their federal theology to their Calvinist religion. Miller points to this problem very precisely when he has Proctor naively demand that he be able to "speak" his "heart." Parris retorts "*in a fury* What, are we Quakers? We are not Quakers here yet, Mr. Proctor. And you may tell that to your followers!" (p. 246). Miller here recalls the antinomian crisis in Puritan New England which, like the witchcraft trials, brought to the surface an inherent tension between the Puritans' strict Calvinist faith and their federal theology; the tension between an invisible covenant between man and God, eternal and unbreakable, and a visible covenant, highly perishable, between God and the people's religious and political institutions. Outward forms, names, and institutions had come to be more cherished than the sanctity of an individual soul, even to the Proctors, who perish as a consequence of what must be viewed not only as apostasy but as human hubris.

How are human beings, in Miller's view, to arrive at moral truth? Tom Driver has argued that:

> Miller's strident moralism is a good example of what happens when ideals must be maintained in an atmosphere of humanistic relativism. There being no objective good or evil, and no imperative other than conscience, man himself must be made to bear the full burden of creating his values and living up to them. The immensity of this task is beyond human capacity.

"Strident moralism," however, is just what Miller is attacking in the play; and he does not leave us in an amorphous chaos of "humanistic relativism" with "no imperative other than conscience." For what he discovers in his investigations of history is a moral order larger and more adaptive than any formulation at which a single individual could arrive, an order which is analogous to the Puritan perception of God, and which is defined first and foremost by a recognition of one's own defective moral faculties and therefore of one's utter dependence upon the charity and good will which issue from God (if one is a Puritan) and/or from a similar recognition about themselves on the parts of others (whether one is a Puritan or a twentieth-century American). Morality, Miller suggests, is dependent upon recognizing and accepting our humanness—an acknowledgement which neither Proctor nor Parris nor any of the Puritans is willing to make. After all, the whole hysteria starts because Parris is incapable of dismissing his daughter's and his niece's juvenile midnight escapade for the child's play that it really is. Proctor's crime mirrors the crime of the children; his relentless accusations of himself are a version of Parris's inhuman persecution of the innocents.

According to Miller, our knowledge of morality, our ability to accommodate the imperfect humanness which defines us all, is to a large extent synonymous with our knowledge of history itself. History for Miller is not a judgemental catalogue of instances of human sinfulness. Rather, it is an exploration of the core reasons for human sinfulness—reasons such as guilt, pride, and the desire to render judgement, to see oneself as one of the elect— which allows sympathy for the human dilemma none the less. Miller searches deep into American history, not to discover a convenient analogy to a contemporary problem, but to indicate the importance of registering the relativity and subjectivity of moral justice within the *absolute* moral principles of charity and humility and forgiveness. "It is as impossible," Miller claims:

> for most men to conceive of a morality without sin as of an earth without "sky." Since 1692 a great but superficial change has wiped out God's beard and the Devil's horns, but the world is still gripped between two diametrically opposed absolutes. The concept of unity, in which positive and negative are attributes of the same force, in which good and evil are relative, ever-changing, and always joined to the same phenomenon— such a concept is still reserved to the physical sciences and to the few who have grasped *the history of ideas*. (p. 248, emphasis added)

History, Miller is claiming, can provide both a sense of moral relativity and a set of values which enable us to behave morally within that relativity. This is what "the history of ideas" gives us, historical consciousness and historical knowledge thus becoming necessary prerequisites for moral behaviour. It is not that Miller does not believe in the devil: "Like Reverend Hale and the others on this stage, we conceive the Devil as a necessary part of a respectable cosmology" (p. 248). As he argues in his "Introduction": "I believe . . . that, from whatever cause, a dedication to evil, not mistaking it for good, but knowing it as evil and loving it as evil, is possible in human beings who appear agreeable and normal. I think now that one of the hidden weaknesses of our whole approach to dramatic psychology is our inability to face this fact—to conceive, in effect, of Iago." But this is the point exactly: that for Miller, evil is more primary than the devil who incorporates it. Satan indeed exists, but as an Iago of the self who is self-created. Thus, Miller puts the emphasis of his play on the importance of self-awareness, the recognition of evil within oneself, and the acknowledgement that this evil may be projected onto others through no fault of theirs.

When Proctor instructs Abby to "[w]ipe it out of mind," and when he falsifies history by claiming that "[w]e never touched," he is already making himself ready prey to the devil's wiles, because he is denying, on a conscious level, the original sin and human fallenness—the evil—which are in fact a part of his nature, and for which, subconsciously, he is already punishing himself. He is, in other words, being dishonest with himself, and with Abby, and with Elizabeth as well, as Elizabeth makes clear for us in their long conversation in Act II. When Proctor thus tries to wipe clean the slate of history and thereby denies to his own consciousness the necessary lessons of his own experience, of his own history, he excludes the possibility for integrated consciousness of his goodness as coexistent with his sinfulness, of his salvation despite his evil.

The situation could not be more dangerous. As a consequence of his black-and-white morality, Proctor does not see that the Puritans' crimes against humanity, against himself, constitute versions of his own crimes against himself. He misunderstands his guilt and therefore misadministers his punishment. Proctor suffers from a misconceived sense of self in which he is either wholly saved or wholly damned. Because he fails to read the historical record, either about himself or about his community, he does not understand that humankind has been defined from the beginning of human history, in the Bible itself, by a curious admixture of good and evil, and that humankind misjudges morality when it ignores the morally vague context of human experience. Since Adam's fall, our relationship with the devil has been much closer than any of us would like to admit, and there are none among us who might not be charged, with a certain degree of truthfulness, with covenanting himself to the devil. This state of affairs is indeed why God has bestowed His grace upon mankind, why He has sacrificed His son.

By writing a historical drama, Miller is asking us to turn to the historical record in order to understand the ambiguous and changing nature of morality. He is evoking our sympathies for characters whose world-view and beliefs are totally different from our own, thus enabling us to do precisely what the Puritans themselves were unable to do—to accept the diversity of opinions, the variety of perceptions, the mixture of bad and good which characterize the human community.

Above all, however, Miller is making a statement about the relationship between objective fact and subjective fiction, or rather, about the existence of subjective fiction within objective fact and vice versa. *The Crucible* not only emphasizes the importance of sympathy in human relationships, but explores why sympathy must be a component of those relationships, not only if we are to see morally, but if we are to see at all. For historical fiction has the unique advantage of insisting upon the realness of the world with which it deals fictively while simultaneously acknowledging that the world which it is now representing is a consequence as much of the readers' or viewers' subjective perceptions as of any objective fact or reality. In historical drama, the paradoxical relationship between fancy and fact is even more vivid than in written fiction, for the realness of actors enacting a history which has been fictionalized and put on the stage has, from Shakespeare on, inevitably raised its own theoretical arguments about the world and the play. "No one can really know what their lives were like," Miller begins the play (p. 226). And yet he proceeds to convince us of exactly what their lives were like, as they themselves confronted what was knowable and unknowable, what was fact and fiction, in life itself.

In the case of a historical drama on the Salem witchcraft trials, the historical and literary interest found a coincidence of purpose and meaning that was startling in the extreme. For the issue of the witchcraft trials is precisely the question of the proportion of fiction to fact in our perceptions of the world; and the lesson is what can happen when individuals forget the limits of their own optical and moral senses, and fail to sympathize with fellow citizens suffering from the same impossibility of separating the imaginary from the real. Furthermore, by casting upon his contemporary audience the spectre of Salem, and pretending that Salem is contemporary America, Miller is asking us to recognize the elements of self within our projections of the devil, the subjectivity which ever colours our knowledge of the objective world.

The Crucible, then, by the very procedures which define its dramatic art, enforces upon us a recognition of the difficulty of distinguishing between the subjective and the objective, between the spectre and the witch. Hence, the play invokes our sympathy for the actors of a tragedy who viewed their lives from much the same complicated perspective by which an audience views a play. The play, in other words, imitates the situation of the Puritans, who witnessed their world as the unfolding of a drama in which external events represented internal realities. But whereas the Puritans failed to recognize the fictionality of that dramatic performance in which their lives consisted, Miller's play, as a play, enforces our awareness of the fiction. It insists that life (i.e., history) and literature are both spectres of consciousness, ours or someone else's, projections of the imagination. The Puritans' principal failing, as it emerges in the play, was their inability to accord to each other, even to themselves, the privacy and individuality which are not simply human rights but inherent features of perception itself. By extending our imaginations over centuries of difference, by identifying with the ghosts which are the past and the ghosts in which the past itself believed, we attain to the sympathetic imaginations, the spiritual charity which the Puritans could not achieve.

JUNE SCHLUETER & JAMES K. FLANAGAN

The Crucible

Though *Death of a Salesman* won Miller a second New York Drama Critics'
Circle Award and a first Pulitzer Prize, before turning to his next original
dramatic effort, *The Crucible*, Miller adapted Ibsen's 1882 play, *An Enemy of
the People*. The drama held several understandable attractions for Miller,
whose own work revealed his respect for Ibsen's technique and who, with
Ibsen, saw drama as an agent of social change. In the preface to his adaptation, Miller celebrates Ibsen's "insistence, his utter conviction, that he is
going to say what he has to say, and that the audience, by God, is going to
listen." Miller's characterization of Ibsen not simply as the creator of a drama
of ideas but as one unwilling to silence or even moderate those ideas suggests
the earlier playwright's kinship with his own characters, those who, despite
all odds and despite all urgings, pursue their individual beliefs. The stub-
bornly insistent Dr. Stockmann, who, with Ibsen, holds on to his megaphone
to announce what he believes is right, is recognizable and repeatable in the
Ibsen canon and is, for Miller, a prototype.

Yet Miller's insistent heroes remain curiously separate from Ibsen's,
who uniformly win an audience's respect. Dr. Stockmann is a character
eminently deserving of admiration, a man of strength and a model of one
unwilling to compromise the truth. Miller's heroes share their predecessor's
personal commitment, but, in the case of both Joe Keller and Willy

From *Arthur Miller*. © 1987 by The Ungar Publishing Company.

Loman—and Eddie Carbone as well—the men are personally wrong. An audience sees their actions against a backdrop of a society that will not accommodate a personal morality that differs from its own but sees as well the heroes' egregious faults. Though Miller's heroes and Ibsen's share the same passion in their personal commitments, an audience assessing their moral position in a societal context scorns in Miller what it admires in Ibsen. Dr. Stockmann's life is a sacrifice; Joe's, Willy's, and Eddie's deaths are a waste.

Miller's wish to adapt *An Enemy of the People* may at least be explained in part by his interest in Ibsen's protagonist, who fits the description Robert Brustein offers in *The Theatre of Revolt*: Stockmann is a "fanatical individualist defending the safety of the community," a "defiant aristocrat of the will worrying over the happiness of the average man." Though Ibsen explains this superiority not as an aristocracy of birth or even of the intellect but of character, Miller still excises those lines:

> I have taken as justification for removing those examples which no longer prove the theme—examples I believe Ibsen would have removed were he alive today. . . . In light of genocide, the holocaust that has swept our world on the wings of the black ideology of racism, it is inconceivable that Ibsen would insist today that certain individuals are by breeding, or race, or "innate" qualities superior to others or possessed of the right to dictate to others.

Having deflated Stockmann's propensity for thinking of himself as the *Übermensch*, Miller is left with an ordinary man who makes an extraordinary choice, a hero of the minority, who stands alone as the strongest man in the world without sacrificing his humanity. For Miller, the moderated Dr. Stockmann is a transitional figure between the pathetically committed Joe Keller and Willy Loman and the idealistic John Proctor of *The Crucible*; between two men who clearly are wrong and one who clearly is right; between two men who attempt to exclude themselves from society's harsh judgment and a man whose personal commitment purposes a greater good; between two characters who can generate only pathos and a character who evokes the admiration and elevation of spirit of the tragically heroic common man.

Miller's hero in *The Crucible*, John Proctor, is a self-aware character who struggles to assert his identity and worth as an individual in the context of public terror and finds himself unexpectedly undergoing a hard reassessment of self. Though clearly a respected man in the community, Proctor's moral code derives from his own conscience, not from the Reverend Mr.

Parris's fire-and-brimstone sermons. Proctor will miss attending church when he is angered by the minister's materialism and will plow his field on Sunday when the land needs working. When interrogated by the Reverend Mr. Hale as to his knowledge of the Commandments, he will forget one yet still not consider himself religiously remiss. Ironically, the Commandment that John's wife, Elizabeth, must remind him of is that concerning adultery, which has been his own sin. As the witchcraft trial intensifies, Proctor knows he will have to expose Abigail Williams as a whore in order to undermine the witch namer's credibility, but in doing so he will have to expose himself as well. And, finally, he will have to make the choice that others make with far greater ease: whether to confess himself a witch and be spared or insist on his innocence and be hanged. For Proctor, the ultimate value, a man's own conscience, prevails.

A prototype of Miller's contemporary hero, who is willing to lay down his life if need be to preserve his dignity, Proctor is a man of extraordinary moral courage. By contrast with those who too readily compromise and by parallel with Rebecca Nurse, who refuses to do so, Proctor becomes one of the few who survive the crucible, though he loses his life in doing so. A common man capable of uncommon moral strength, Proctor endorses values his neighbors fearfully deny. Though he softens on the day of his execution, not only confessing to witchcraft but signing a document of confession as well, he will not name names, and, finally, he will not permit the confession to be posted in public. Reneging, he agrees to death to preserve for his sons the honor of his name.

For Proctor, a name is a man's public self; to bring dishonor to his name is to bring social death to himself and his sons. As he fights to preserve the respect for the integrity of the individual, he frequently refers to the symbolic importance of names. In opposing the beginnings of the witch-hunt, he rebukes one of the primary advocates of the investigation, Thomas Putnam, pressuring Parris to follow Putnam's lead: "You cannot command Mr. Parris. We vote by name in this society, not by acreage." When he confesses to lechery, he tells Danforth, "I have made a bell of my honor! I have rung the doom of my good name." To explain why his wife lies to protect him from the guilt of lechery, he explains, "She only thought to save my name!" When he is torn between saving his family by confessing to witchcraft and preserving the integrity of his name, his public self, he is caught in a dilemma. In confessing, he avoids seeing the others who refuse to confess because "they think to go like saints. I like not to spoil their names." In refusing, at first, to sign a written confession to be publicly displayed, he cries out, "I have confessed myself! Is there no good penitence but it be public? God does not need my name nailed upon the church! God sees my name; God knows how black my sins are! It is enough!" Finally, in refusing, he calls out, as Miller's stage direction has it, "with a cry of his whole soul": "Because it is my name! Because I cannot have another in my life! Because I lie and sign myself to lies! Because I am not worth the dust on the feet of them that hang! How may I live without my name? I have given you my soul; leave me my name!"

Others in the community who do not possess the sense of identity one's name provides are persuaded by the court that confession offers the only possibility of redemption. Not only do they admit to trafficking with the devil, but they name others as well. Parris's Barbados slave, Tituba, begins the naming when she herself is questioned and accused. At Mary Putnam's urging, Tituba had gone into the forest with a number of girls and, through her native magic, attempted to conjure Goody Putnam's dead babies, all seven of whom had died at birth. Tituba's imagination becomes especially active when, threatened with hanging, she hears Parris and Hale, the imported authority on demonology, tell her she is an agent of God, who will help in cleansing the village. Her example prompts Abigail to plead for the light of God and to add names to the list Tituba has begun. Parris's daughter, Betty, who has been in a trance—or feigning a trance—since her father came upon the dancing girls in the forest, joins the choral assignation of guilt to the respectable women and men of Salem. The hysterical litany of names that closes the first act and resonates throughout the trial is a terrifying incrimination of the New England theocracy that murdered in the name of God.

Abigail, who had once worked in the home of John and Elizabeth Proctor and to whom Proctor's lust had yielded, becomes the sustaining power behind the continuing obsession with witch-hunting that begins in the spring of 1692 and continues through the summer and the fall. A "strikingly beautiful girl, an orphan, with an endless capacity for dissembling," Abigail originally acts out of self-protection, as so many others in the community will do later. A shrewd opportunist, she turns her own violation of Salem law into an occasion for naming those for whom she has little liking and, in so doing, transforms herself into a local heroine. As a participant in Tituba's forest ceremony, Abigail drank blood, believing the ritual would curse Elizabeth Proctor, who, seven months earlier, suspecting her husband and Abigail, released the girl from their service. It is clear from a private conversation between Abigail and Proctor in act 1 that, though Proctor considers their affair over, Abigail still longs for him.

As Abigail takes center stage in the witchcraft hearings, John understands that she wants to dance with him on his wife's grave and that to do so she will orchestrate the unconscionable finger pointing that condemns to death a congeries of God-fearing citizens and forces innocent women to their knees in confession. Ready to believe Abigail and her teenage followers, the court indicts and summarily tries everyone the girls name, including Proctor's wife. But Elizabeth, whose goodness remains constant, will not confess; she is, ironically, spared death for a year so the unborn child she carries may be born.

Perhaps uncomfortable with his portrayal of Abigail as so unrelenting and unconscionable a young woman, Miller created a curious addition in an alternate version, moderating her vindictiveness, paralleling her commitment with that of the court officials, and alluding to the purgative process of the crucible. In this scene (2.2), which takes place in the forest, Abigail appears as a maddened religious fanatic whose mission is to expose the demons around her. She attributes her vision and zeal to Proctor, to whom she explains:

> Why, you taught me goodness, therefore you are good. It were a fire you walked me through, and all my ignorance was burned away. It were a fire, John, we lay in fire. And from that night no woman dare call me wicked anymore but I knew my answer. I used to weep for my sins when the wind lifted up my skirts; and blushed for shame because some old Rebecca called me loose. And then you burned my ignorance away. As bare as some December tree I saw them all—walking like saints to church, running to feed the sick, and hypocrites in their hearts! And God gave me strength to call them liars, and God made men to listen to me, and by God I will scrub the world clean for love of Him! Oh, John, I will make you such a wife when the world is white again!

John, of course, has no intention in either version of marrying Abigail. When Elizabeth suspected a relationship between her husband and Abigail, he was overwhelmed by guilt and confessed the truth. Though he has had difficulty enduring Elizabeth's continuing judgment and the coldness of personality that existed even before the transgression, John's experiences with Abigail and with the Salem court have only increased his awareness of Elizabeth's goodness. When John humbles himself before the court, confessing to lechery in hopes that Abigail's exposure as a whore will end the readiness to believe her accusations, the court calls the honest Elizabeth from her cell for confirmation of John's claim. But if John was willing to sacrifice himself for his wife, Elizabeth is willing to sacrifice herself for her husband's good name. Publicly lying, she denies that her husband is a lecher.

The abiding goodness and respect that characterizes the relationship between John and Elizabeth expresses itself most forcefully in the final act, when John seeks Elizabeth's counsel. If John confesses, he will be saved; if he does not, he will hang that day. "What would you have me do?" he asks his wife, but she will not judge him: "As you will, I would have it." During the interview, Elizabeth tells her husband of Rebecca Nurse's imminent hanging and Giles Corey's pressing to death with stones, because he would not plead. She admits she wants him living, but she reminds him it is his soul, not hers. And she acknowledges her own sin in not knowing how to "say" her love. John cannot yield to dishonest confession; though it means he will hang, he tears up the document he has signed.

The Crucible is patterned in a detailed and accurate manner upon the historical records of the Salem witchcraft trials of 1692. As a consequence of the fanaticism that characterized those trials, nineteen women and men and two dogs were hanged, one man was pressed to death for refusing to plead, and 150 were imprisoned; they were awaiting trial when a Boston court finally declared the evidence insufficient to warrant the death sentence. Communal participation in the witch-hunts was in response to the testimony of a group of girls and young women, aged nine to twenty, who fainted and cried out in hysteria as they named their prey. In "A Note on the Historical Accuracy of This Play," Miller observes that the fates of the characters in *The Crucible* coincide with those of their historical counterparts. In order to shape the historical material to suit his dramatic purpose, however, he made a number of minor alterations, at times representing several characters as one or two, as with the court officials, Hathorne and Danforth; reducing the number of girls involved in the witch naming; and, to make credible the invented relationship between Abigail Williams and John Proctor, turning a preadolescent girl into a seventeen-year-old.

Miller speaks as well of the historical characters and circumstances in Salem through a lengthy narrative beginning act 1 and through interruptive narrations throughout that act. The historical Parris, a fatherless widower with little understanding of or love for children, "cut a villainous path," apparently the consequence of a persecution complex. Thomas Putnam, son of the richest man in Salem, sought restitution for the village's rejection of his candidate for minister and contested his father's will when it favored his younger brother; Putnam's name appeared on a number of historical documents, characterizing him as an embittered, vindictive man. Francis Nurse was a frequent arbitrator in Salem, a man apparently capable of impartial judgment; he was, however, involved in a land dispute with his neighbors, including Putnam, and in the campaign for the ministerial candidate in opposition to Putnam's. It was Putnam who initiated the document accusing the highly respected Rebecca Nurse, Francis's wife, of witchcraft, and Putnam's young daughter who pointed hysterically and accusingly at the old woman at the hearing. Giles Corey, a man in his eighties at the time of the hearings, was the village misfit; careless of public opinion and casual about religion, he was the first to be suspected when a cow was missing or a fire blazed. And John Proctor, a farmer, was "the kind of man—powerful of body, even-tempered, and not easily led—who cannot refuse support to partisans without drawing their deepest resentment. In Proctor's presence a fool felt his foolishness instantly—and a Proctor is always marked for calumny therefore." But none of the personal animosities and motives of those involved in the purge at Salem seemed to be the concern of the court, which pursued its cause with a dedication and a zeal that repeatedly endorsed Salem's heritage of "self-denial," "purposefulness," "suspicion of all vain pursuits," and "hard-handed justice."

Miller knew his dramatization of the Salem trials portrayed society at its tyrannical worst, polarizing good and evil so that, for his audience, those who opted to save their lives were clearly moral cowards and those who hanged were heroes. Abigail, absent the idealism she expressed in the forest, was unquestionably a fraud, whose missionary zeal, though in tune with the genuine zeal of the court, was unconscionable. And the court's officials as well, guardians of a misguided society's propensity for purity, carried out their grim task with an energy and a dedication that a contemporary audience could only associate with animated evil. Danforth and Hathorne, who presided over the court, and the early Hale possessed and perpetuated a simplistic mentality that functioned in polarities and in the assurance of right.

Though such insistence upon absolute evil diminishes the complexity of moral decision, Miller, in reflecting on *The Crucible*, was sorry he did not emphasize the polarities even more:

> I think now, almost four years after the writing of it, that I was wrong in mitigating the evil of this man [Danforth] and the judges he represents. Instead, I would perfect his evil to its utmost and make an open issue, a thematic consideration of it in the play. I believe now, as I did not conceive then, that there are people dedicated to evil in the world; that without their perverse example we should not know the good. (*CP*, p. 43)

The occasion for Miller's writing of *The Crucible* was clearly the specter of McCarthyism that possessed America at the time. In 1950, Senator Joseph McCarthy of Wisconsin publicly charged that 205 communists had infiltrated the state department. Though he could not name a single card-carrying communist, McCarthy transformed his strident voice into a national mania. Before he was censured in late 1954 by his own Senate colleagues, he had assassinated the characters and ruined the professional lives of a host of Americans, whom he accused of having communist sympathies. The zealous guardian of the public good led a vulnerable country through one of the darkest chapters in its history.

The analogy between the McCarthy communist hunt and the Salem witch-hunt was clearly fundamental to Miller's dramatic strategy. But despite the effectiveness of the strategy—not to mention the artistic courage such a political action endorsed—Eric Bentley saw the analogy as erroneous; writing in 1953, he noted that, unlike witchcraft, "communism is not . . . merely a chimera." Indeed, no one knew this better than Miller, who not only made the same acknowledgment in his narrative in the play but who was himself called before the House Committee on Un-American Activities three years after the opening of *The Crucible*. Facing an investigative process similar to that in Salem, Miller, unlike many of his contemporaries, survived professionally, escaping involvement in the ritualistic terror of exposing names of so-called communist subversives.

In the introduction to *Collected Plays*, Miller observed that the climate in this country immediately preceding McCarthyism was one of a "new religiosity," an "official piety" that created new sins monthly and "above all horrors . . . accepted the notion that conscience was no longer a private matter but one of state administration" (*CP*, p. 40). But his attraction to the Salem witchcraft trials preceded his writing of *The Crucible* by some years. More than the specific, contemporary political madness, Miller saw in the Salem witch-hunts a model of the subtle but devastating usurpation of political purity by the religious mentality. The Salem affair was emblematic of a presiding communal and personal guilt that the hysteria did not create but unleashed. A repressive society, Salem endorsed an austere life of self-denial that was enforced by communally created laws dedicated to preserving order and public authority.

But individual, personal guilt figured strongly in Miller's drama as well. If the historical Salem court ignored personal animosity, Miller's play repeatedly suggests impure motives, creating quarrels between Proctor and Parris over whether the minister's firewood should be included in his salary and between Proctor and Putnam over a piece of land, creating jealousy on the part of Abigail over Elizabeth and suspicion on the part of Elizabeth over her husband and Abigail. Abigail's animosity toward Elizabeth is a clear example of a vindictiveness that Abigail has been unable, for seven months, to express any more effectively than in her response to Parris's early query. There she imputed hatred and bitterness to Abigail, defending her own good name and calling Goody Proctor a "gossiping liar." Through Tituba's confession, Miller more subtly suggests the extent to which repressed desire found a forum in the Salem witchhunts. When forced to admit her relationship with the devil, Tituba immediately charges the devil with discrediting Parris, coaxing her into killing him, just as, the confession implies, Tituba might have liked to have done.

As Miller points out, the witch-hunt was "a long overdue opportunity for everyone so inclined to express publicly his guilt and sins, under the cover of accusations against the victims" (*CP*, p. 229). For those who confessed to trafficking with the devil, the witchcraft hearings provided both an opportunity to articulate guilt in a specific form and a forum for expression. In a society that nurtures through its repressiveness an abiding sense of personal guilt, there is freedom in falling to one's knees and agreeing to the most heinous of sins, face-to-face communion with evil. It is not difficult to imagine members of the Salem community secretly hoping their names would be the next to be called, for in such a climate people not only want others to be guilty, they want their own guilt recognized as well, even as they fear the consequence.

Like Ibsen, Miller has always been interested in the question of guilt; in *All My Sons*, he examined the toxic consequences of hidden culpability on the part of the head of a family. But Joe Keller is guilty of a specific crime of commission; for other Miller characters, including many in *The Crucible*, guilt is a less specific quality of mind. When urged into communal expression by a public forum, such guilt acquires enormous power. Dennis Welland rightly observes that "in the life of a society evil is occasioned less by deliberate villainy than by the abnegation of personal responsibility," by the failure of the individual to assert and define his sense of self-worth. Such guilt, which Miller will repeatedly acknowledge and examine in his subsequent work, greatly inhibits that defense.

ISKA ALTER

Betrayal and Blessedness:
Explorations of Feminine Power in The Crucible,
A View from the Bridge, and After the Fall

It hardly needs to be argued that Arthur Miller is preeminently a play-wright concerned with exploring the dimensions of male authority and defining the constituents of male identity within patriarchal systems of culture: Joe Keller, Willy Loman, John Proctor, Eddie Carbone, Quentin, and the Franz brothers are proof enough. However, the extent to which Miller also possesses a complex vision of female power, albeit one inevitably determined by masculine necessity, has been scarcely recognized. Critics have simplified the position women occupy in Miller's plays at the very least; some ignore the feminine presence entirely because women, as a rule, do not act in that public arena which seems so frequently to regulate Miller's theatrical geography. Of this evasion, the author himself is aware:

> Critics generally see them as far more passive than they are. . . .
> The women characters in my plays are very complex. They've
> been played somewhat sentimentally, but that isn't the way they
> were intended. There is a more sinister side to the women char-
> acters . . . they both receive the benefits of the male's mistakes
> and protect his mistakes in crazy ways: They are forced to do
> that. So the females are victims as well.

From *Feminist Rereadings of Modern American Drama.* © 1989 by Associated University Presses, Inc.

Miller would have us acknowledge that his women are complicitous in sustaining patriarchy; that they are capable of manipulating its ideology to achieve the power they have; and that they can offer a limited, treacherously ambiguous escape from its most oppressive constraints. They are not only the source of betrayal, guilt, and self-destructive fragmentation but are also the genesis of blessedness, sensual liberation, and generativity. Throughout his work, Miller evolves an elaborate palimpsest of feminine authority, derived from presumptive archetypes representing modes of generalized human behavior, social forms enclosing individual action, and psychoanalytic explanations of personal response.

Central to this intricate design of nurture and treason, shaping Miller's view of the female imperium, is the role of the mother, primary author of the fall into consciousness, into knowledge of praise and subversion, of loyalty and rebellion, of desire and guilt: "It was of course the mother . . . actually the concept of her in a most primordial sense that perhaps only the boy-child, half-lover and half-rebel against her domain, really knows in his mythifying blood." The ineluctable doubleness of the maternal poisons the wellspring of male sexuality just as it explodes the family, transforming the ideal of edenic safety into the battleground of conflicting impulses: "The family is, after all, the nursery of all our neuroses, and it is the nursery of our hopes, our capacity to endure suffering."

Carrying into maturity a self divided by these unresolved Oedipal paradoxes, the male, according to Miller, first attempts to heal such divisions through the traditional machinery of duty and responsibility, the invariable agents of a repressive community. But duty and responsibility are finally insufficient to control the demanding contradictory energies released by psychic breakdown. Instead, the instrumentality by which the shattered masculine self can be integrated and made whole is the redemptive, even sanctifying, possibility of female sexuality. Seeking to live authentically, independent of custom and social orthodoxy, the male invests the women of his childhood with extraordinary power rooted in sensual openness and instinctive spontaneity. Yet this liberating desire cannot by its definition be contained within a stable, enduring monogamy; nor can its anarchic immediacy be tempted, postponed, or curbed by normative institutional arrangements. Rather, active feminine sensuality undermines hypocrisy, nullifies convention, and directly challenges the standard definitions of mutuality. Miller describes the frightening revolutionary potential of such expressive eroticism:

> . . . perhaps it was simply that when the sight of her [Marilyn Monroe] made men disloyal and women angry with envy, the ordinary compromises of living seemed to trumpet their fraudulence

and her very body was a white beam of truth. She knew she could roll into a party like a grenade and wreck complacent couples with a smile, and she enjoyed this power, but it also brought back the old sinister news that nothing whatsoever could last.

The mystery of ecstatic unity apparently proclaimed by woman's blessedness dissolves once again into the familiar if dissonant pattern of nurture and treason to be denied or disguised by the claims of ordinary existence.

The increasingly tangled conception of female authority is further complicated by the playwright's insistent identification of the oppositional tensions inherent in the feminine impulse with the origins of his own imaginative and artistic generativity ("The muse has always been a sanctifying woman, God help her"):

> I wanted to stop turning away from the power my work had won for me, and to engorge experience forbidden in a life of disciplined ambition. . . . Cautiously at first, . . . I let the mystery and blessing of womankind break like waves over my head. . . . Fluidity and chance soon poured in to swamp all law, that of the psyche as well as the courts. . . .
>
> the chaos within remained; a youth was rising from a long sleep to claim the feminine blessing that was the spring of his creativity. . . .

But the turbulent contraries of sexual desire—the life force itself, if you will—that Miller finally names as the ultimate source of feminine blessedness and female endowment must be subjugated to the orderliness and predictability of the everyday. The roles of mother, wife, and daughter that patriarchy uses to control woman's rulebreaking threat instead produce the inevitable betrayals and ongoing treacheries that for Miller describe the nature of experience.

From *The Crucible* through *A View from the Bridge* to *After the Fall*, Miller's characters are forced to behave according to the terms dictated by this ambiguous contradictory model of feminine authority, increasingly seen by the dramatist as the inherited condition of human existence. Initially, Miller creates separate characters who seem to embody the self's interior antagonisms: those who betray and those who nurture, while Miller attempts to dispose of the traitors through dramatic action. But the protagonists seem eventually to learn that, to eliminate these externalized combatants, emblems of the unavoidable rifts and cracks of selfhood, is to retreat into murderous innocence. As each play enacts its particular dilemma, the various figures come to recognize to a greater or lesser degree that the divided consciousness—a feminine legacy, as Miller would have it—is the quintessential defining paradox of the individual and as such must be acknowledged and accepted; that blessedness and betrayal emerge from the same psychic matrix; and that betrayal necessarily signifies blessedness because it removes the destructive expectations of deceiving innocence.

I

There is no need to rehearse again the many discussions of the political significance of *The Crucible*. Nor do I wish to deny either its historical importance as a theatrical document bearing witness to the destructive terrors of the nineteen fifties, America's plague years, or its value as a continuing and vital protest against any nation's scoundrel time. I would, however, like to remind the critics that what originally provokes the events of *The Crucible* is not a matter of principle or conscience but rather the experience of sexual desire translated by a repressive patriarchal establishment first into criminal behavior and then into acts of public rebellion. Although an earlier version of the play suggests additional socioeconomic reasons for the communal hostilities driving the prosecutions, and the residue of these explanations remains in its present form, Miller himself attests to the centrality of the sexual, frequently identified with modes of female sensuality, that Puritanism would have equated with demonic agency. Miller reads into Salem's texts presumptive adultery and construes the testimony as an illustration of

> the sexual theme, either open or barely concealed; the Devil himself . . . was almost always a black man in a white community, and of course the initial inflammatory instance that convinced so many that the town was under Luciferian siege was the forced confession of the black slave Tituba. . . . almost all the bewitched women were tempted by a warlock, a male witch. Night was the usual time to be subverted from dutiful Christian behavior, and dozens were in their beds when through window or door, as real as life, a spectral visitor floated in and lay upon them or provoked them to some filthy act like kissing. . . . The relief that came to those who testified was orgasmic; they were actually encouraged in open court to talk about sharing a bed with someone they weren't married to. . . .
>
> Here was guilt, the guilt of illicit sexuality.

To enhance further this interpretation, Miller alerts historical circumstances: for example, he raises the age of Abigail Williams from eleven to seventeen while lowering that of Mary Warren from twenty to seventeen in order to represent emergent desire and to justify susceptibility; he pushes the Putnams into early middle age to place the couple beyond the possibility of reproduction; he omits any mention of Tituba's husband in order to underscore her isolation and to emphasize her sensual particularity.

The design of *The Crucible* attempts to make visible two discrete, self-contained and antagonistic expressions of female power to test their legitimacy as authentic definitions of sexual desire. The externalized contest between the impulse that betrays, embodied in the group of accusers led by Abigail Williams, and the force that nurtures, personified by the figures of Rebecca Nurse and Elizabeth Proctor, shapes the choices made by John Proctor on his road to martyrdom. This schematic moral division is clearly drawn. The young women compelled by the anarchic strength of the erotic destroy the righteous and the dutiful for whom instinct is disciplined or submerged in service to family and community. But as the play unfolds, its melodramatic absolutism collapses under the pressure of Puritan authority suspicious of both views, because any knowledge of desire is potentially a transgression; and the too easily assumed virtue that seemed to inform John Proctor's decisions grows darker, more complex and more difficult.

There is no question that the girls—Betty Parris, Ruth Putnam, Mercy Lewis, Mary Warren, and, most especially, Abigail Williams—are suspect and possibly dangerous. Their sexually charged presence in the forest, the Puritan landscape of nightmare, is an explicit violation of publicly affirmed communal norms as well as private standards of right conduct insisted upon by a male-authorized social order sustained by a patriarchal, woman-fearing theology:

> *Parris.* Now look you, child, your punishment will come in its time. But if you have trafficked with spirits in the forest I must know it now. . . .
> *Abigail.* But we never conjured spirits. . . .
> *Parris.* . . . my own household is discovered to be the very center of some obscene practice. Abominations are done in the forest—
> *Abigail.* It were sport, uncle!
> *Parris.* [*Pointing at Betty.*]. You call this sport?. . . I saw Tituba waving her arms over the fire when I came upon you. Why was she doing that? And I heard a screeching and gibberish coming from her mouth. She was swaying like a dumb beast over that fire!

Abigail. She always sings her Barbados song, and we dance.

Parris. I cannot blink what I saw, Abigail. . . . I saw a dress lying
on the grass.

Abigail. [*Innocently.*]. A dress?

Parris. [*It is very hard to say.*]. Aye, a dress. And I thought I saw—
someone naked running through the trees!

Abigail. [*In terror.*]. No one was naked! You mistake yourself,
uncle!

Parris. [*With anger.*]. I saw it!

Having named desire as unnatural, this repressive culture has
condemned an inherent, normal biological process as aberrant, criminal, or,
worse yet, as profoundly evil, the essential principle of demonic command.
The journey into the woods, undertaken as an attempt to deal with and
manage the consequences of inchoate sexuality, renders these young women
outlaws. Within the dramatic action of the play, the sexually fallen Abigail
particularly represents the release of this insurgent, destabilizing horrific
energy:

Betty. You drank blood, Abby! You didn't tell him that! . . . You
drank a charm to kill John Proctor's wife! You drank a charm
to kill Goody Proctor!

Abigail, smashes her across the face. Shut it! Now shut it! . . . Now
look you. All of you. We danced. And Tituba conjured Ruth
Putnam's dead sisters. And that is all. And mark this. Let either
of you breathe a word, or the edge of a word, about the other
things, and I will come to you in the black of some terrible
night and I will bring a pointy reckoning that will shudder
you. And you know I can do it; I saw Indians smash my dear
parents' heads on the pillow next to mine, and I have seen
reddish work done at night, and I can make you wish you had
never seen the sun go down! (238)

As distrusted adolescents, motherless or poorly mothered, servants, and
female, their status is rendered even more equivocal; so they accuse to maintain a measure of control over their societal identities, their passional selves,
and the structures of Puritan male dominance that determined their place.

To redeem their problematic illegitimacy, the girls first denounce
communal pariahs enacting transgressions that cannot be protected,
contained, or disguised by the institutional machinery governing Salem

society: the black slave Tituba, whose concupiscent Devil "be pleasure man in Barbados" (313); Goody Osburn, sleeping "in ditches, and so very old and poor. . . . beggin' bread and a cup of cider" (267); "*a bundle of rags*"—Sarah Good (312); and Bridget Bishop "that lived three year with Bishop before she married him" (316).

The effects of denunciation are, ironically, empowering for the accusers, as they forge an alternative if troubling center of matriarchal authority. Abigail's sexuality becomes publicly useful and needs no longer to be hidden:

> *Abigail.* . . . She comes to me while I sleep; she's always making me dream corruptions! . . . Sometimes I wake and find myself standing in the open doorway and not a stitch on my body! I always hear her laughing in my sleep. I hear her singing her Barbados songs and tempting me with—(256–57)

while Mary Warren's is curiously revolutionary:

> *Mary Warren, hysterically, pointing at Proctor, fearful of him.* My name, he want my name. "I'll murder you," he says, "if my wife hangs! We must go and overthrow the court," he says! . . . He wake me every night, his eyes were like coals and his fingers claw my neck, and I sign, I sign . . . (310)

Even the condemned are oddly liberated by their indictments, because it allows them to utter possibilities that ordinarily would have been restrained by judgment and discretion:

> *Tituba, suddenly bursting out.* Oh, how many times he bid me kill you, Mr. Parris!
> *Parris.* Kill me!
> *Tituba, in a fury.* He say Mr. Parris must be kill! Mr. Parris no goodly man, Mr. Parris mean man and no gentle man, and he bid me rise out of my bed and cut your throat! *They gasp.* But I tell him "No! I don't hate that man. I don't want kill that man." . . . then he come one stormy night to me, and he say, "Look! I have white people belong to me." (258–59)

Awakened by her illicit relationship with John Proctor to the instinctive, rule-dissolving vitality of desire, Abigail recognizes that the function of piety, responsibility, and duty—the conventions of the respectable—is to deny the amoral authority of nature; that behind all legitimate acts of copulation sanctioned by patriarchy to ensure its continued existence is the same driving, rebellious, potentially threatening sexuality:

> *Abigail, in tears.* I look for John Proctor that took me from my sleep and put knowledge in my heart! I never knew what pretense Salem was, I never knew the lying lessons I was taught by all these Christian women and their covenanted men! And now you bid me tear the light out of my eyes? I will not, I cannot! (241)

Puritanism has transformed this risky sexuality into witchcraft, thereby conceding the danger at the heart of feminine power, and has made putative witches out of the entire community, creating the revolution it had thought to contain.

> *Danforth.* . . . You have heard rebellion spoken in the town?
> *Hale.* Excellency, there are orphans wandering from house to house; abandoned cattle bellow on the highroads, the stink of rotting crops hangs everywhere, and no man knows when the harlots' cry will end his life—and you wonder yet if rebellion's spoke? Better you should marvel how they do not burn your province! (318–19)

By challenging the apparently decent men and women of Salem, the young women, led by the knowing Abigail, act to scourge hypocrisy, punish its practitioners, and exact revenge for their socially determined impotence. Rebecca Nurse, for example, is attacked because she seems able to control and direct nature's fecundity ("You think it God's work you should never lose a child, nor grandchild either" [245]); and Elizabeth Proctor because her righteousness seems an instrument for the denial of her fundamental sensuality. For both women, the condemnation demands a necessary reevaluation of the assumptions that conditioned their lives. Rebecca, who has never known suffering, accepts her pain, therefore granting that she cannot master the ambiguous force of natural energy and welcoming her martyrdom. Elizabeth Proctor confesses her complicity in her husband's downfall. ("I have read my heart this three month, John. . . . I have sins' of my own to count. It needs a cold wife to prompt lechery" [323]). She finds blessing in acknowledging her participation in a series of complex betrayals provoked by erotic uncertainty, and, with curious irony, Elizabeth is permitted to survive her adulterous if heroic husband because of a pregnancy that in the most obvious fashion reaffirms the sexuality she initially has chosen to repudiate.

In a world shattered by the radical effects of the systemic rejection of women's power signified by the repudiation of nature and the resultant criminalizing of desire, John Proctor, the uncertain, divided protagonist, equivocal in his allegiance to Puritan patriarchal rule, has to discover what constitutes right moral action, then choose to act appropriately. To do so, he must not only accept the insurrectionary strength of the sexual impulse, but he also must publicly indicate his responsibility for the disruptive social consequences of delegitimized private behavior (albeit in the same condemnatory rhetoric used by the dominant and dominating culture—the only language he has been given):

> *Proctor.* How do you call Heaven! Whore! Whore! . . .
> *Danforth.* You will prove this! This will not pass!
> *Proctor, trembling, his life collapsing about him.* I have known her, sir. I have known her.
> *Danforth.* You—you are a lecher! . . . In—in what time! In what place?
> *Proctor, his voice about to break, and his shame great.* In the proper place—where my beasts are bedded. On the last night of my joy, some eight months past. She used to serve me in my house, sir. . . . She thinks to dance with me on my wife's grave! And well she might, for I thought of her softly. God help me, I lusted, and there is a promise in such sweat. (304–5)

The respectable citizen has become a malefactor, as proof of personal and communal conscience is seen to reside in the acknowledged inevitability of desire.

Because his wife's confession of instinct denied makes her a culpable third partner in the adultery, he recognizes that goodness is neither absolute, nor unitary, nor prohibited by guilt derived from the violation of culturally determined normative conduct:

> *Elizabeth.* You take my sins upon you, John—
> *Proctor, in agony.* No. I take my own, my own!
> *Elizabeth.* John, I counted myself so plain, so poorly made, no honest love could come to me! Suspicion kissed you when I did; I never knew how I should say my love. It were a cold house I kept! . . . But let none be your judge. There is no higher judge under Heaven than Proctor is! Forgive me, forgive me, John—I never knew such goodness in the world! (323)

Finally, and not without considerable irony, Proctor learns that the price of survival might well betray its worth. He will confess to his own disorderly sins of sexuality, "for sending your spirit out upon Mary Warren" (326); but he refuses to indict the female principle—Goody Nurse, Mary Easty, Martha Corey—at least in its maternal incarnation; nor will he allow his confession to be exploited to justify the validity of their presumptive crimes, "You will not use me! . . . I blacken all of them when this is nailed to the church the very day they hang for silence!" (327). His masculinity, his identity, his name is preserved by his willingness to sustain some vision of female authority.

As John Proctor goes to his martyrdom, the melodramatic structure of *The Crucible* seems to reassert itself although the subtextual content of the play tempers our pleasure at the victory of principle with a curious indeterminacy. After all, notwithstanding the heroic manner of his death, the transgressing adulterous male is punished most severely. The sexually active women remain triumphantly alive: Abigail Williams and Mary Lewis, ironic terrorists of instinct and desire, escape; and honest Elizabeth Proctor, whose one lie, apparently uttered to preserve both her husband's and her own reputations, condemns him, is saved by her pregnancy, surely the most visible sign of the source of female power.

II

If Miller's exploration of the contradictory, male-determined ideology of feminine power in *The Crucible* is dictated by the claims of historical specificity, then *A View from the Bridge*, in both its one-act and two-act versions, attempts to dramatize the tyrannical authority of the primitive formulae of blood and desire identified with the archetypal female imperium hidden in the local and the particular, drawing the Italian community of Red Hook, Brooklyn, back into its tribal past. As Miller describes the genesis of the play:

> You see that story . . . is age-old. I didn't know it when I heard it the first time, but just telling it around a few times to people who lived on the waterfront where I used to live, it was quite obvious that—in its details it was a little different but basically the orphan girl or the niece who is not quite a blood relation living in the house is a stick of dynamite which always ends badly and the betrayal by an individual in a passion—his betrayal of some group is part of it, generally. It had a myth-like resonance for me. I didn't feel I was making anything up, but

rather recording something old and marvellous. . . . Raf Vallone has toured Italy three times with it and especially in the small southern towns the people, he tells me, react to it almost as a rite.

Unlike the articulate self-consciousness of the earlier drama, in which the Puritan "not only felt, but constantly referred his feelings to concepts, to codes and ideas of social and ethical importance," *A View from the Bridge* recovers the inexplicable. Alfieri, the lawyer-narrator who must negotiate among the conflicting demands of the law of matriarchal nature, the rules of the tribe, and the legalisms of civilization, comments on the anarchic force of ancient definitions of the sexual impulse:

> —and yet . . . every few years there is still a case, and as the parties tell me what the trouble is, the flat air in my office suddenly washes in with the green scent of the sea, the dust in this air is blown away and the thought comes that in some Caesar's year, in Calabria perhaps or on the cliff at Syracuse, another lawyer, quite differently dressed, heard the same complaint and sat there as powerless as I, and watched it run its bloody course. (379)

Indeed, it seems as if only the very structure of the work—the balance "between the play's formal, cool classicism and the turmoil of incestuous desire and betrayal within it"—guarded by the interpretive rhetoric of Alfieri can contain the unloosened flood of instinct and passion masquerading as destiny.

The first version of *A View from the Bridge* presents Eddie Carbone's sexual obsession with his niece Catherine as the mythic "awesomeness of a passion which, despite its contradicting the self-interest of the individual it inhabits, despite every kind of warning, despite even its destruction of the moral beliefs of the individual, proceeds to magnify its power over him until it destroys him." The playwright gives his audience as well as his protagonist "an unbreakable series of actions that went to create a closed circle impervious to all interpretation" (47–48). There is no effort to explain Eddie's psychology, nor to offer a contextual justification for his mutinous, life-denying sexuality, nor to provide theatrically for "a conventional investigation in width which would necessarily relax that clear, clean line of his catastrophe." The characters exist "purely in terms of their action . . . because they are a kind of people who, when inactive, have no new significant definition as people."

Notwithstanding the fact that female seductiveness and maternity are essential to enacting Eddie's story, the women are curiously adjunctive participants in the events. Catherine seems almost an arbitrary trigger of desire. The fact that she is Eddie's niece is surely structurally necessary for the tragedy, but Miller concedes only that static necessity. One weakness of this initial version is that Catherine appears too knowing and too aggressive to accept so passive a role as unconscious provocateur. Beatrice, on the other hand, remains unconvincingly naïve as the impotent wife, vaguely disturbed but not allowed by the exigencies of authorial insistence on dramatic inevitability to account for the single-minded trajectory of Eddie's ruin or to intervene in its progress toward devastation. For Miller, the story is Eddie's alone and "to cleave to his story was to cleave to the man."

The two-act revision, or the play as we presently know it, arises from the playwright's recognition that excluding the communal ethos into which Eddie Carbone is bound deprives its protagonist of humanity even as it seems to elevate his presumptive mythic authority:

> The mind of Eddie Carbone is not comprehensible apart from its relation to his neighborhood, his fellow workers, his social situation. His self-esteem depends upon their estimate of him, and his value is created largely by his fidelity to the code of his culture. . . .
>
> In other words, once Eddie had been placed squarely in his social context, among his people, the mythlike feeling of the story emerged of itself, and he could be made more human and less a figure, a force.

Once he re-creates Eddie as less a phenomenon than an individual determined by complex sociocultural ideologies rooted perhaps in the powerful archetypal tensions of an earlier tribal sense of society, Miller also can refashion the presence of the feminine as a significant instrumentality driving the action of the play. He introduces "the autonomous viewpoints of his wife and niece," which are no longer "muted counterpoints to the march of Eddie's career" but have become "involved forces pressing him forward or holding him back and eventually forming, in part, the nature of disaster" (51). More important, however, Miller has reconceived the ways sexuality operates through the characters and events of the play, dramatizing its dangerous unpredictable authority by locating it once again within the oppositional possibilities of the feminine principle. By embodying the insurgent energies of the archetypal matriarchy in Catherine's destructive innocence and B.'s knowing maternity, he has restored the disruptive centrality of female power to the mythic design elaborated in *A View from the Bridge*.

Granted innocence, Catherine's erotic vitality becomes an unconscious element of character. In this play, however, such innocence is costly. Because Miller defines this sensuality as inherent, an innate component of female selfhood, and therefore beyond awareness, Catherine is freed not only from responsibility for its consequences but also from its guilts. That such a formula can be neither satisfactory nor persuasive is clear enough if we are meant to accept B.'s later attempt to impose collective accountability:

> *Catherine.* . . . In the garbage he belongs! . . .
> *Beatrice.* . . . *To Catherine.* Then we all belong in the garbage.
> You, and me too. . . . Whatever happened we all done it, and
> don't you ever forget it, Catherine. (436)

Although she is seventeen (the same age of sexual maturity as those troublesome young women of Salem), she remains "Baby," "Katie baby," or "kid" to both Beatrice and Eddie—notwithstanding B.'s increasing discomfort with and Eddie's urgent, compulsive insistence on such a characterization. This process of infantilization, surely a method for defusing and inhibiting Catherine's emergent sexuality, is strengthened by Eddie's frequent recourse to the word *madonna* to describe her conditional naiveté ("With your hair that way you look like a madonna, you know that? You're the madonna type. . . . You wanna go to work, heh, Madonna?" [386]), which finally controls her eroticism by recasting it in suppressive religious terms.

Because her childlikeness has been encouraged, particularly by Eddie's fearful needs, she seems unable to recognize the seductive subtext of her gestural affection that confuses the actions of daughter, wife, and lover, although Eddie certainly can define its absence when those gestures are transferred to Rodolpho:

> *Catherine.* You like sugar?
> *Rodolpho.* Sugar? Yes! I like sugar very much!
> *Eddie is downstage, watching as she pours a spoonful of sugar into his
> cup, his face puffed with trouble.* . . . (397)

Ironically named "the blessed one," given the treacherous wisdom she imparts to her niece, only Beatrice, whose awareness has been sharpened by sexual experience and sexual deprivation, can begin the necessary explanations to Catherine of the explosive archetypal power she contains:

> *Beatrice.* . . . you gotta be your own self more. You still think
> you're a little girl, honey. . . .

Catherine. Yeah, but how am I going to do that? He thinks I'm a
baby.

Beatrice. Because *you* think you're a baby. I told you fifty times
already, you can't act the way you act. You still walk around in
front of him in your slip—

Catherine. Well I forgot.

Beatrice. Well you can't do it. Or like you sit on the edge of the
bathtub talkie' to him when he's shavin' in his underwear. . . .
if you act like a baby and he be treatin' you like a baby. Like
when he comes home sometimes you throw yourself at him
like when you was twelve years old.

Catherine. Well I like to see him and I'm happy so I—

Beatrice. Look, I'm not tellin' you what to do honey, but—

Catherine. No, you could tell me, B.! Gee, I'm all mixed up. See,
I—He looks so sad now and it hurts me.

Beatrice. Well look Katie, if it's goin' to hurt you so much you're
gonna end up an old maid here. . . . I'm tellin' you, I'm not
makin' a joke. I tried to tell you a couple of times in the last
year or so. That's why I was so happy you were going to go out
and get work, you wouldn't be here so much, you'd be a little
more independent. I mean it. It's wonderful for a whole family
to love each other, but you're a grown woman and you're in
the same house with a grown man. So you'll act different now,
heh? . . . Because it ain't only up to him, Katie, you understand? (405)

Catherine's awakening to the treasonous demands of desire continues
when her own passions become conscious and explicit, aroused by a
presumptively acceptable male and sanctioned by those conventions that
exist to domesticate the unruly impulses of sexuality. This instinctual release
allows her to voice the troublesome ambiguities embedded in her relationship with Eddie, using language that emphasizes the equivocal by blurring
once again the distinctions among mother, wife, and lover:

Catherine. . . . I've been here all my life. . . . Every day I saw him
when he left in the morning and when he came home at night.
You think it's so easy to turn around and say to a man he's
nothin' to you no more? . . . I'm not a baby, I know a lot more
than people think I know. . . . I can tell a block away when he's
blue in his mind and just wants to talk to somebody quiet and
nice. . . . I can tell when he's hungry or wants a beer before he

even says anything. I know when his feet hurt him, I mean I know him and now I'm supposed to turn around and make a stranger out of him? I don't know why I have to do that, I mean.

Rodolpho. Catherine. If I take in my hands a little bird. And she grows and wishes to fly. But I will not let her out of my hands because I love her so much, is that right for me to do? I don't say you must hate him; but anyway you must go, mustn't you? (420–21)

However, as the rhetoric of Catherine's speeches of discovery indicate, she does not resolve these tensions until her uncle's incestuous betrayal and homoerotic fixation collapse the normative categories of gender behavior and familial order. Yet her resolution does little to change the determined course of action. Because as a woman she simply is a figuration of the erotic, her influence operates independently of personal choice, so that she can neither alter nor regulate Eddie's obsessional responses; and the arc of his fate impelled by the frightening ineluctable power of female sexuality drives Eddie Carbone to his death.

If the adolescent Catherine embodies the innocence that unwittingly kills, then the mature Beatrice is a version of the archetypal mother, the Great Goddess who knows, and perhaps is, the darkness as well as the redemptive light, the source of Miller's belief in the inevitability of both betrayal and blessedness.

Because her knowledge encompasses the disorderly contradictions that fuel sexual desire, and she understands their threatening power, Beatrice attempts to manage these rebellious forces as they emerge and enclose the knotted relationships among niece, husband, and immigrant cousins. That she fails is not from want of recognizing that she cannot succeed: not only is she aware of the autonomous warrant of the erotic, but she also realizes that as a woman she is an inevitable circumstantial source of the oppositional energies that generate the tragic action.

Beatrice's maternity dictates that she warn Catherine of the dangerous consequences of her childishness, although she knows that her criticism might be stained by sexual jealousy, the result of the niece's unconscious erotic empowerment:

Beatrice . . . She reaches over to Catherine's hand; with a strained smile. You think I'm jealous of you, honey?
Catherine. No! It's the first I thought of it.
Beatrice, with a quiet sad laugh. Well, you should have thought of it before . . . but I'm not. (406)

She seeks to alleviate the problem of Eddie's physical withdrawal by confronting it:

> *Beatrice.* When am I gonna be a wife again, Eddie?
> *Eddie.* I ain't been feelin' good. They bother me since they came.
> *Beatrice.* It's almost three months you don't feel good: they're only here a couple of weeks. It's three months, Eddie
> *Eddie.* I don't know, B. I don't want to talk about it.
> *Beatrice.* What's the matter, Eddie, you don't like me, heh?
> *Eddie.* What do you mean, I don't like you? I said I don't feel good, that's all.
> *Beatrice.* Well, tell me, am I doing something wrong? Talk to me.
> *Eddie—Pause. He can't speak, then.* I can't. I can't think about it.
> *Beatrice.* Well tell me what—
> *Eddie.* I got nothin' to say about it! (399)

Yet her barely suppressed anger at the loss of sexual recognition undercuts her genuine concern and makes the confrontation ironic just as it intensifies Eddie's inner divisions, forces him into silence, and further dissolves his public and private allegiances.

Beatrice seems to accept the structure of traditional marriage that denies the sexual source of female power, but to Eddie her acceptance becomes frighteningly provisional as each independently asserted opinion or speech of dissatisfaction is interpreted as a direct challenge to the increasingly unstable determinants of patriarchal authority and male identity:

> *Eddie.* You used to be different, Beatrice. You had a whole different way.
> *Beatrice.* I'm no different.
> *Eddie.* You didn't used to jump me all the time about everything. The last year or two I come in the house I don't know what's gonna hit me. It's a shootin' gallery in here and I'm the pigeon.
> *Beatrice.* Okay, okay.
> *Eddie.* Don't tell me okay, okay, I'm tellin' you the truth. A wife is supposed to believe the husband. (426–27)

As John Proctor's case indicated, and as *A View from the Bridge* verifies in representing the trajectory of Eddie Carbone's destruction, it is the male and the male principle that is defeated by this inexplicable, revolutionary surge of desire generated by female presence. Eddie, "as good a man as he had to be in a life that was hard and even" (390), has lived within the unequivocal categories, the clear definitions, and the precisely conceived roles imposed by patriarchy. He knows what it means to be a wife, an uncle/father, and a man. But when "passion . . . moved into his body, like a stranger" (406), the carefully contrived design that controlled his knowledge and ruled his experience unravels. The more powerful and destabilizing his desire becomes, however, the more urgently Eddie needs to maintain the governing distinctions of his life; and the more he is driven to maintain those distinctions, the less he is able to do so.

The wifely B. is re-created as the shrewish Beatrice, whose fearful truths must be denied at all cost:

> *Beatrice.* . . . What's gonna mean somethin'? Eddie, listen to me. Who could give you your name? . . . if Marco'll kiss your hand outside, if he goes on his knees, what is he got to give you? That's not what you want.
> *Eddie.* Don't bother me!
> *Beatrice.* You want somethin' else, Eddie, and you can never have her! . . .
> *Eddie, shocked, horrified, his fists clenching.* Beatrice! . . .
> *Beatrice, crying out weeping.* The truth is not as bad as blood, Eddie! I'm tellin' you the truth—tell her good-by forever!
> *Eddie, crying out in agony.* That's what you think of me—that I would have such a thoughts? *His fists clench his head as though it will burst.* (437–38)

Any recognition of Catherine's adulthood must be dismissed, just as any admission of her active sexuality, symbolized by her wedding, must be repudiated. Rodolpho's masculinity—his blond hair (ironically ascribed to the sexual consequences of the Danish invasion of Sicily), tenor voice, ability to cook and sew, inadequacy as a boxer—must be established as signifiers of homosexuality ("If I tell you that guy ain't right don't tell me he is right" [427]) to reduce his desirability. But such a metamorphosis is dangerous, because it not only sustains Eddie's sense of maleness but also undermines it: if Rodolpho is feminized and still arouses Catherine, then Eddie's potency is rendered problematic. Having subverted personal relationships and disrupted familial order, this incomprehensible, rule-breaking desire finally compels Eddie to a last, self-destructive act of communal betrayal.

Although the concluding moments of the play offer an image of reconciliation or blessedness,

> *Eddie.* Then why—Oh, B.!

> *Beatrice.* Yes, yes!
> *Eddie.* My B.!
> *He dies in her arms, and Beatrice covers him with her body.* (439),

it cannot annul or replace the betrayals that are the consequence of the insurrectionary struggle inherent in the feminine archetype that has doomed Eddie Carbone.

A View from the Bridge, like *The Crucible*, ends with a singleminded absoluteness that disguises a certain discomfort with the subtext of the play's resolution. But if *The Crucible* depends on the consciousness of its characters and culture for its impact, then *A View from the Bridge* dramatizes a story that is contingent on lack of awareness and helplessness. Indeed, Miller insists, through the language and structure of the play, that Eddie is overtaken by a force he neither understands nor controls; that Catherine cannot be held responsible for an erotic power that is inherent in her identity and is, undoubtedly, a defining condition of femaleness itself; and that Beatrice sees and understands but is unable to intervene in halting the course of events. Yet Beatrice asserts that all are culpable for creating the situation of Eddie's betrayal. That collective guilt is an inappropriate response when there is no consciousness or responsibility, and no control may account for the residual ambiguities that remain embedded in the mythic conventions of *A View from the Bridge*. It is also the crucial issue that greatly disturbs the action of *After the Fall*.

III

Unlike the necessary historicism of *The Crucible* and the tribal ethnicity of *A View from the Bridge* as those forces shape the ambiguous dramatic representations of matriarchal power and female desire, *After the Fall* relies on the causative particularity of the autobiographical. In this play, Quentin's problematic litany attempts to understand and perhaps to control the agents of destructive innocence, inevitable betrayal, and the tentative possibilities of reconciliatory blessedness issuing from the various modalities of feminine authority. Although Miller seems more conscious of the governing archetypes that embody the rule-annihilating impulses of the female imperium and uses these mythic patterns as the structural determinants of the protagonist's confessional fable, *After the Fall* remains a troubled and troublesome depiction of woman's equivocal dominion despite the playwright's increased awareness and qualified optimism.

Throughout *After the Fall*, Quentin's voice, often synonymous with patriarchal convention, establishes the linguistic terms and the behavioral signs describing feminine power and defining its limits as he denounces the genre-fixed categories he has created for the cultural disruption and personal disintegration that fuel such action as the play contrives. Miller's knowing use of the self-exposing monologue organizes Quentin's responses to the demanding complexity of feminine force as enacted by the three women (and their acolytes) who have made, shattered, and recorded his existence: Mother, defined by primary function rather than by individuating name; Maggie, the erotic signifier and the sexually signified; and Holga, balanced and integrated, the completed female self. These women are not only distinct, potentially oppositional figurations of patriarchy's need for and belief in a concept of unitary femaleness that embraces, contains, and disciplines the insurrectionary energies of contradiction. They also are enabling representatives of the quintessential dualism of matriarchal nurture and subversion that support the instruments of communal repression and equate acts of private culpability and shame with forms of public treason, transforming murderous thoughts into an ideology of collected guilt, that final ironic evasion of responsibility.

Echoing the male-generated vocabulary of psychoanalysis, laden with blame and desire, *After the Fall* offers a clear paradigm of emasculating maternal sovereignty in addition to presenting the most obvious statement of the disruptive Oedipal tensions that had been a covert source of the confrontational theatrical strength in the earlier plays:

> *Quentin.* . . . Why is the world so treacherous? Shall we lay it all to mothers? You understand? The sickness is much larger than my skull; aren't there mothers who keep dissatisfaction hidden to the grave, and do not split the faith of sons until they go in guilt for what they did not do?

Quentin's mother is the primary maternal actor in the mythic Oedipal drama that, in part, determines the action of *After the Fall*. In his reconstructive memory, "so many of my thoughts of her degenerate into some crime" (212), usually murder, including an imagined matricide that erupts into Quentin's violent attempt to kill Maggie's imprisoning hold over him. Mother almost always appears in conjunction with the re-emergence from darkness of the concentration camp tower, the play's most emphatic symbol of human complicity and historic evil. However, because we know within moments that she has died months before her son's testimony, we are necessarily conscious that her residual influence will be enclosed and diminished. Indeed, just as we learn early in the play of Mother's death, in the same way we also discover Maggie's end and Quentin's decision regarding Holga. There is no question that possessing such information reduces significantly the anguished seriousness of Quentin's complaint and minimizes the conflicts that explode *The Crucible* and *A View from the Bridge*. This method of decreasing the play's emotional intensity functions as the technical means of superintending the insurgent claims of the feminine will that would annul social order and dissolve individual repression.

Within the limits constituted by the dramatic machinery, the playwright restricts further the matriarchal warrant by contriving a representative of matriarchal tyranny that we must condemn. She is conceded to be a figure of betrayal even before she actively enters Quentin's edgy recollections when her death is perceived as the abandonment of a hospitalized and needy husband infantilized over the years by a wife who has maintained her embittering ascendancy by re-establishing and exploiting modes of childhood dependence:

> *Dan.* . . . How can we walk in and say, "Your wife is dead?" It's like sawing off his arm. . . . Kid, the woman was his right hand. Without her he was never very much, you know. He'll fall apart. (133)

The initial paternal response to the news—"*Father's hand grips his abdomen as though he were stabbed*" (135)—is a reactive gesture to deliberately inflicted pain repeating the physical sign—"*as though stabbed*" (146)—that marked his reply to the first act of traumatic maternal disloyalty that Quentin witnesses. But although we observe the lingering authority of the matriarchal agent, it is presented again in circumscribed fashion. Quentin's father not only survives the presumed devastation of his wife's death, he is allowed the limited triumph of delayed adulthood as he participates for the first time in the traditionally public world of masculine power.

> *Quentin.* . . . Still, a couple of months later he bothered to register and vote. . . . Well, I mean . . . it didn't kill him either, with all his tears. (136)

Quentin is also granted a qualified victory during this early episode because he, not his brother Dan, becomes the advocate (albeit an ambivalent one) for the certainty, even the inevitability of paternal strength. Only after we have seen the scope of maternal jurisdiction contained are we finally permitted to view the extent of her manipulations and to know the weight of her control.

Although Mother surely has been victimized by male-derived systems of culture,

> *Mother.* . . . God, I'll never forget it, valedictorian of the class with a scholarship to Hunter in my hand—*A blackness flows into her soul*—and I come home, and Grandpa says, "You're getting married!" It had never come into my mind! I was like . . . like with small wings, just getting ready to fly; I slept all year with the catalogue under my pillow. To learn, to learn everything! (144–45),

such knowledge offers no reason for sympathy because she ultimately achieves her problematic empowerment through the psychic mutilation of others. She becomes adept at using the patriarchal gender system and the roles assigned within it to subvert their legitimacy. She humiliates the father, undermines the family, and makes Quentin a guilty, resentful accomplice in the process of destabilization.

Mother first appears in a complex re-enactment in which sexual awareness, the failure of capitalism, and the privileging of literacy are knotted together as the contradictory Oedipal sources of wisdom, danger, and complicity. As Quentin remembers, we watch as he is transformed into a reluctant maternal partisan and an unwilling paternal competitor through a manipulative account of his mother's life that both elevates and diminishes his father's potency. Although he is sexually desirable and financially successful—a paradigmatic figure to imitate and envy—he is also illiterate, an emasculating legacy of another mother's betrayal, unlike his son who is learning the empowering force of language at his mother's insistence:

> *Mother.* . . . Why don't you practice your penmanship . . . ? You write like a monkey, darling.

> *   *   *   *

> *Mother.* . . . *With a strange and deep fear*: Please, darling, I want you to *draw* the letters, that scribbling is ugly, dear. . . . (143, 144)

Throughout this play, the ownership of the words, identified with matriarchal supremacy, renders Quentin an accessory, a guilty and shamed parricide:

> *Mother.* . . . And two weeks after the wedding, Papa hands me the menu. To *read*!

Quentin. Huh! Yes! And to a little boy . . . who knows how to
   read; a powerful reader, that little boy!
Mother. I want your handwriting beautiful, darling; I want you to
   be . . .
Quentin. . . . an accomplice! (157)

The remaining action of the episode, noted by Quentin through "*a
sharp shaft of light*" suggesting a slightly open door, reinforces his divided and
warring allegiances as his father is stripped of his wealth by the Depression
and his sexual presence ("*Father is gradually losing his stance, his grandeur. . . .
He sits, closing his eyes, his neck bent*" [146–47]) by his wife's harsh words. All
that is left is the defeated illiterate, vanquished by an embittered woman for
whom the patriarchal contract has collapsed:

   Mother. . . . *Breaks off; open horror on her face and now a growing
   contempt.* You mean you saw everything going down and you
   throw good money after bad? Are you some kind of moron?
   . . . I should have run the day I met you! . . . I should have
   done what my sisters did, tell my parents to go to hell and
   thought of myself for once! I should have run for my life! . . . I
   ought to get a divorce! . . . But your last dollar? *Bending over, into
   his face*: You are an idiot! (146–47)

It is this term *idiot* that resonates during *After the Fall* as an incantatory
summons invoking the mutinous anger of feminine rebellion until Holga's
visionary balance reconstructs its meaning to signify an acceptance of the
human condition.

   Each additional appearance of Mother emerging from the overdetermined associations that drive Quentin's memory is not only a recapitulation
of maternal seduction, betrayal, or abandonment but also an uncomfortable
reminder of the ongoing authority of the female imperium. Such moments
of matriarchal assertion further widen the cracks and fissures within his
oppositional consciousness. He becomes increasingly unable to control the
murderous impulses embedded in his unresolved Oedipal dilemma until he
is forced to enact them and recognize their residual strength before he can
acknowledge that all we possess is after the Fall.

   Even the other votaries of matriarchy such as Elsie and Louise in
their collateral roles as wives practice the treacheries of female seduction
and disloyalty, reproducing the first mother's betrayal. Elsie, for example,
has compelled Lou (Quentin's professional mentor/father and, therefore,
the embodiment of the precarious value of the Law) into his initial act of

dishonesty that has made conditional his sense of adult masculinity.

> *Mickey*. . . . and I remember who made you throw your first
> version into my fireplace! . . . I saw you burn a true book and
> write another that told lies! Because she demanded it, because
> she terrified you, because she has taken your soul! (163–64)

She then denies him the opportunity to recover his identity through the
restorative action of self-denying work:

> *Lou*. . . . but Elsie feels . . . I'd just be drawing down the light-
> ning again to publish now. She even feels it's some uncon-
> scious wish for self-destruction on my part. And yet, if I put
> the book away, it's like a kind of suicide to me. . . . with this
> book of mine, I want to be true to myself. . . .
> *Elsie appears, approaching, hearing.*
> *Elsie*. Lou, I'm quite surprised. I thought we'd settled this. . . .
> You certainly don't think he ought to publish.
> *Quentin*. But the alternative seems—
> *Elsie, with a volcanic, suppressed alarm.* Paul dear, that's the *situa-
> tion*! Lou's not like you. . . . He's *incapable* of going out and . . .
> *Lou*. . . . Well, dear, I'm not all that delicate, I—
> *Elsie—a sudden flash of contempt; to Lou.* This is hardly the time for
> illusions! (151–52)

Only when he seems a despairing failure (largely because of Elsie's interven-
tion) does she nurture and comfort:

> *Quentin*. . . . *He turns to Elsie, who is lifting Lou to his feet and kisses
> him.* How tenderly she lifts him up—now that he is ruined.

It should be no surprise, given the design of the play's gender relationships,
that as surrogate mother/lover she also would attempt to seduce Quentin,
re-enacting yet again the traditional Oedipal triad.

Although Quentin, with a narcissist's unpersuasive attempt at honesty,
often concedes the validity of Louise's analyses of their personal and marital
difficulties, he consigns her to the ranks of "These goddamned women" who
"have injured me" (131). But her treason, if it is such, is more apparent than
real, as Miller imposes a characterization on Louise that is not borne out by
her dramatic experience or ours to justify Quentin's over-determined
emotionalism.

Quentin demands from Louise a presumed sensitivity that his own Oedipally conditioned gender behavior cannot return ("Never forget it, dear, you're a man, and a man has all the choices" [143]). Although he expects her to understand the causes and tolerate the excuses for his sexual adventurism, he would prefer normative feminine exclusivity, notwithstanding his smug, unconvincing qualification:

> *Louise.* . . . Supposing I came home and told you I'd met a man—
> a man on the street I wanted to go to bed with . . .
> *He hangs his head, defeated.*
> because he made the city seem full of lovers. What would you feel? Overjoyed for my discovery?
> *Quentin—pause; struck.* I understand. I'm sorry. I guess it would anger me too. *Slight pause.* But if you came to me with such a thing, I think I would see that you were struggling. And I would ask myself—maybe I'd even be brave enough to ask you—how I had failed. (182)

He resents her contained, disciplined sexuality, perceiving the only reasons for her withdrawal to be punishment, a mode of repressive familial control, and a function of that dangerous surety that defines innocence as unacceptable. He also insists that Louise acknowledge responsibility for the flawed marriage in encounters that echo the pattern of the initial episode of primal treachery, although the evidence of the dramatic action substantiates the greater extent of Quentin's liability:

> *Louise.* Quentin, you are full of resentment; you think I'm blind?
> *Quentin.* What I resent is being forever on trial, Louise. Are you an innocent bystander here? I keep waiting for some contribution you might have made to what I did, and I resent not hearing it. . . . How much shame do you want me to feel? I hate what I did. But I think I've explained it—I felt like nothing; I shouldn't have, but I did, and I took the only means I knew to—
> *Louise.* This is exactly what I mean, Quentin—you are still defending it. Right now.
> *He is stopped by this truth.*
> And I know it, Quentin.
> *Quentin.* And you're . . . not at all to blame, heh?
> *Louise.* But how?

Quentin. Well, for example . . . you never turn your back on me
   in bed?
Louise. I never turned my—
Quentin. You have turned your back on me in bed, Louise. I am
   not insane!
Louise. Well what do you expect? Silent, cold, you lay your hand
   on me?
Quentin, fallen. Well, I . . . I'm not very demonstrative, I guess.
   (167)

It becomes increasingly clear, however, that certitude, absolution, and
the recovery of an unfallen world are the problematic concerns of Quentin's
investigative recall, the consequences of which are associated with his reaction to all gestures of separation that mark the play but especially with his
fear-laden attitude toward his wife's efforts to establish an independent feminine self. Louise's desire for an identity apart from the culturally designated
roles that bind her to Quentin forces him to realize grudgingly that every
separation, each feminine betrayal, is a mimic Fall, replicating the primary
maternal treachery—withdrawal of the nourishing breast—dissolving the
unity of nurturing mother and feeding child and losing Eden forever. Whatever its symbolic significance (this world is a broken image of what has been
forfeit), its psychological results (the persistence of guilt, rage, and frustration), or its socioideological outcome (the disempowerment of women as
cause of the forfeit, guilt, rage, and frustration), the process is biologically
inevitable—the necessary, painful severance that transforms child into adult,
betrayal into blessedness.

   Like the knowing Abigail and the innocent Catherine, Maggie also is
the emblem of the insurrectionary power of sexuality—the quintessential
element of femaleness, a basic constituent of matriarchal authority, another
face of the Great Goddess, as reconstructed by the necessities of the patriarchal imagination. Like them, Maggie becomes an instrument of social and
personal destruction once the anarchic eroticism that she embodies has been
thwarted by the ideological requirements of patriarchy, as it is initially
exploited, contained, and finally suffocated.

   Maggie is an obvious representation of life's complex cyclical energies;
throughout the play, her symbolic and actual presence is signified by the sounds
of her breathing; when those energies fail, her respiration becomes labored; and
she dies of barbiturate poisoning that kills "by suffocation. And the signal is a
kind of sighing—the diaphragm is paralyzed" (240). From the first, Quentin
describes her as "a truth; symmetrical, lovely skin, undeniable" (170). She is
defined as a physically encoded being, a figuration of the female sexual principle:

> *Quentin.* . . . I met a girl tonight. . . . but one thing struck me, she
> wasn't defending anything, upholding anything, or accusing—
> she was just there, like a tree or a cat. And I felt strangely
> abstract beside her. (181)

Given the insurgent force of Maggie's authority, this linguistic objecti-
fication has the curious effect of confining rather than merely identifying her
power. The hermeneutic enclosure of her erotic generativity transforms
Maggie into a singular icon to be controlled and used, lest her rule-denying
sexuality subverts the conservative structures of patriarchy. Quentin,
consciously using the illusionary language of limitless love—"a love not even
of persons but blind, blind to insult, blind to the spear in the flesh, like justice
blind" (225)—Quentin acquires Maggie as an archetypical gender transac-
tion, believing that possessing her is synonymous with restoring the primal
unity irrecoverably lost by maternal betrayal:

> *Quentin.* . . . You ever felt you once saw yourself—absolutely
> true? I may have dreamed it, but I swear I feel that somewhere
> along the line—with Maggie I think—for one split second I
> saw my life, what I had done, what had been done to me and
> even what I ought to do (190)

But possession is the exercise of tyranny, not an act of love, and yet another
betrayal, although it takes a second expression of near-murderous guilt for
Quentin to realize the extent of his treachery and Maggie's complicity:

> *Quentin.* . . . and God's power is love without limit. But when a
> man dares reach for that. . . . he is only reaching for the power.
> Whoever goes to save another person with the lie of limitless
> love throws a shadow on the face of God. (233)

That Maggie is complicitous in her own fate, if not a willing victim
then one who needs victimization for the creation of selfhood, is a liberating
recognition for Quentin. As Miller writes of the genesis of Maggie's character from an earlier theatrical probe:

> For she appeared so trusting in her candor, and as strong and
> non-judgmental as a fine animal, while within she felt painfully
> illicit, a kind of freak whose very candor brought her little but
> disguised contempt in the serious opinion of the world. And so,
> bewildered and overwhelmed, she secretly came to side against

herself, taking the world's part as its cynicism toward her ground
down her brittle self-regard, until denial finally began its work,
leaving her all but totally innocent of insight into her own collab-
oration as well as her blind blows of retaliation.

But the consequences of such a position, whether it be Quentin's or
Miller's, are disturbing and dramatically irresponsible eventually discrediting
the play's qualified optimism. If Maggie is emblematic sexuality, the physical
incarnation of the claims of eros as defined by the man who "loved" her, the
patriarchal culture that exploited her, and the playwright who fashioned her,
then her identity will always be contingent and tentative, depending for
completion on the male other, the very agency that has determined her existence and fixed her meaning. Maggie can never be a whole separate person—
her creators have seen to that. Under such circumstances and with
considerable unwitting irony, suicide becomes both the final gesture of
despair and the first act of the self's independence.

If, as Arthur Ganz has observed, *"After the Fall* . . . show[s] a genuine
alteration of temper and attitude," then the reasons for such a change seem to
be embedded in the aptly named character Holga. Although Miller may have
"turned from the celebration of innocence to a search for the roots of guilt,"
Holga's presence in this essentially grim theatrical enterprise oddly infuses the
play with a comic sensibility, if by comedy we mean that generic form that
promises renewal and subscribes to recovery in limited proportions.

Although she is not a convincing figure—she is balanced too schemat-
ically between the extremes of Mother and Maggie which diminishes her
dramatic power to support Quentin's symbolic function—she does offer this
pathologically troubled character a methodology of hope. As an archeologist,
she puts together shards of the past to explain the rise and fall of civilizations.
Because she has both studied and experienced the indeterminacy of history,
she neither requires consistency nor values certainty:

> *Quentin.* . . . I swear I don't know if I have lived in good faith.
>   And the doubt ties my tongue when I think of promising
>   anything again.
> *Holga.* . . . But how can one ever be sure of one's good faith?
> *Quentin, surprised.* God, it's wonderful to hear you say that. All
>   my women have been so goddamned sure!
> *Holga.* But how can one ever be? (140)

She can take Quentin to a concentration camp, then offer him *The Magic
Flute*, knowing and accepting the apparent contradiction; as a survivor, she

reminds her lover that "no one they didn't kill can be innocent again" (148). Holga teaches him the necessary lesson that guilt, loss, and betrayal are not punishments to be avoided but inevitable signs of the human condition:

> *Holga.* . . . And for a long time after I had the same dream each night—that I had a child, and even in the dream I saw that the child was my life; and it was an idiot. And I wept, and a hundred times I ran away, but each time I came back it had the same dreadful face. Until I thought, if I could kiss it, whatever in it was my own, perhaps I could rest. And I bent to its broken face, and it was horrible . . . but I kissed it.
> *Quentin.* Does it still come back?
> *Holga.* At times. But it somehow has the virtue now . . . of being mine. I think one must finally take one's life in one's arms, Quentin. (148)

This reconciliatory embrace becomes, finally, the process of the play and the content of Quentin's education. By using the rhetoric of nurturing matriarchy, Holga reconstitutes the significance of the term idiot, incorporating even the negative resonances, and permits Quentin to redeem both the paternal legacy and the maternal embrace:

> *Quentin.* . . . To know, and even happily that we meet unblessed not in some garden of wax fruit and painted trees, that lie of Eden but after, after the Fall, after many, many deaths. Is the knowing all? And the wish to kill is never killed, but with some gift of courage one may look into its face when it appears, and with a stroke of love—as to an idiot in the house—forgive it; again and again . . . forever? (241)

While *The Crucible* operates within the circumscribed events of a verifiable past and *A View from the Bridge* occurs with the primitive designs of transcultural archetypes, *After the Fall*, interiorizing both historical awareness and mythic perception, remains firmly placed within the interpretive flow of an individual memory. The social concerns—the Depression, the Holocaust, the treacherous fifties—and the archetypal energies emerge from the overdetermined activity of a single unconscious, reflecting psychoanalytic narcissism.

Although the play appears committed to developing a flexible methodology of affirmation based on a balanced unitary vision of feminine wisdom, unlike the earlier works, with their enclosed movement, *After the Fall* also seems to possess an uncomfortable subtext. Perhaps the containment inherent in the play's central structural device can create only problematic optimism and suspect hope. Certainly neither the imagined matricide nor Mother's actual death can resolve the persistent Oedipal tensions issuing from Quentin's obsessive sense of maternal betrayal. His apparent adoption of "the idiot in the house," however sentimentally pleasing the rhetorical gesture, is not entirely convincing. Quentin's response to Maggie's suicide, the ultimate denial of her erotic power and insurrectionary sexuality, seems less conditioned by his liberated, if smug, sensitivity than by the fear of its residual seductiveness.

Yet reconciliation continues to be a possibility even within the limits imposed by Quentin's restrictive consciousness. Holga's truths are no less truths because they are confined by dramatic circumstances; and self-righteousness does not negate the discovery that to ensure our humanity, we must all live as if after the Fall.

MICHELLE I. PEARSON

John Proctor and the Crucible of Individuation in Arthur Miller's The Crucible

In his introduction to his *Collected Plays*, Arthur Miller says that "[e]ach of these plays, in varying degrees, was begun in the belief that it was unveiling a truth already known but unrecognized as such" (11). *The Crucible* focuses on just such a truth, the truth that an individual must find and be true to his essential self. However, most early criticism of *The Crucible* focuses on the socio/political aspects of the play's development. For example, many early scholars criticize the play's lack of historical authenticity in dealing with the material on the Salem witchcraft trials (Warshow, Levin). They point out that the judges in the play are not accurately portrayed (Levin), nor are the girls who "cry out" against the accused witches (Martin). Miller responds to this criticism by saying that he did not intend for the play to be a history, but rather a drama based on history. In other cases, scholars focus on the possible allegory between events in Salem during the seventeenth century and the McCarthy trials during the 1950's (Douglas, Warshow, Nathan). Miller willingly acknowledges his association of these two topics, explaining that he was both fascinated and horrified by the parallels.

More recent studies have begun to re-examine Miller's characterization, especially in the case of John Proctor. Some see Proctor as a classic tragic hero whose tragic flaw is his adulterous relationship with Abigail (Walker, Popkin). Others see him as an agrarian hero whose work ethic and

From *Studies in American Drama 1945–Present* 6:1 (1991). © 1991 by the Ohio State University Press.

ties to the land elicit the sympathy of the audience (Porter). Still others view Proctor's conflict as a clear case of the individual as a victim of the social system (Ferres, Meserve). Finally, one critic even views Proctor as a villain, expressing shock that American audiences (the critic is French) can sympathize with this man who obviously seduces an "innocent" girl, tries to hide his shame, and eventually tries to redeem himself by saving his wife at the cost of the girl's reputation (Ayme). Most of these critics analyze Proctor in terms of a static character, showing little or no development through the play. Patricia Schroeder, however, analyzes Proctor's decision-making process in terms of his learning "to accept public responsibility for the repercussions of even his most private actions" (83). Michael O'Neal adds that Proctor's forced involvement in events that he tries to remain aloof from leads to the personal crucible "in which he discovers his essential 'goodness'" (114). Rather than remain a static character, Proctor must go through this decision making process, this personal crucible, in order to reach his final decision to die rather than sacrifice his name. Thus Proctor's development in the play takes the form of a search for his essential self, classically illustrating Carl Jung's process of individuation.

According to Jung's theory, developed in *The Archetypes and the Collective Unconscious*, each individual possesses certain archetypes, images of the repressed aspects of one's personality. During the process of individuation, an individual moves from the superficial level of the persona, which is the mask shown to society, to the deepest, most inner archetype. In order to individuate successfully, a person must confront and accept these archetypal images. Frieda Fordham points out that the unconscious contains innumerable archetypes; therefore we can become somewhat familiar only with those "which seem to have the greatest significance and most powerful influence on us" (59). While the contents of the unconscious are infinite, the most powerful archetypes confronted during individuation are the shadow, the anima/animus, the wise old man/earth mother, and the self. The first of these four powerful archetypes, the shadow, represents the animal urges, uncivilized desires, uncontrolled emotions, and other feelings that we repress because society does not accept them (Fordham 49–50). The second archetype, the anima/animus figure, differs for men and women. For a man, the anima portrays the complementary elements of the feminine personality while a woman's animus portrays elements of the masculine personality. Third, the wise old man/earth mother figure represents wisdom from within. After confronting and accepting these three images, the archetypal self unifies these dissimilar elements of the personality (Fordham 62). Having accepted these repressed personality traits, the individualized person can act not simply as a surface persona, but as a complete individual reconciled to all aspects of life.

In *The Crucible*, John Proctor individuates from the persona he shows to his society, through the archetypes represented by other characters in the play, finally to the self, reached when he decides to die an honorable death. Fordham explains the persona as the mask worn by an individual to signify the role being played in society. The persona displays those traits expected of a person in a certain position (48). Proctor, a farmer and land-owner, displays a strong, respectable persona. Miller describes him as having a "steady manner," a "quiet confidence," and an "unexpressed, hidden force" (18). A hard-working man, Proctor explains that he occasionally must plow even on Sunday in order to make his land produce. The people of Salem respect Proctor, as evidenced when Giles Corey and Francis Nurse look to him for help when their wives are arrested, as well as Parris's explanation late in the play that hanging Proctor could cause rebellion in Salem: "John Proctor is not Isaac Ward that drank his family to ruin. . . . these people have great weight in the town (122). Finally, according to Miller, Proctor does not tolerate hypocrisy or foolishness, judgments that prevent him from always being popular (18). From the beginning of the play, Proctor recognizes the falseness of his persona, having "come to regard himself as a kind of a fraud" (18). While the people of Salem look at Proctor and see a strong, hard-working, no-nonsense man, Proctor himself knows that he is an adulterer, a lecher, and that he drives himself to try to be free of his guilt. Not until faced with a crisis, however, will he leave the persona behind and begin the process of individuation.

The Reverend Samuel Parris, the overbearing minister of the Salem parish, represents Proctor's archetypal shadow. The shadow figure contains desires and emotions which are "incompatible with . . . our ideal personality, all that we are ashamed of, all that we do not want to know about ourselves" (Fordham 50). Fordham also explains that the shadow is often personified in people we dislike because we may dislike a quality of our own in that person (49–50). Parris exhibits two qualities, rigid authority and hypocrisy, that Proctor clearly does not wish to acknowledge within himself. Since Proctor is ashamed of the authoritarian and hypocritical aspects of his own personality, he intensely dislikes Parris. Parris covets a position of authority in the Salem community, a position he feels should automatically be his as minister of the parish. He resents his parishioners' lack of respect: "In meeting, he felt insulted if someone rose to shut the door without first asking his permission" (1). Believing that his authority comes from God, and therefore ought to be respected absolutely, Parris tells the townspeople, "You people seem not to comprehend that a minister is the Lord's man in the parish; a minister is not to be so lightly crossed and contradicted . . . There is either obedience or the church will burn like Hell is burning!" (27). Clearly, Parris believes disobedience to his authority should have dire consequences.

Proctor, on the other hand, is more covertly authoritarian. While he does not explicitly demand obedience, he commands other characters and clearly expects them to obey. Early in the play, he orders Abigail not to speak against Elizabeth, and when she continues, he threatens a whipping. Later he commands Elizabeth to "judge me not" (53), but his guilt weakens his "authority" over Elizabeth. Proctor's commands are not confined to those who are younger or female. He even says to Giles Corey, "Now come along, Giles, and help me drag my lumber home" (29). Finally, he is most authoritative over Mary Warren, his servant-girl. He forbids her to go to Salem, orders her to bed, threatens to whip her, and finally forces her to go to court and confess the fraud of her crying out.

Unconsciously coveting authority for himself, Proctor resists Parris's authority, declaring, "I like not the smell of this 'authority'" (28). He openly admits his willingness to join an opposing faction within the parish, if such a faction indeed exists. Walter Meserve points out that Proctor rebels against Parris's authority, but in general respects authority, partly because authority is a part of his own character (129). It is the authority "without inner sanction" (Ferres 9), the potential abuse of authority, which Proctor resists. Parris clearly abuses his position of authority, and Proctor is capable of abusing authority also, as evidenced in his frequent threats to whip those who disobey.

Parris's blatant hypocrisy is even more significant to his development as Proctor's shadow figure. Miller reveals almost instantly that Proctor has "a sharp and biting way with hypocrites" (18), but also that he considers himself a fraud. Clearly, the hypocrisy he so sharply criticizes in Parris is the very trait within himself that he wishes to deny. Parris demonstrates his hypocrisy throughout the play. During the first scenes, as Betty lies inexplicably ill, perhaps dying, Parris worries more about his reputation in the community than his daughter's health" . . . now my ministry's at stake, my ministry and perhaps your cousin's [Betty's] life" (9). Ferres notes Parris's "grasping materialism, hypocritically concealed behind a facade of piety" (9), symbolized for Proctor in Parris's insistence on having golden candlesticks (instead of the former pewter ones) for the altar. Finally, Parris displays the ultimate hypocrisy during the scenes surrounding the hangings. As dawn of execution day approaches, Parris pleads with Deputy Governor Danforth to postpone the hangings, giving time for at least one of the accused to confess. His pleas, however, are not for the lives of the accused witches, but for his own. Parris recognizes that the hanging of well-respected citizens carries the potential for riot, and even for his own murder. In fear for his life, he begs Danforth, "You cannot hang this sort. There is danger for me. I dare not step outside at night!" (123). To the end, he pleads with Proctor to confess falsely, ignoring Proctor's spiritual needs in favor of saving his own life.

Proctor's hypocrisy surrounds his dealings with and about Abigail. In committing adultery with Abigail, Proctor has sinned "not only against the moral fashion of the time, but against his own vision of decent conduct" (18). He wishes, however, to deny this sin both to himself and to others. To Abigail he says to "[w]ipe it out of mind. We never touched, Abby . . . we did not" (21). To Elizabeth he contends that he has no feelings for Abby, that theirs was a totally physical relationship: "The promise that a stallion gives a mare I gave that girl!" (60). Nevertheless, he hesitates to testify in court that Abigail lies in her accusations of witchcraft against the townspeople. Elizabeth logically surmises that Abby still holds an attraction for John: "She has an arrow in you yet, John Proctor, and you know it well!" (60). Indeed Proctor does know it well, but he will not be able to admit it until he successfully acknowledges his own propensity toward hypocrisy and abuse of authority, thereby incorporating the shadow figure.

In addition to hypocrisy and abuse of authority, Proctor has repressed other character traits, some of them traditionally feminine characteristics. The second archetype encountered in the journey of individuation, the anima or animus, represents complementary characteristics from the opposite gender of the individual in question. Traditionally feminine attributes, such as emotion and intuition, become part of a man's anima, while stereotypically masculine traits, such as analytical thinking, constitute a woman's animus. Thus a man projects his anima, his "complementary feminine element" (Fordham 52), first onto his mother and then onto other women. Fordham explains of the anima that "[s]he is also two-sided or has two aspects, a light and a dark, corresponding to the different types of women; on the one hand the pure, the good, the noble goddess-like figure, on the other the prostitute, the seductress or the witch" (54). As Priscilla McKinney has discussed, "Abby symbolizes the lowest stage" of the anima or the dark side, while "Elizabeth . . . represents the mature 'anima'—which is wise, pure, and transcendent" (51).

Abigail, Proctor's partner in adultery, represents the dark side of the anima, displaying characteristics of uncontrolled passion, manipulation and lying, and evil in her words and actions. Passion led to Abby's situation at the beginning of the play, and Abby both shows and admits this passion as soon as she has contact with John Proctor. She is described as "absorbing his presence" (19), she remembers his strength, and she reminds him of the passion they shared, begging for a "soft word" (19). Acknowledging her passion, she tells John that "a wild thing [such as herself] may say wild things" (20).

Early in the play we learn that Abigail, along with several other girls, has been discovered dancing in the forest, a sign of association with the devil in the eyes of the Puritan community. She says whatever is necessary, with no regard for the truth, to cover up her sin. To her uncle (Samuel Parris) she denies having conjured spirits or danced naked, but later with the girls she discusses these same events. As the leader of the group of girls, Abby threatens them with the consequences of not corroborating her lies:

> Now look you. All of you. We danced. And Tituba conjured Ruth Putnam's dead sisters. And that is all. And mark this. Let either of you breathe a word, or the edge of a word, about the other things, and I will come to you in the black of some terrible night and I will bring a pointy reckoning that will shudder you. And you know I can do it; I saw Indians smash my dear parents' heads on the pillow next to mine, and I have seen some reddish work done at night, and I can make you wish you had never seen the sun go down! (17)

Obviously, Abby's most significant lies, and her most significant manipulation, involve the "crying out" against the alleged witches. Tituba, the Barbados slave who has been "conjuring" in the forest with the girls, is the easiest scapegoat. Abigail blames all that has happened on Tituba, saying that Tituba was trying to win their souls for the Devil. Tituba surmises very quickly that confession is her only hope for survival; she admits having consorted with the Devil and names others in Salem whom she has "seen" with the Devil. Abigail, watching these proceedings, sees that Tituba is forgiven and looked upon as an instrument of God in the fight against evil. Suddenly, Abby too wants to confess: "I danced for the Devil; I saw him; I wrote in his book; I go back to Jesus; I kiss His hand. I saw Sarah Good with the Devil! I saw Bridget Bishop with the Devil!" (45). Without interruption, Betty picks up the chant, naming those whom she has seen with the Devil. What began as the relatively harmless sport of dancing in the forest and playing the forbidden games that attract all children swells into accusations of witchcraft. Abigail's lies and manipulation will hang innocent people. In the courtroom scene, Abby manipulates through hysteria. Threatened with discovery by means of Mary Warren's testimony, Abigail stares in fear at a threatening "bird" in the rafters, begging Mary not to attack. Instantly, the other girls in the courtroom pick up her cue and join the hysteria, eventually rising to a pitch which overwhelms Mary and causes her to "confess" her treachery and name John Proctor as an instrument of the Devil. In controlling the other girls, Abby displays her propensity for lying, manipulation and evil. As Porter explains, Abby's real evil lies in the means to her ends: "She is willing to sacrifice the community and everyone in it, to subvert the function of the Law, in order to gain her objectives" (187). Abby knows that she fakes, but she does it so well that she can bring on "fits" in the other children (Porter 188).

Elizabeth Proctor represents the light side of Proctor's anima in her qualities of goodness, honesty, and love. Proctor emphasizes the quality of goodness throughout the play, associating it with Elizabeth, but not with himself. When they argue about his affair with Abigail, Proctor accuses Elizabeth of being judgmental: "Let you look sometimes for the goodness in me, and judge me not" (53), to which Elizabeth immediately responds that she does not judge him, he judges himself, and that she believes him to be "a good man" (53). Later, after Elizabeth's arrest, Proctor proclaims "[m]y wife will never die for me! . . . that goodness will not die for me!" (77–78). While Proctor asserts Elizabeth's goodness, he cannot accept that any such trait exists within himself, not until he successfully individuates at the end of the play.

Proctor maintains that, as well as being good, Elizabeth is inherently honest. He explains to the court that Elizabeth "have never lied. There are them that cannot sing, and them that cannot weep—my wife cannot lie" (107). Again, while Proctor insists upon Elizabeth's honesty, he knows himself to be a liar. "John . . . sees only Elizabeth's goodness, feeling that she is incapable of lying, while viewing his own mendacity as evidence of his sinful nature" (McKinney 51–52). Puritan belief that "God damns all liars" (97) shows the importance of honesty throughout the play. For John and Elizabeth, it is an ironical pattern. Proctor believes himself to be a sinful liar, but tells his most damning truth in an attempt to save Elizabeth. Elizabeth, believed incapable of lying, tells the only lie in her life (believing that by doing so she is damning her soul) when her honesty would save her husband. While Proctor sees both goodness and honesty in his wife, he finds neither of these qualities in himself, which he admits when trying to decide whether to confess: "My honesty is broke, Elizabeth; I am no good man" (130).

Proctor recognizes love in Elizabeth, a love he feels unworthy of and helpless to reciprocate. He has tried, he says, to win back her trust in the months since Abigail left their house, telling her "I mean to please you, Elizabeth" (48). When she is arrested, he tries desperately to protect her, first ripping up the arrest warrant, then refusing to let her be taken, finally telling her to "fear nothing" (75) because he will bring her home soon. Penelope Curtis points out that Elizabeth and John "share a passionate desire for trust and wholeness, for a mutual growth in self-knowledge" (267). Elizabeth proves her love for John by lying to save his name, while he shows his love by sacrificing his name to try to save Elizabeth.

While Proctor needs to incorporate the negative personality aspects personified by Parris and the feminine traits represented by Elizabeth, he also must find wisdom and courage. The third archetypal figure, the wise old man or the earth mother, represents wisdom from within. For Proctor, Giles Corey personifies this archetype. Corey engenders respect and affection from Proctor throughout the play, as seen in the good-natured word play between the two men in Act 1, where Proctor points out that Corey takes men to court on an all-too-regular basis: "Is it the Devil's fault that a man cannot say you good morning without you clap him for defamation? You're old, Giles, and you're not hearin' so well as you did" (29). Later, as the action becomes intense, Corey provides a model of behavior for Proctor. Attempting to save their wives, Francis Nurse, Giles Corey, and John Proctor go before the court with evidence of various sorts. Corey accuses one of the girls who is "crying out" of lying, because her father can profit by his neighbors being hanged so that he can obtain their land. His proof of this claim is secondhand: "I have it from an honest man who heard Putnam say it! The day his [Putnam's] daughter cried out on Jacobs, he said she'd given him a fair gift of land" (92). Deputy Governor Danforth demands the name of this "honest man," information which Corey refuses to supply. He knows by this time that anyone who opposes the system endangers himself, and he will not endanger another by naming him. Proctor follows this model later when he refuses to name other conspirators with the Devil as part of his confession.

Finally, Corey's heroic death shows Proctor a model for courage. Stubborn to the end, Corey refuses either to confess or deny being a wizard, thereby dying a Christian and legally leaving his farm to his sons. Attempting to force either a confession or a denial, the authorities have him pressed: "Great stones they lay upon his chest until he plead aye or nay. . . . They say he give them but two words. 'More weight,' he says. And died" (130). Proctor hears of Corey's death from Elizabeth, during the crucial scene where he must decide his own fate. Perceiving saintliness in Giles's death, Proctor explains to Elizabeth that he is not a saint: "I cannot mount the gibbet like a saint. It is a fraud. I am not that man" (130). He has seen the wisdom and courage of the wise old man, but has not yet been able to incorporate these attributes into his own character.

Assimilating the shadow-figure Parris, the light and dark animas Elizabeth and Abigail, and the wise old man Giles Corey, John Proctor begins the process of individuating toward the archetypal self. Proctor is initially dominated by the persona. He knows some of his inconsistencies, but is not yet ready to confront the archetypal representations of these traits. A crisis, the arrest of Elizabeth, begins the process leading to Proctor's individuation.

As Act II ends, just after Elizabeth has been led away in chains, Proctor proclaims to Mary that "all our old pretense is ripped away . . . we are only what we always were, but naked now" (78). The persona will be stripped away, allowing Proctor to confront and integrate the archetypes. Proctor confronts the shadow figure in front of Deputy Governor Danforth, who will eventually decide the fate of both Proctors. When questioned concerning his religious practices, Proctor insists that he is a Christian, but admits that he has no love for Parris, thereby acknowledging his dislike for the shadow figure. Soon will follow his own abandonment of both authority and hypocrisy as he treats Mary gently in the court (holding her hand and reassuring her) and admits his adultery in front of the court.

Confronting the dark side of the anima figure is undoubtedly the most difficult for Proctor. To prove, however, that Abigail is lying in her accusations of witchcraft, Proctor must shed doubt on her character, thus incriminating his own. Although he has resisted the need to do so, Proctor now realizes that he must name Abigail for what she is—"It is a whore!" (105)—and prove it by admitting his liaison with her. In doing so, he admits within himself the very traits which Abby as the dark anima represents—the unbridled passion, the evil, the mendacity: "She thinks to dance with me on my wife's grave! And well she might, for I thought of her softly. God help me, I lusted, and there *is* a promise in such sweat" (106). This confrontation leads to Proctor's own arrest, and the remainder of his individuation takes place in jail, on the morning of his execution.

Confronting the light side of the anima presents difficulty, not because Proctor resists seeing the feminine qualities of Elizabeth, but because he is unable to see them in himself. Elizabeth insists on making him see her anima's qualities in himself. She explains to him that the adultery, which has been their stumbling block, was not his fault alone, saying "I have sins of my own to count. It needs a cold wife to prompt lechery" (131). By taking some of the blame for Proctor's lechery, Elizabeth tries to help him see that he is a good man, capable of deciding his fate for himself: "Do what you will. But let none be your judge. There be no higher judge under Heaven than Proctor is! . . . I never knew such goodness in the world!" (132). The crisis concerning the anima figure involves Proctor's decision to confess, which he immediately recognizes as evil, a lie which Elizabeth would be incapable of uttering: "Would you give them such a lie? Say it. Would you ever give them this? You would not; if tongs of fire were singeing you you would not! It is evil. Good, then—it is evil, and I do it!" (132). At this point Proctor has confronted the light anima, but denies the existence of its qualities within himself.

Again, in the case of the wise old man figure, Proctor is unable to assimilate the character traits immediately. When he learns of Corey's heroic death, Proctor reaches a crisis in his indecision. Elizabeth describes Giles as a "fearsome man," but Proctor has no reaction. Instead ("with great force of will, but not quite looking at her"), he says, "I have been thinking I would confess to them, Elizabeth" (130). Now Proctor has confronted the shadow, the dark anima, the light anima, and the wise old man, but, while he has integrated the shadow and the dark anima, he denies the light anima and the wise old man. Tempted to return to the persona, he would give up the insights he has gained from confronting the archetypes. Feeling that giving the judges what they want—his confession—is meaningless, he therefore tries to convince himself that it is harmless. In this crisis of indecision, Proctor can no longer face anyone who represents for him the archetypes he has denied. He turns from Elizabeth in anguish as he makes the statement that will lead to his confession, "I want my life" (132), He feels trapped; if he goes to the gallows like a saint, he believes himself a fraud, but if he confesses he is a liar. Agonized, he paces in a "tantalized search" (132), a search for the soul he can find only when he accepts the archetypes. When Rebecca Nurse is brought in, she serves as a reminder of Giles Corey, for she will die a heroic death just as he did. Ashamed of the decision he has made, Proctor "turns his face to the wall" (134) and is unable either to face or acknowledge Rebecca. Again, having denied the wise old man, Proctor cannot face anyone who represents this figure for him.

Finally, Proctor is confronted with the self, that archetype that unifies all the others, which "unites all the opposing elements in man and woman, consciousness and unconsciousness, good and bad, male and female" (Fordham 62). For Proctor, the self is represented by the name, not just for himself, but also for others. Michael O'Neal explains "name magic" as the name's being more than a mere symbol of a person, actually the person. For example, signing one's name in the black book of the Devil is equivalent to signing away one's soul; "crying out" against witches simply involves naming them (116-18). Trying to return to the persona, Proctor moves toward a false confession, as this is behavior the persona can maintain—it is what society wants and accepts, regardless of Proctor's inner turmoil. He balks increasingly at the process as it comes closer to threatening names, both his own and others. First he questions why the confession must be in writing, then refuses to name others whom he has "seen" with the Devil; finally he hesitates when the confession must be signed. As Sheila Huftel asserts, "a man's name is his conscience, his immortal soul, and without it there is no person left" (131). Making a verbal confession is in keeping with the persona, but indicting others and signing his name are behaviors that the persona cannot maintain. Ferres explains this battle between the essential self and the social disguises one must wear, or, in Jungian terms, the conflict between the self and the persona:

Miller believes a man must be true to himself and to his fellows, even though being untrue may be the only way to stay alive. Out of the ordeal of his personal crucible . . . [he] comes to know the truth about himself. In order to confront his essential self, to discover that self in the void between being and seeming, a man must strip away the disguises society requires him to wear. (8)

Only by turning from the persona, that which tells him to confess and live, can Proctor accept the light anima (his good qualities) and the wise old man (his heroic qualities) and successfully individuate to self. All of these things happen in the scene where he cries out for his name and destroys his confession. Proctor wishes for Danforth simply to "spread the word" that he has confessed, rather than post his written confession, a wish Danforth cannot comprehend.

> DANFORTH (*with suspicion*): It is the same, is it not? If I report it or you sign to it?
> PROCTOR (*he knows it is insane*): No, it is not the same! What others say and what I sign to is not the same!
> DANFORTH: Why? Do you mean to deny this confession when you are free?
> PROCTOR: I mean to deny nothing!
> DANFORTH: Then explain to me, Mr. Proctor, why you will not let—
> PROCTOR (*with a cry of his whole soul*): Because it is my name! Because I cannot have another in my life! Because I lie and sign myself to lies! Because I am not worth the dust on the feet of them that hang! How may I live without my name? I have given you my soul; leave me my name! (137–38)

Having confronted the archetypes, Proctor cannot simply return to the naivete of the persona; he must continue the individuation. In crying out for his name, Proctor cries out for his archetypal self, thus integrating the light anima and the wise old man. His actions following this "cry of his whole soul" stand in stark contrast with his previous actions. Although he weeps as he destroys the confession, it is "weeping in fury" (138), and he stands erect. Now, having accepted his essential self, Proctor can stand tall and proud, as opposed to the shame he felt when tempted to return to the persona. In his final emotional speech, he fully integrates the archetypes:

> I can [hang]. And there's your first marvel, that I can. You have

made your magic now, for now I do think I see some shred of goodness in John Proctor. Not enough to weave a banner with, but white enough to keep it from such dogs . . . Give them no tear! Tears pleasure them! Show honor now, show a stony heart and sink them with it! (138)

In his statement that he can indeed face death, he acknowledges his tie to Giles Corey. His recognition of goodness within himself integrates the light anima figure represented by Elizabeth. He even notes the goodness as being white, a symbol of the purity of the anima. His admonition to Elizabeth to be brave shows that he has fully left behind the persona: neither he nor Elizabeth will give the officials what they want and accept—John will not confess and he does not want Elizabeth to cry for his death. Finally, in showing his complete individuation, Proctor passionately kisses Elizabeth, and walks toward his death, in the meantime catching the faint Rebecca Nurse as they exit. He is able to face Elizabeth and Rebecca because, as a fully individuated character, he can show passion as well as compassion.

Fordham explains that the self "brings a feeling of 'oneness,' and of reconciliation with life, which can now be accepted as it is, not as it ought to be" (63). When Proctor cries out for his name and fully individuates, he reconciles himself to his need to die an honest death rather than live a lie. His death is his choice over accepting the label of society, a "kind of triumph, an affirmation of the individual" (Weales 89). Miller was later to explain that *The Crucible*'s real and inner theme was "the handing over of conscience to another . . . and the realization that with conscience goes the person, the soul immortal, and the 'name'" ("Introduction" 47). When Proctor hands over his conscience, his false confession, to Danforth, he is attempting to retain the persona. But having come this far in the process of individuation, having confronted the shadow, the dark anima, the light anima, and the wise old man, Proctor cannot simply return to a superficial persona. He successfully individuates when he cries out for his self, represented by his name, and destroys his false confession. In the final scene of the play, Elizabeth emphasizes Proctor's successful individuation when she stands in the window with the new morning sun shining on her face and cries, "He have his goodness now. God forbid I take it from him" (139).

WENDY SCHISSEL

Re(dis)covering the Witches in Arthur Miller's The Crucible: *A Feminist Reading*

Arthur Miller's *The Crucible* is a disturbing work, not only because of the obvious moral dilemma that is irresolutely solved by John Proctor's death, but also because of the treatment that Abigail and Elizabeth receive at Miller's hands and at the hands of critics. In forty years of criticism very little has been said about the ways in which *The Crucible* reinforces stereotypes of *femme fatales* and cold and unforgiving wives in order to assert apparently universal virtues. It is a morality play based upon a questionable androcentric morality. Like Proctor, *The Crucible* "[roars] down" Elizabeth, making her concede a fault which is not hers but of Miller's making: "It needs a cold wife to prompt lechery," she admits in her final meeting with her husband. Critics have seen John as a "tragically heroic common man," hu*manly* tempted, "a just man in a universe gone mad," but they have never given Elizabeth similar consideration, nor have they deconstructed the phallologocentric sanctions implicit in Miller's account of Abigail's fate, Elizabeth's confession, and John's temptation and death. As a feminist reader of the 1990s, I am troubled by the unrecognized fallout from the existential hu*man*ism that Miller and his critics have held dear. *The Crucible* is in need of an/Other reading, one that reveals the assumptions of the text, the author, and the reader/critic who "is part of the shared consciousness created by the [play]." It is time to reveal the vicarious enjoyment that Miller and his critics

From *Modern Drama* 37:3 (Fall 1994). © 1994 by the University of Toronto.

have found in a cathartic male character who has enacted their sexual and political fantasies.

The setting of *The Crucible* is a favoured starting point in an analysis of the play. Puritan New England of 1692 may indeed have had its parallels to McCarthy's America of 1952, but there is more to the paranoia than xenophobia—of Natives and Communists, respectively. Implicit in Puritan theology, in Miller's version of the Salem witch trials, and all too frequent in the society which has produced Miller's critics is gynecophobia—fear and distrust of women.

The "half dozen heavy books" (36) which the zealous Reverend Hale endows on Salem "like a bridegroom to his beloved, bearing gifts" (132) are books on witchcraft from which he has acquired an "armory of symptoms, catchwords, and diagnostic procedures" (36). A 1948 edition of the 1486 *Malleus Maleficarum* (*Hammer of Witches*), with a foreword by Montague Summers, may have prompted Miller's inclusion of seventeenth-century and Protestant elucidations upon a work originally sanctioned by the Roman Church. Hale's books would be "highly misogynic" tomes, for like the *Malleus* they would be premised on the belief that "'All witchcraft comes from carnal lust which in women is insatiable.'" The authors of the *Maleus*, two Dominican monks, Johan Sprenger and Heinrich Kraemer, were writing yet another fear-filled version of the apocryphal bad woman: they looked to Ecclesiasties which declares

> the wickedness of a woman is all evil . . . there is no anger above
> the anger of a woman. It will be more agreeable to abide with a
> lion and a dragon, than to dwell with a wicked woman . . . from
> the woman came the beginning of sin, and by her we all die.
> (25:17, 23, 33)

The Crucible is evidence that Miller partakes of similar fears about wicked, angry, or wise women; even if his complicity in such gynecophobia is unwitting—and that is the most generous thing we can accord him, a "misrecognition" of himself and his reputation-conscious hero John as the authors of a subjectivity which belongs exclusively to men—the result for generations of readers has been the same. In Salem, the majority of witches condemned to die were women. Even so, Salem's numbers were negligible compared with the gynocide in Europe: Andrea Dworkin quotes a moderate estimate of nine million witches executed at a ratio of women to men of as much as 100 to 1. Miller assures us in one of his editorial and political (and long and didactic) comments, that despite the Puritans' belief in witchcraft, "there were no witches" (35) in Salem; his play, however, belies his claim, and so do his critics.

The Crucible is filled with witches, from the wise woman/healer Rebecca *Nurse* to the black woman Tituba, who initiates the girls into the dancing which has always been part of the communal celebrations of women healers/witches. But the most obvious witch in Miller's invention upon Salem *history* is Abigail Williams. She is the consummate seductress; the witchcraft hysteria in the play originates in *her* carnal lust for Proctor. Miller describes Abigail as *"a strikingly beautiful girl . . . with an endless capacity for dissembling"* (8–9). In 1953, William Hawkins called Abigail "an evil child"; in 1967, critic Leonard Moss said she was a "malicious figure" and "unstable"; in 1987, June Schlueter and James Flanagan proclaimed her "a whore," echoing Proctor's "How do you call Heaven! Whore! Whore!" (109); and in 1989, Bernard Dukore suggested that "if the *'strikingly beautiful'* Abigail's behaviour in the play is an indication, she may have been the one to take the initiative."

The critics forget what Abigail cannot: "John Proctor . . . took me from my sleep and put knowledge in my heart!" (24). They, like Miller, underplay so as not openly to condone the "natural" behaviour of a man tempted to adultery because of a young woman's beauty and precociousness, her proximity in a house where there is also an *apparently* frigid wife, and the repression of Puritan society and religion. Abigail is a delectable commodity in what Luce Irigaray has termed a "dominant scopic economy." We are covertly invited to equate John's admirable rebellion at the end of the play—against the unconscionable demands of implicating others in a falsely acknowledged sin of serving that which is antithetical to community (the Puritans called that antithesis the devil)—with his more self-serving rebellion against its sexual mores. The subtle equation allows Miller not only to project fault upon Abigail, but also to make what is really a cliched act of adultery on John's part much more interesting. Miller wants us to recognize, if not celebrate, the individual trials of his existential hero, a "spokesman for rational feeling and disinterested intelligence" in a play about "integrity and its obverse, compromise." Mary Daly might describe the scholarly support that Miller has received for his fantasy-fulfilling hero as "The second element of the Sado-Ritual [of the witchcraze] . . . [an] erasure of responsibility."

No critic has asked, though, how a seventeen-year-old girl, raised in the household of a Puritan minister, can have the knowledge of how to seduce a man. (The only rationale offered scapegoats another woman, Tituba, complicating gynecophobia with xenophobia.) The omission on Miller's and his critics' parts implies that Abigail's sexual knowledge must be inherent in her gender. I see the condemnation of Abigail as an all too common example of blaming the victim.

Mercy Lewis's reaction to John is another indictment of the sexual precociousness of the girls of Salem. Obviously knowledgeable of John and Abigail's affair, Mercy is both afraid of John and, Miller says, *"strangely titillated"* as she *"sidles out"* of the room (21). Mary Warren, too, knows: "Abby'll charge lechery on you, Mr. Proctor" (80), she says when he demands she tell what she knows about the "poppet" to the court. John is aghast: "She's told you!" (80). Rather than condemning John, all these incidents are included to emphasize the "vengeance of a little girl" (79), and, I would add, to convince the reader who is supposed to sympathize with John (or to feel titillation himself) that no girl is a "good girl," free of sexual knowledge, that each is her mother Eve's daughter.

The fact is, however, that Salem's young women, who have been preached at by a fire and brimstone preacher, Mr. Parris, are ashamed of their bodies. A gynocritical reading of Mary Warren's cramps after Sarah Good mumbles her displeasure at being turned away from the Proctor's door empty-handed is explainable as a "curse" of a more periodic nature:

> But *what* does she mumble? You must remember, Goody Proctor. Last Month—a Monday, I think—she walked away, and I thought my guts would burst for two days after. Do you remember it? (58)

The "girls" are the inheritors of Eve's sin, and their bodies are their reminders. Though, like all young people, they find ways to rebel—just because adolescence did not exist in Puritan society does not mean that the hormones did not flow—they are seriously repressed. And the most insidious aspect of that repression, in a society in which girls are not considered women until they marry (as young as fourteen, or significantly, with the onset of menses), is the turning of the young women's frustrations upon members of their own gender. It is not so strange as Proctor suggests for "a Christian girl to hang old women!" (58), when one such Christian girl claims her position in society with understandable determination: "I'll not be ordered to bed no more, Mr. Proctor! I am eighteen and a woman, however single!" (60). Paradoxically, of course, the discord only serves to prove the assumptions of a parochial society about the jealousies of women, an important aspect of this play in which Miller makes each woman in John's life claim herself as his rightful spouse: Elizabeth assures him that "I will be your only wife, or no wife at all!" (62); and Abigail makes her heart's desire plain with "I will make you such a wife when the world is white again!" (150). To realize her claim Abigail has sought the help of voodoo—Tituba's and the court's—to get rid of Elizabeth, but not without clear provocation on John's part.

Miller misses an opportunity to make an important comment upon the real and perceived competitions for men forced upon women in a patriarchal society by subsuming the women's concerns within what he knows his audience will recognize as more admirable communal and idealistic concerns. The eternal triangle motif, while it serves many interests for Miller, is, ultimately, less important than the overwhelming nobility of John's Christ-like martyrdom; against that the women's complaints seem petty indeed, and an audience whose collective consciousness recognizes a dutifully repentant hero also sees the women in his life as less sympathetic. For Abigail and Elizabeth also represent the extremes of female sexuality—sultriness and frigidity, respectively—which test a man's body, endanger his spirit, and threaten his "natural" dominance or needs.

In order to make Abigail's seductive capability more believable and John's culpability less pronounced, Miller has deliberately raised Abigail's age ("A Note on the Historical Accuracy of This Play") from twelve to seventeen. He introduces us to John and Abigail in the first act with John's acknowledgement of her young age. Abby—the diminutive form of her name is not to be missed—is understandably annoyed: "How do you call me child!" (23). We already know about his having "clutched" her back behind his house and "sweated like a stallion" at her every approach (22). Despite Abigail's allegations, Miller achieves the curious effect of making *her* the apparent aggressor in this scene—as critical commentary proves. Miller's ploy, to blame a woman for the Fall of a good man, is a sleight of pen as old as the Old Testament. There is something too convenient in the fact that "legend has it that Abigail turned up later as a prostitute in Boston" ("Echoes Down the Corridor"). Prostitution is not only the oldest profession, but it is also the oldest evidence for the law of supply and demand. Men demand sexual services of women they in turn regard as socially deviant. Miller's statement of Abigail's fate resounds with implicit forgiveness for the man who is unwittingly tempted by a fatal female, a conniving witch.

Miller's treatment of Abigail in the second scene of Act Two, left out of the original reading version and most productions but included as an appendix in contemporary texts of the play, is also dishonest. Having promised Elizabeth as she is being taken away in chains that "I will fall like an ocean on that court! Fear nothing" (78)—at the end of the first scene of Act Two—John returns to Abigail, alone and at night. The scene is both anticlimactic and potentially damning of the hero. What may have begun as Miller's attempt to have the rational John reason with Abigail, even with the defense that Elizabeth has adjured him to talk to her (61)—although that is before Elizabeth is herself accused—ends in a discussion that is dangerous to John's position in the play.

Miller wants us to believe, as Proctor does "*seeing her madness*" when she reveals her self-inflicted injuries, that Abigail is insane: "I'm holes all over from their damned needles and pins" (149). While Miller may have intended her madness to be a metaphor for her inherent evil—sociologists suggest that madness replaced witchcraft as a pathology to be treated not by burning or hanging but by physicians and incarceration in mental institutions—he must have realized he ran the risk of making her more sympathetic than he intended. Miller is intent upon presenting John as a man haunted by guilt and aware of his own hypocrisy, and to make Abigail equally aware, even in a state of madness, is too risky. Her long speech about John's "goodness" cannot be tolerated because its irony is too costly to John.

> Why, you taught me goodness, therefore you are good. It were fire you walked me through, and all my ignorance was burned away. It were a fire, John, we lay in fire. And from that night no woman dare call me wicked any more but I knew my answer. I used to weep for my sins when the wind lifted up my skirts; and blushed for shame because some old Rebecca called me loose. And then you burned my ignorance away. As bare as some December tree I saw them all—walking like saints to church, running to feed the sick, and hypocrites in their hearts! And God gave me strength to call them liars, and God made men to listen to me, and by God I will scrub the world clean for the love of Him! (150)

We must not forget, either, when we are considering critical commentary, that we are dealing with an art form which has a specular dimension. The many Abigails of the stage have no doubt contributed to the unacknowledged view of Abigail as siren/witch that so many critics have. In Jed Harris's original production in 1953, in Miller's own production of the same year (to which the later excised scene was first added), and in Laurence Olivier's 1965 production, Abigail was played by an actress in her twenties, not a young girl. The intent on each director's part had to have been to make *Abigail's* lust for John believable. Individual performers have consistently enacted the siren's role:

> The eyes of Madeleine Sherwood, who played Abigail in 1953, glowed with lust . . . [but] Perhaps the most impressive Abigail has been that of Sarah Miles in 1965. A "plaguingly sexy mixture of beauty and crossness" . . . Miles "reeks with the cunning of suppressed evil and steams with the promise of suppressed passion."

Only the 1980 production of *The Crucible* by Bill Bryden employed girls who looked even younger than seventeen. Dukore suggests that Bryden's solution to the fact that John's "seduction of a teenage girl half his age appears not to have impressed [critics] as a major fault" was "ingenious yet (now that he has done it) obvious."

Abigail is not the only witch in Miller's play, though; Elizabeth, too, is a hag. But it is Elizabeth who is most in need of feminist reader-redemption. If John is diminished as Christian hero by a feminist deconstruction, the diminution is necessary to a balanced reading of the play and to a revised mythopoeia of the paternalistic monotheism of the Puritans and its twentieth-century equivalent, the existential mysticism of Miller.

John's sense of guilt is intended by Miller to act as salve to any emotional injuries given his wife and his own conscience. When his conscience cannot be calmed, when he quakes at doing what he knows must be done in revealing Abigail's deceit, it is upon Elizabeth that he turns his wrath:

> Spare me! You forget nothin' and forgive nothin'. Learn charity, woman. I have gone tiptoe in this house all seven month since she is gone. I have not moved from there to there without I think to please you, and still an everlasting funeral marches round your heart. I cannot speak but I am doubted, every moment judged for lies. as though I come into a court when I come into this house. (54–55)

What we are meant to read as understandably defensive anger—that is if we read within the patriarchal framework in which the play is written—must be re-evaluated; such a reading must be done in the light of Elizabeth's logic—paradoxically, the only "cold" thing about her. She is right when she turns his anger back on him with "the magistrate sits in your heart that judges you" (55). She is also right on two other counts. First, John has "a faulty understanding of young girls. There is a promise made in any bed" (61). The uninitiated and obviously self-punishing Abigail may be excused for thinking as she does (once again in the excised scene) that he is "singing secret hallelujahs that [his] wife will hang!" (152) Second, John *does* retain some tender feelings for Abigail despite his indignation. Elizabeth's question reverberates with insight: "if it were not Abigail that you must go to hurt, would you falter now? I think not" (54). John has already admitted to Abigail—and to us—in the first act that "I may think of you softly from time to time" (23), and he does look at her with *"the faintest suggestion of a knowing smile on his face"* (21). And John's use of wintry images of Elizabeth and their home in Act Two—"It's winter in her yet" (51)—echoes the imagery used by Abigail in Act One. John is to Abigail "no wintry man," but one whose "heat" has drawn her to her window to see him looking up (23). She is the one who describes Elizabeth as "a cold, snivelling woman" (24), but it is Miller's favoured imagery for a stereotypically frigid wife who is no less a witch (in patriarchal lore) than a hotblooded sperm-stealer like Abigail. Exacerbating all of this is the fact that John lies to Elizabeth about having been alone with Abigail in Parris's house; Miller would have us believe that John lies to save Elizabeth pain, but I believe he lies out of a rationalizing habit that he carries forward to his death.

Miller *may* want to be kind to Elizabeth, but he cannot manage that and John's heroism, too. Act Two opens with Elizabeth as hearth angel singing softly offstage to the children who are, significantly, never seen in the play, and bringing John his supper—stewed rabbit which, she says, "it hurt my heart to strip" (50). But in the space of four pages Miller upbraids her six times. First, John "is not quite pleased" (49) with the taste of Elizabeth's stew, and before she appears on stage he adds salt to it. Second, there is a "certain disappointment" (so) for John in the way Elizabeth receives his kiss. Third, John's request for "Cider?" made *"as gently as he can"* (51) leaves Elizabeth *"reprimanding herself for having forgot"* (51). Fourth, John reminds Elizabeth of the cold atmosphere in their house: "You ought to bring flowers in the house . . . It's winter in here yet" (51). Fifth, John perceives Elizabeth's melancholy as something perennial: "I think you're sad *again*" (51, emphasis added). And sixth, and in a more overtly condemning mood, John berates Elizabeth when he discovers that she has allowed Mary Warren to go to Salem to testify: "It is a fault, it is a fault, Elizabeth—you're the mistress here" (52). Cumulatively, these criticisms work to arouse sympathy for a man who would *season* his meal, his home, and his *amour*, a man who is meant to appeal to us because of his sensual awareness of spring's erotic promise: "It's warm as blood beneath the clods" (50), and "I never see such a load of flowers on the earth. . . . Lilacs have a purple smell. Lilac is the smell of nightfall" (51). We, too, are seasoned to believe that John really does "[aim] to please" Elizabeth, and that Elizabeth is relentless in her admonishing of John for his affair, of which she is knowledgeable. It is for John that we are to feel sympathy when he says, "Let you look to your own improvement before you go to judge your husband more" (54). Miller has informed us of several ways in which Elizabeth could improve herself.

Neil Carson claims that "Miller intends the audience to view Proctor ironically" in this scene; Proctor, he says, is "a man who is rationalising in order to avoid facing himself," and at the beginning of Act Two "Proctor is as guilty as any of projecting his own faults onto others." While I find much in Carson's entire chapter on *The Crucible* as sensitive a criticism of the play as any written, I am still uncomfortable about the fact that a "tragic victory" for the protagonist necessarily means an admission of guilt for his wife— once again, it seems to me, a victim is being blamed.

No critic, not even Carson, questions Miller's insistence that Elizabeth is at least partly to blame for John's infidelity. Her fate is sealed in the lie she tells for love of her husband because she proves *him* a liar: "as in *All My Sons*," says critic Leonard Moss, "a woman inadvertently *betrays* her husband." John has told several lies throughout the play, but it is Elizabeth's lie that the critics (and Miller) settle upon, for once again the lie fits the stereotype woman as liar, woman as schemer, woman as witch sealing the fate of man the would-be hero.

But looked at another way, Elizabeth is not a liar. The question put to her by Judge Danforth is "Is [present tense] your husband a lecher!" (113). Elizabeth can in good conscience respond in the negative for she knows the affair to be over. She has no desire to condemn the man who has betrayed her, for she believes John to be nothing but a "good man . . . only somewhat bewildered" (55). Once again, though, her comment condemns her because an audience hears (and Miller perhaps intends) condescension on her part. The patriarchal reading is invited by John's ironic response: "Oh, Elizabeth, your justice would freeze beer!" (55). What seems to be happening is that Goody Proctor is turned into a goody two-shoes, a voice of morality. Why we should expect anything else of Elizabeth, raised within a Puritan society and a living example of its valued "good woman," escapes me. I find it amazing that the same rules made but not obeyed by "good" men can be used to condemn the women who do adhere to them.

The other thing which Miller and the critics seem unwilling to acknowledge is the hurt that Elizabeth feels over John's betrayal; instead, her anger, elicited not specifically about the affair but about the incident with the poppet, following hard upon the knowledge of Giles Corey's wife having been taken, is evidence that she is no good woman. Her language condemns her: "[Abigail] is murder! She must be ripped out of the world!" (76). Anger in woman, a danger of which Ecclesiastes warns, has been cause for locking her up for centuries.

After Elizabeth's incarceration, and without her persistent logic, Miller is able to focus on John and his sense of failure. But Elizabeth's last words as she is taken from her home are about the children: "When the children wake, speak nothing of witchcraft—it will frighten them. *She cannot go on.* . . . Tell the children I have gone to visit someone sick" (77–78). I find it strange that John's similar concerns when he has torn up the confession—"I have three children—how may I teach them to walk like men in the world, and I sold my friends?" (143)—should be valued above Elizabeth's. Is it because the children are boys? Is it because Elizabeth is expected to react in the maternal fashion that she does but for John to respond thus is a sign of sensitive masculinity? Is it because the communal as defined by the Word is threatened by the integrity of women? And why is maintaining a name more important than living? At least alive he might attend to his children's daily needs—after all, we are told about the sad situation of the "orphans walking from house to house" (130).

It would be foolish to argue that John does not suffer—that, after all, is the point of the play. But what of Elizabeth's suffering? She is about to lose her husband, her children are without parents, she is sure to be condemned to death as well. Miller must, once again, diminish the threat that Elizabeth offers to John's martyrdom, for he has created a woman who does not lie, who her husband believes would not give the court the admission of guilt "if tongs of fire were singeing" her (138). Miller's play about the life and death struggle for a *man's* soul, cannot be threatened by a woman's struggle. In order to control his character, *Miller* impregnates her. The court will not sentence an unborn child, so Elizabeth does not have to make a choice. Were she to choose to die without wavering in her decision, as both John and Miller think she would, she would be a threat to the outcome of the play and the sympathy which is supposed to accrue to John. Were she to make the decision to live, for the reasons which Reverend Hale stresses, that "Life, woman, life is God's most precious gift; no principle, however glorious, may justify the taking of it" (132), she would undermine existential integrity with compromise.

I am not reading another version of *The Crucible*, one which Miller did not intend, but rather looking at the assumptions inherent in his intentions, assumptions that Miller seems oblivious to and which his critics to date have questioned far too little. I, too, can read the play as a psychological and ethical contest which no one wins, and of which it can be said that both John and Elizabeth are expressions of men and women with all their failings and nobility, but I am troubled by the fact that Elizabeth is seldom granted even that much, that so much is made of Elizabeth's complicity in John's adultery, and that the victim of John's "virility," Abigail, is blamed because she is evil and/or mad. I do want to question the gender stereotypes in the play and in the criticism that has been written about it.

Let me indulge finally for a moment in another kind of criticism, one that is a fiction, or more precisely, a "crypto-friction" that defies "stratifications of canonical thought" and transgresses generic boundaries of drama/fiction and criticism. Like Virginia Woolf I would like to speculate on a play written by a fictional sister to a famous playwright. Let us call Arthur

Miller's wide-eyed younger sister, who believes she can counter a scopic economy by stepping beyond the mirror, *Alice* Miller. In Alice's play, Elizabeth and John suffer equally in a domestic problem which is exacerbated by the hysteria around them. John does not try to intimidate Elizabeth with his anger, and she is not described as cold or condescending. Abigail is a victim of an older man's lust and not inherently a "bad girl"; she is not beautiful or if she is the playwright does not make so much of it. Her calling out of witches would be explained by wiser critics as the result of her fear and her confusion, not her lust. There is no effort made in Alice's play to create a hero at the expense of the female characters, or a heroine at the expense of a male character. John is no villain, but—as another male victim/hero character, created by a woman, describes himself—"a trite, commonplace sinner," trying to right a wrong he admits without blaming others.

Or, here is another version, written by another, more radical f(r)ictional sister, *Mary* Miller, a real hag. In it, all the witches celebrate the death of John Proctor. The idea comes from two sources: first, a question from a female student who wanted to know if part of Elizabeth's motivation in not pressing her husband to confess is her desire to pay him back for his betrayal; and second, from a response to Jean-Paul Sartre's ending for the film *Les Sorcieres de Salem*. In his 1957 version of John Proctor's story, Sartre identifies Elizabeth "with the God of prohibiting sex and the God of judgment," but he has her save Abigail, who tries to break John out of jail and is in danger of being hanged as a traitor too, because Elizabeth realizes "'she loved [John].'" As the film ends, "Abigail stands shocked in a new understanding."

In Mary Miller's version Elizabeth is not identified with the male God of the Word, but with the goddesses of old forced into hiding or hanged because of a *renaissance* of patriarchal ideology. Mary's witches come together, alleged seductress and cold wife alike, not for love of a man who does not deserve either, but to celebrate life and their victory over male character, playwright, and critics, "'men in power' . . . who create and identify with the roles of both the victimizers and the victims," men who Mary Miller would suggest "vicariously enjoyed the women's suffering."

STEPHEN MARINO

Arthur Miller's "Weight of Truth" in The Crucible

One of the more intriguing historical events Arthur Miller included in *The Crucible* was Giles Corey's refusal to answer his indictment for witchcraft in order to preserve his land for his sons' inheritance. In punishment, Corey was pressed with great stones, still refusing to confess to witchery. Corey died, still in defiance, uttering as his last words, "More Weight." Miller assigns great significance to Corey's words for he uses them in Act Four at a decisive moment for his protagonist, John Proctor. In hearing about Giles's death, Proctor repeats Corey's words, as if to consider their meaning for himself. In fact, Miller intimately connects the word "weight" to the theme of the play by employing it ten times throughout the four acts. Tracing the repetition "weight" in *The Crucible* reveals how the word supports one of the play's crucial themes: how an individual's struggle for truth often conflicts with society.

Some critics have conducted similar language studies of *The Crucible*. In "Setting, Language and the Force of Evil in *The Crucible*," Penelope Curtis maintains that the language of the play is marked by what she calls "half-metaphor," which Miller employs to suggest the themes. For example, she examines the interplay of language between Elizabeth and Abigail which indicates reputation, such as "something soiled," "entirely white," "no blush about my name." John Prudhoe, in "Arthur Miller and the Tradition of

From *Modern Drama* 38:4 (Winter 1995). © 1995 by the University of Toronto.

Tragedy," notes how the characters use Biblical imagery in their language because "a large context of traditional beliefs gives meaning to their words." Stephen Fender, in "Precision and Pseudo-Precision in *The Crucible*," refutes Prudhoe's analysis and argues that the language of the Salemites actually reveals "the speech of a society totally without moral referents." Leonard Moss, in "Arthur Miller and the Common Man's Language," discusses how Miller as a playwright has a "talent for expressing inward urgency through colloquial language." Among the articles which discuss the importance of "name" in the language of the play are Ruby Cohn in *Dialogue in American Drama*, Gerald Weales in "Arthur Miller: Man and His Image," and Michael J. O'Neal in "History, Myth and Name Magic in Arthur Miller's *The Crucible*." The only critic who makes a similar linguistic analysis is Edward Murray. In *Arthur Miller, Dramatist*, Murray examines how in *The Crucible* Miller "in a very subtle manner, uses key words to knit together the texture of action and theme." He notes, for example, the recurrent use of the word "soft" in the text.

Certainly the struggle for truth is at the center of the play's conflicts. Jean Selz believes "the avatars of truth" are the most important of the underlying themes: "We see truth—at first forceful and sure of itself—get enmeshed in the ways of uncertainty, falter and grow pale and transform itself little by little into a mean and sorry thing. . . . whom everyone refuses to accept." Selz argues that truth is at odds with the very people, the judges and ministers, who are supposed to discern it. "Those impostors who call themselves judges," Selz thinks, are particularly indictable because they force truth to become the "invisible heroine" of the play. Similarly, Miller's thematic use of weight is intimately connected to the conflicts that occur when an individual's struggle to know truth opposes society's understanding of it. For the dramatic tension of the play is based on the clashes of truth between those characters who profess to speak it, those who profess it, those who live it and those who die for it.

Miller's initial use of "weight" in the first scene immediately connects it with truth. Reverend Parris, trying to discover the cause of his daughter Betty's unnatural sleeping fit, pleads with, and then threatens, his niece Abigail:

> Now tell me true, Abigail. And I pray you feel the weight of truth upon you, for now my ministry's at stake, my ministry and perhaps your cousin's life. (11)

The "weight of truth" Parris implores Abigail to consider operates on a number of levels both in this scene and in the rest of the play. Obviously,

Parris wants to discover the literal truth about the abominations that Abigail, Betty, and the other girls, led by Tituba, are alleged to have performed in the forest. However, the "weight of truth" which Parris begs Abigail to consider more importantly encompasses all of its figurative meanings: seriousness, heaviness, gravity, importance, burden, pressure, influence—all of which are connected to religion and law, the foundations upon which the theocracy of Salem village is built. For clearly *The Crucible* questions the meaning of truth in this theocratic society and the weight that that truth bears on an individual and on the society itself.

Thus, Parris's appeal to Abigail to "feel the weight of truth" contains many thematic implications. On one level, Parris's use of weight as "importance" or "seriousness" appeals to Abigail on a personal level, since her uncle's ministry and her cousin's life are at stake. On another level, because Parris invokes his ministry in connection with the "weight of truth," the religious connotation is clear. If Abigail felt the weight of religious truth, she would confess to Parris about the abominations performed in the forest, thereby releasing her from the heaviness of falsehood, sin, guilt, and the power of Satan. On another level, Miller clearly establishes negative connotations of the "weight of truth." For there is no doubt that Parris threatens Abigail with all the heaviness of his ministry, and the severe power of theocracy that it represents for Abigail and the inhabitants of Salem village—a power whose weight and truth we see unleashed in the play.

When Reverend Hale enters, Miller expands the thematic implications with the second use of "weight." Hale carries half a dozen heavy books:

HALE Pray you, someone take these!
PARRIS, *delighted* Mr. Hale! Oh! it's good to see you again!
    Taking some books: My, they're heavy!
HALE, *setting down his books*: They must be; they are weighted
    with authority. (36)

In these lines Miller significantly connects the literal heaviness of the texts to their figurative meaning, something even Hale as a character is aware of. For later in the act Hale explains their significance as the authoritative texts on witchcraft:

Here is all the invisible world, caught, defined and calculated. In these books the Devil stands stripped of all his brute disguises. Here are all your familiar spirits—your incubi and succubi; your witches that go by land, by air, and by sea; your wizards of the night and of the day. (39)

Hale's mission is to use these texts to discover the truth of the alleged witch-craft in Salem village. Thus, his mission is equally connected to the same religious "weight of truth" as Parris's.

However, Hale's mission is not the same as Parris's. What marks Hale's mission and his importance as a character is that he truly believes in the books' authority. The author's notes explain at length Hale's serious devotion to his grave task. Hale comes to Salem village as an outside observer, an examiner with not only the expertise but also the objectivity to discover the truth. Thus, his eventual judgment that private vengeance fuels many of the witchcraft accusations illustrates the difference between the truth of religion and the truth of law. Hale and his texts, weighted so heavily with the authority of religion, become at odds with the civil authority of the law, an irony in this theocracy where Church and State law are intertwined.

On this level, the reader and audience readily perceive the growing conflict between Church and State in the play. For the modern audiences, the religious authority of incubi and succubi, with which Hale believes his books are weighted, clearly does not exist. We see the hypocrisy of a religious system which bases the truth on nothing but the words of young girls. We see that actual authority and weight lie in the secular law that these religious texts are going to put in motion to crush innocent people. Thus, the first two uses of "weight" in the play significantly intertwine the "weight of truth" and the "weight of authority." For the "crying out" is about to begin, and the audience already knows the "sport" (11) that the witchcraft rumors are based on, as Abigail has told both John and Parris. Furthermore, the audience has already witnessed the personal squabbles of the Salem villagers over land, meetinghouse, and minister, and the personal intimacies between Abigail and John. The weight and authority of religious truth that Hale so reverences quickly turns into the weight and authority of law.

The third reference to weight does not occur until Act Two, and it significantly connects the word to the law. Elizabeth Proctor relates to John how their servant girl, Mary Warren, is now a witness to the court that has been convened:

> PROCTOR Court! What court?
> ELIZABETH Aye, it is a proper court they have now. They've sent four judges out of Boston, she says, weighty magistrates of the General Court, and at the head sits the Deputy Governor of the Province. (52)

With this line, Miller intertwines the religious connotations that "weight" had in Parris's and Hale's lines with the disposition of that religious law in

Massachusetts Bay Colony. Indeed, the weighty power of the magistrates' civil law is based on the truth of religious dogma. This connection between law and religion is reinforced by Mary Warren herself a few lines later when she comes home after spending a long day at the court proceedings:

> PROCTOR You will not go to court again, Mary Warren.
> MARY WARREN I must tell you, sir, I will be gone every day
> now. I am amazed you do not see what weighty work we do.
> (58)

In this line, "weighty" possesses all of the figurative connotations of both law and religion. Clearly, the exposure of witches to the community is the work of God and religion, but it is equally the work of the community in its legal entity to dispose of such witchcraft. Thus, the "weight of truth" that Parris uses in all its ramifications and the "weight of authority" that Hale so reverences are both dispensed by the weight of the law.

Ironically, in the entire play the word "weight" never directly describes the law. In Act Two, after Hale's examination of the Proctors, Ezekiel Cheever comes to arrest Elizabeth, a significant scene in Hale's realization that the weight of the court and law is now outweighing the weight of his authority. Cheever says:

> Now believe me, Proctor, how heavy be the law, all its tonnage I
> do carry on my back tonight. . . . I have a warrant for your wife.
> (72)

What is implied by the fact that "weight" is not employed in this line? Perhaps it shows how the law is now operating on its own, without the benefit of the religious "weight of truth" or "weight of authority": the arrests of Elizabeth and others do occur without Hale's authority and knowledge. Perhaps it also suggests that in a theocracy there must be a balance between law and religion or the results will be tragic. Certainly, Hale, as the outside observer, ultimately discovers the truth about Proctor's character and the falseness of Abigail's. Thus, describing the law as "heavy," as opposed to "weighty," removes the religious association and endows it with the power to suppress, pressure, and crush whoever opposes it, accurately foreshadowing what will happen to Giles Corey, Rebecca Nurse, and John Proctor. At this point in the play, we understand that the "tonnage" that Cheever carries will ultimately break the lives of the characters and the back of theocracy in Massachusetts.

The character who best signifies the power of the law is Judge

Danforth. In Act Three, when Proctor and Francis Nurse are attempting to prove the falseness of the accusations against their wives, Nurse remarks to Danforth: "I never thought to say it to such a weighty judge, but you are deceived" (87). Nurse's description of Danforth as a "weighty" judge occurs at a crucial moment in the play in terms of Miller's use of it. For Danforth in his role as Deputy Judge represents the height of power in Massachusetts. Francis's words exhibit how Danforth should be the arbiter of religious and civil truth, discerning between the accusations and defenses that are made. However, this scene illustrates how tenuous is the relationship between law and religion, and how the law has superseded religion. At this crucial point in the play the audience perceives the hypocrisy of the religious and legal truth. Danforth uses the weight and power of the law to crush dissent, as when he declares Corey in contempt, proclaims court in session, and calls for the arrest and examination of those people who have signed depositions as character witnesses for Martha Corey, Rebecca Nurse, and Elizabeth Proctor. Ironically, after Danforth spouts the "invisible crime" speech (100), the audience perceives how this "weighty judge" is indeed deceived.

We see how the "weight of truth" has changed from its initial association with religion. Danforth, as the personification of the law, is in marked contrast to Reverend Hale. Hale and Danforth best represent the tension between the truth as discerned by law and the truth as discerned by religion. The conflict between Hale as a "minister of the Lord" and Danforth as the "arbiter of justice" reaches a climax in this scene, since Hale has increasingly come to doubt the truth of the girls' claims. This scene culminates with Hale's realization that the civil law is out of control, and he denounces the proceedings after the examination and arrest of Proctor by Danforth.

Interestingly, Hale's plea to Danforth to let a lawyer argue on behalf of John includes "weight":

HALE Excellency, a moment. I think this goes to the heart of the matter.
DANFORTH, *with deep misgivings* It surely does.
HALE I cannot say he is an innocent man; I know him little. But in all justice, sir, a claim so weighty cannot be argued by a farmer. In God's name, sir, stop here; send him home and let him come again with a lawyer—
DANFORTH, *patiently* Now look you, Mr. Hale—
HALE Excellency, I have signed seventy-two death warrants; I am a minister of the Lord, and I dare not take a life without there be a proof so immaculate no slightest qualm of conscience may doubt it.

DANFORTH Mr. Hale, you surely do not doubt my justice. (99)

Hale's application of "weighty" to Proctor's claim indicates a crucial and marked shift of the word's use in the play. David Levin in "Salem Witchcraft in Recent Fiction and Drama" discusses how Miller uses the Salem Witch Trials to show how people are blinded to the truth. Levin maintains that Miller "has his characters turn the truth upside down." He cites as examples the change in Hale from his belief in truth in the beginning of the play to his remorseful plea to the innocent victims to confess falsely. Levin also points out the irony of how Abigail's lies are taken as the truth, and how Proctor's truths are taken as lies. Miller uses a similar movement in the play to shift the meaning of "weight." The first five references associate weight with the religion and law of the Salem theocracy, whose truth, power, and authority the audience perceives as false, unjust and hypocritical for destroying innocent people. However, Hale's reference to Proctor's claim as "weighty" shifts the application of the word—from the state and religion to those innocent characters who are accused, and then destroyed, by the false weight and authority of religious and civil truth: Proctor, Giles, Rebecca. Thus, "weight" can be traced as it moves from theological truth to legal truth, and finally to the truth of individual conscience.

How ironic that Parris, who first gives the word its thematic significance also indicates the shift in its usage. In Act Four, he exhibits his fear at the impending executions of Proctor and Rebecca Nurse:

PARRIS Judge Hathorne—it were another sort that hanged till now. Rebecca Nurse is no Bridget that lived three year with Bishop before she married him. John Proctor is not Isaac Ward that drank his family to ruin. *To* DANFORTH: I would to God it were not so, Excellency, but these people have great weight yet in the town. Let Rebecca stand upon the gibbet and send up some righteous prayer, and I fear she'll wake a vengeance on you. (127)

On one level, the weight that Parris refers to is the influence that Proctor and Nurse have because of their social status in the community. On another level, their weight connotes the religious weight of truth that Parris earlier has invoked. The irony lies in the "righteous prayer" he fears Rebecca could send. For the audience now understands the falseness of Parris's weight of truth, and that Rebecca and John have been empowered with their own weight of truth and righteousness. Parris fears Rebecca's weight will carry some vengeance, but the audience understands that vengeance is only the tactic of those preaching and administering falseness. The weight of Rebecca and John becomes the threat to Parris.

The most historically accurate use of "weight" occurs later in Act Four, a scene which is significant for Proctor's connection to the theme of truth. Confronted with his pending execution, he is tempted to confess falsely in order to save his life. Elizabeth relays to John the details of Giles Corey's death:

> ELIZABETH Great stones they lay upon his chest until he plead aye or nay. *With a tender smile for the old man*: They say he give them but two words. "More weight," he says. And died.
> PROCTOR, *numbed—a thread to weave into his agony* "More weight."
> ELIZABETH Aye. It were a fearsome man, Giles Corey. (135)

In Giles's last words, "weight" connects with both its literal and figurative meanings as it did with Hale's books. Obviously, the great weight of the stones literally crushed Giles to death. However, the literal and figurative are intimately intertwined here. For even if Giles used the words only to end his torture, in the context of the play the symbolic importance of Corey's words and the weight which pressed him to death is crucial. Those great stones represent the power, heaviness, seriousness, and gravity of a Massachusetts theocracy which crushed the life out of Giles. Despite this power, Corey refused to answer his indictment so that his sons could inherit his property. Thus, the words "More weight" liberate the individual conscience of the defiant Corey from the law of society. They become the weight of truth that he, Nurse, and Proctor possess.

In this scene, the same weight is about to crush John Proctor as well. In his repetition of Corey's words he seems to understand their significance for Giles, yet struggles to understand their significance for himself. Proctor's personal struggle in the play is at a crisis in this scene. Because of his affair with Abigail and its effect on his relationship with Elizabeth, his Christian character, his soul and his conscience, he does not consider himself the fearsome man like Corey or the saint like Rebecca. He is willing to confess because he does not think he possesses the great weight they have.

Ultimately, John discovers the "shred of goodness" (144) in himself: the weight of truth of his name and character. Significantly, Parris applies the word "weight" to Proctor's name after John has confessed:

> It is a great service, sir. It is a weighty name; it will strike the village that Proctor confess. I beg you, let him sign it. . . . (141)

Proctor comes to understand not the weightiness of his name for the village, but the weightiness of it for himself. His unwillingness to have his confession signed for posting on the church door is connected to his name. His name is the only truth that Proctor knows; it is the only item that he knows still bears weight, as Parris has indicated. Yet the weight that Parris assigns to Proctor's name is not the same that Proctor himself assigns. For Proctor, a man's name represents the weight of his existence in the world. A name is not connected to his piety or his spirituality. For Proctor, a man cannot live without the weight of his name; he cannot teach his sons to be men without it. "How may I live without my name? I have given you my soul; leave me my name!" (143). Thus, he dies with the goodness and weight of his name. Note that his last words to Elizabeth connect to the power of weight: "Show honor now, show a stony heart and sink them with it" (144). The weight of truth sets Proctor, Elizabeth, and Massachusetts free.

Chronology

1915   Arthur Miller born on October 17 in Harlem, New York City, the second son of Isadore Miller, a manufacturer of women's clothing, and Augusta Barnett Miller. Characters in several of Miller's plays would be modeled on his older brother, Kermit.

1921   Joan Miller is born. She will become an actress with the stage name Joan Copeland.

1928   Father's business fails and family moves to Brooklyn. Attends James Madison High School; injury received playing football later keeps him from military service.

1930   Transfers to Abraham Lincoln High School.

1933   Graduates from high school and becomes interested in literature after reading Dostoevsky's *The Brothers Karamazov*. Refused admission to University of Michigan because of poor grades; works for his father in family's new garment business. Writes a short story, never published, "In Memorium," about the difficult life of a salesman.

1934   Admitted to University of Michigan after writing persuasive letter to the dean. Meets Mary Grace Slattery, who will be his first wife. Studies playwriting.

1936   *No Villain* wins Avery Hopwood Award.

1937   *Honors at Dawn* wins Avery Hopwood Award.

1938   *They too Arise* (revision of *No Villain*, revised again that year as
            The Grass Still Grows) wins the Theater Guild National Award.
            Writes *The Great Disobedience*; graduates.

1939   Returns to New York and participates in the New York Federal
            Theater Project; coauthors *Listen My Children* with Norman
            Rosten.

1940   Federal Theater Project ends and Miller goes on relief;
            completes *The Golden Years*. Marries Mary Grace Slattery on
            August 5. She works as a waitress and as an editor to support
            them while Miller writes.

1941   Completes two radio scripts: *The Pussycat and the Expert Plumber
            Who Was a Man* and *William Ireland's Confession*. Works in box
            factory, as scriptwriter in bond drives, and as shipfitter's helper at
            the Brooklyn Navy Yard.

1942   Writes *The Four Freedoms*, a radio play.

1943   Completes *The Half-Bridge*. Becomes interested in Marxism and
            attends a study course. *That They May Win*, a one-act play in
            support of the war effort, produced by a Brooklyn community
            theater group.

1944   Jane Miller born on September 7. *The Man Who Had All the Luck*,
            his first Broadway play, closes after six performances and is
            published in *Cross-Section: A Collection of New American Writing*;
            Situation Normal, interviews with American servicemen,
            published.

1945   *Focus*, a novel about anti-Semitism; *Grandpa and the Statue*, a
            radio play; and *That They May Win* published. In article in *New
            Masses*, attacks Ezra Pound for supporting fascism.

1946   "The Plaster Masks," a short story, published.

1947   Robert Miller born on May 31. *All My Sons* opens on Broadway;
            auctions off manuscript to support Progressive Citizens of
            America. "It Takes a Thief" published in *Collier's*; *The Story of Gus*

included in *Radio's Best Plays*, and his adaptation of Ferenc Molnar's *The Guardsman* appears in *Theater Guild on the Air*; an essay, "Subsidized Theater," published in the *New York Times*.

1949   *Death of a Salesman* opens on Broadway; wins New York Drama Critics Circle Award and the Pulitzer Prize. "Tragedy and the Common Man," and "Arthur Miller on 'The Nature of Tragedy'" published.

1950   Meets Marilyn Monroe. *Death of a Salesman* closes after 742 performances; Miller's version of Ibsen's *An Enemy of the People* runs for thirty-six performances.

1951   *An Enemy of the People* published; a short story, "Monte Saint Angelo," appears in *Harper's*; writes screenplay, *The Hook*.

1953   *The Crucible* opens on Broadway.

1955   One-act version of *A View from the Bridge* and *A Memory of Two Mondays* produced on Broadway. Contracted to write film script for New York City Youth Board; dropped from project after *New York Herald Tribune* publishes article attacking his leftist political connections.

1956   Divorced from Mary Grace Slattery; marries Marilyn Monroe; subpoenaed to appear before House Un-American Activities Committee (HUAC); cited for contempt of Congress when he refuses to name names. Two-act version of *A View from the Bridge* opens in London and runs for 220 performances.

1957   Blacklisted after convicted for contempt of Congress. "The Misfits," a short story, published in *Esquire*. Rewrites "The Misfits" as screenplay for Marilyn Monroe. Publishes *Collected Plays*.

1958   *The Misfits* is filmed. Miller's contempt conviction reversed.

1959   "I Don't Need You Any More," a short story, published in *Esquire*.

1960   "Please Don't Kill Anything," a short story, published in *Noble Savage*.

1961   Marilyn Monroe applies for Mexican divorce. Miller's mother dies in March. "Please Don't Kill Anything" published in *Redbook*; "The Prophecy" published in *Esquire*; Italian operatic version of *A View from the Bridge* produced in Rome, Italy, as *Una Sguardo dal Ponte*; New York City Opera Company performs Robert Ward's version of *The Crucible*.

1962   Marries Ingeborg Morath, a photographer, in February. Marilyn Monroe commits suicide in August. "Glimpse at a Jockey" published in *Noble Savage*.

1963   Begins *After the Fall*; publishes children's story, *Jane's Blanket*. Daughter Rebecca Miller born in September.

1964   *After the Fall* performed by Lincoln Center Repertory Theater; *Incident at Vichy* opens at Lincoln Center. Attends Nazi trials at Frankfurt, Germany, as special commentator for the *New York Herald-Tribune*.

1965   *Incident at Vichy* published. Miller elected president of International PEN.

1966   *Death of a Salesman* produced for television. "The Recognitions" published in *Esquire*; "Search for a Future" published in the *Saturday Evening Post*.

1967   Collection of short stories, *I Don't Need You Anymore*, published; *The Crucible* produced for television; *Una Sguardo dal Ponte* performed at the Philadelphia Lyric Opera.

1968   *The Price* opens on Broadway; millionth copy of *Death of a Salesman* sold. Attends Democratic National Convention as delegate for Eugene McCarthy. Petitions Soviet government to lift ban on works of Aleksandr Solzhenitsyn.

1969   *The Price* closes after 425 performances. Refuses to allow publication of his works in Greece in protest of oppression of writers. *The Reason Why*, an anti-war allegory, filmed; with Inge Morath, publishes *In Russia*.

1970   Receives Creative Arts Award Medal from Brandeis University. Two, one-act plays, *Fame* and *The Reason Why*, run for twenty performances at New York's New Theater Workshop. Soviet Union, in response to *In Russia*, bans all Miller's works.

1971   *The Price* and *A Memory of Two Mondays* produced for television. Miller's version of *An Enemy of the People* opens at Lincoln Center for brief run; elected to American Academy of Arts and Letters; *The Portable Arthur Miller*, a collection of writings, published.

1972   All-black production of *Death of a Salesman* opens in Baltimore; *The Crucible* revived at Lincoln Center; a comedy, *The Creation of the World and Other Business* opens to poor reviews and closes after twenty performances.

1973   *The Creation of the World and Other Business* published. Appointed adjunct professor in residence at the University of Michigan, 1973–74.

1974   *After the Fall* produced for television.

1975   *Death of a Salesman* produced in New York at Circle in the Square. Denounces United Nations' policies toward Israel; protests treatment of writers in Iran; appears on panel before Senate to support freedom of writers throughout the world.

1976   *The Crucible* produced at Stratford, Connecticut; *The Archbishop's Ceiling* produced in New Haven. "Ham Sandwich" and *The Poosidin's Resignation* appear in the *Boston University Quarterly*. Participates in symposium on Jewish culture and Jewish writers.

1977   *In the Country*, with photographs by Inge Morath, published; *The Archbishop's Ceiling* opens for limited run at Kennedy Center, Washington, to poor reviews. Joins in letter to Czech head of state to protest oppression of Czech writers.

1978   *Fame* produced for television; *The Theater Essays of Arthur Miller* published. Participates in protest over arrests of Soviet dissidents. Miller and Inge visit the People's Republic of China.

1979   *The Price* revived on Broadway to critical and financial success. Writes screenplay for Fania Fenelon's *Playing for Time*; criticized for his support of Vanessa Redgrave for the leading role. A film, *Arthur Miller on Home Ground*, shown in New York; *Chinese Encounters*, with Inge Morath, published.

1980   Presents "Theater in Modern China" with Cao Yu, China's most prominent dramatist, at Columbia University. *The American Clock* opens to critical praise. Signs letter with other American Jews protesting Israel's expansion on the West Bank; supports Polish Soidarity movement. *Playing for Time* shown on television to critical acclaim. *The American Clock* opens on Broadway for twelve performances.

1981   *Collected Plays, Volume Two* and *Playing for Time* published; narrates concert version of *Up From Paradise* at Whitney Museum, New York.

1982   *Elegy for a Lady* and *Some Kind of Love Story* produced in New Haven; *The American Clock* published.

1983   *A View from the Bridge* revived on Broadway; *Death of a Salesman* produced in Beijing, China; *Up From Paradise* revived off-Broadway. Receives Bobst Medal Award and $2,500 stipend from New York University.

1984   Publishes *"Salesman" in Beijing*, with photographs by Inge Morath, and revised version of *The Archbishop's Ceiling*. *Death of a Salesman* revived on Broadway. He and Inge awarded honorary doctorates from the University of Hartford.

1985   *The Price* revived on Broadway. Announces that he is writing his autobiography. Travels to Istanbul with Harold Pinter in support of Turkish writers. *Death of a Salesman* shown on television.

1986   *The Crucible* revived at Trinity Repertory Company in New York, *All My Sons* in New Haven. *The American Clock* and *The Archbishop's Ceiling* revived in London. *Danger: Memory!*, *I Don't Remember Anything*, and *Clara* published.

1987   *All My Sons* revived on television; *Danger: Memory!* opens at Lincoln Center; *All My Sons* revived on Broadway and wins Tony award; Miller's autobiography, *Timebends: A Life*, published.

Contributors

HAROLD BLOOM is Sterling Professor of Humanities at Yale University and Professor of English at New York University. His works include *Shelley's Mythmaking* (1959), *The Visionary Company* (1961), *The Anxiety of Influence* (1973), *Agon: Towards a Theory of Revisionism* (1982), *The Book of J* (1990), *The American Religion* (1992), and *The Western Canon* (1994). His forthcoming books are a study of Shakespeare and *Freud, Transference and Authority*, which considers all of Freud's major writings. A MacArthur Prize Fellow, Professor Bloom is the editor of more than thirty anthologies and general editor of five series of literary criticism published by Chelsea House.

SHEILA HUFTEL has published articles on Dorothy Wordsworth, Samuel Taylor Coleridge, and dramatist Nathan Field in *Contemporary Review*.

STEPHEN FENDER is Professor of American Studies at the University of Sussex, England, and Director of the Postgraduate Centre in the Humanities. His published works include *Plotting the Golden West: American Literature and the Rhetoric of the California Trail* (1981), *American Literature in Context: 1620–1830* (1983), and *Sea Changes: British Emigration and American Literature* (1992). He is the editor of *Henry David Thoreau* (1997).

THOMAS E. PORTER was Dean of the College of Liberal Arts at the University of Texas at Arlington, where he also taught in the departments of English, philosophy, fine arts, and the honors program. He was for many years a Jesuit priest. He has published essays on the works of Arthur Miller,

G.K. Chesterton, and William Shakespeare, and is the author of *Myth and Modern American Drama* (1969).

ROBERT A. MARTIN is Emeritus Professor of English at the University of Michigan at Ann Arbor. He has published articles and reviews on American literature and drama in *Modern Drama, Educational Theatre Journal, Michigan Quarterly Review, Studies in American Fiction,* and *The CEA Critic.* He is the editor of *The Theater Essays of Arthur Miller* (1977) and *Critical Essays on Tennessee Williams* (1997).

WILLIAM T. LISTON is the editor of *Francis Quarles' Divine Fancies: A Critical Edition* (1992), a volume in the series, *The Renaissance Imagination.*

E. MILLER BUDICK is a Senior Lecturer in the Departments of American Studies and English Literature at The Hebrew University of Jerusalem. Among his published works are essays on Edgar Allan Poe, William Cullen Bryant, Emily Dickinson, and Nathaniel Hawthorne.

JUNE SCHLUETER is Provost of Lafayette College in Easton, Pennsylvania. Her published works include *Metafictional Charaters in Modern Drama* (1979), *Modern American Drama: The Female Canon* (1990), and *Dramatic Closure: Reading the End* (1995).

ISKA ALTER is Assistant Professor of English at Hofstra University. She is the author of *The Good Man's Dilemma: Social Criticism in the Fiction of Bernard Malamud* (1981) and *The World Well Lost: Women and the Problematic of Assimilation in the Fiction of Anzia Yezierska* (1992), and essays on Shakespeare, modern drama, and Jewish-American fiction.

WENDY SCHISSEL is Co-President of St. Peter's College in Muenster, Saskatchewan, an affiliate college of the University of Saskatchewan. She teaches English and Women and Gender Studies. She is the author of *The Keepers of Memory: Canadian Mythopoeic Poets and Magic Realist Painters* (1992) and *The Landscape of Loneliness: Ambiguity in Ethel Wilson's Fiction* (1984).

STEPHEN MARINO recently completed a doctorate at Fordham University, in New York. His dissertation examines Arthur Miller's use of language in his major plays. He teaches and conducts creative writing workshops at Saint Francis College, Brooklyn. His poetry has appeared in *Echos, The Lowell Pearl,* and *Poems That Thump in the Dark.*

Bibliography

Bergeron, David M. "Arthur Miller's *The Crucible* and Nathaniel Hawthorne: Some Parallels," *English Journal* 58:1 (1969): 47–55.

Bergman, Herbert. " 'The Interior of a Heart': *The Crucible* and *The Scarlet Letter*," *University College Quarterly* 15:4 (1970): 27–32.

Calarco, Joseph. "Production as Criticism: Miller's *The Crucible*," *Educational Theatre Journal* 29 (1977): 354–61.

Carson, Neil. *Arthur Miller.* New York: Grove Press, 1982. 60–76.

DelFattore, Joan. "Fueling the Fire of Hell: A Reply to Censors of *The Crucible*," *Censored Books: Critical Viewpoints*. Nicholas Karolides, et al, eds. Metuchen, NJ: Scarecrow Press, 1993.

Ditsky, John. "Stone, Fire, and Light: Approaches to *The Crucible*," *North Dakota Quarterly* 46:2 (1978): 65–72.

Douglas, James W. "Miller's *The Crucible*: Which Witch is Which?" Renascence 15 (1963): 145–51.

Ferres, John H. *Twentieth-Century Interpretations of* "The Crucible." Englewood Cliffs, NJ: Prentice-Hall, 1972.

Griffin, John and Alice. "Arthur Miller Discusses *The Crucible*," *Theatre Arts* 37 (October 1953): 34.

Levin, David. "Salem Witchcraft in Recent Fiction and Drama," *New England Quarterly* (December 1955): 537–42.

Meserve, Walter. "*The Crucible*: 'This Fool Am I'," *Arthur Miller: New Perspectives*. Robert A. Martin, ed. and intro. Englewood Cliffs, NJ: 1982.

Nathan, George Jean. "*The Crucible*," *Theatre Arts* 37 (April 1953): 24–26.

Popkin, Henry. "Arthur Miller's *The Crucible*," *College English* 26 (November 1964): 141.

———. "Arthur Miller: The Strange Encounter," *Sewanee Review* 68 (Winter 1960): 34–60.

Walker, Philip. "Arthur Miller's *The Crucible*: Tragedy or Allegory?" *Western Speech* 20 (1956): 222–24.

Warshow, Robert. "The Liberal Conscience in *The Crucible*," *Commentary* 15 (1953): 265–71.

Weales, Gerald, ed. *The Crucible: Text and Criticism.* New York: Viking, 1971.

Acknowledgments

"The Crucible" by Sheila Huftel from *Arthur Miller: The Burning Glass* by Sheila Huftel. Copyright © 1965 by The Citadel Press. Reprinted by permission.

"Precision and Pseudo Precision in *The Crucible*" by Stephen Fender from *Journal of American Studies* 1:1 (April 1967). Copyright © 1967 by Cambridge University Press. Reprinted by permission.

"The Long Shadow of the Law: *The Crucible*" by Thomas E. Porter from *Myth and Modern American Drama* by Thomas E. Porter, reprinted in *Critical Essays on Arthur Miller*, edited by James J. Martine. Copyright © 1969 by Wayne State University Press. Reprinted by permission.

"Arthur Miller's *The Crucible:* Background and Sources" by Robert A. Martin from *Modern Drama* 20 (1977), reprinted in *Critical Essays on Arthur Miller*, edited by James J. Martine. Copyright © 1977 by the University of Toronto. Reprinted by permission.

"John Proctor's Playing in *The Crucible*" by William T. Liston from *The Midwest Quarterly* 20:4 (Summer 1979). Copyright © 1979 by Pittsburg State University. Reprinted by permission.

"The Crucible of History: Arthur Miller's John Proctor" by William J. McGill, Jr., from *The New England Quarterly* 54:2 (June 1981). Copyright © 1981 by The New England Quarterly. Reprinted by permission.

"History, Myth, and Name Magic in Arthur Miller's *The Crucible*" by Michael J. O'Neal from *CLIO* 12:2 (Winter 1983). Copyright © 1983 by Robert H. Canary and Henry Kozicki. Reprinted by permission.

"History and Other Spectres in Arthur Miller's *The Crucible*" by E. Miller Budick from *Modern Drama* 27:4 (December 1985). Copyright © 1985 by the University of Toronto. Reprinted by permission.

"The Crucible" by June Schlueter and James K. Flanagan from *Arthur Miller* by June Schlueter and James K. Flanagan. Copyright © 1987 by The Ungar Publishing Company. Reprinted by permission.

"Betrayal and Blessedness: Explorations of Feminine Power in *The Crucible, A View from the Bridge,* and *After the Fall*" by Iska Alter from *Feminist Rereadings of Modern American Drama;* ed., June Schlueter. Copyright © 1989 by Associated University Presses, Inc. Reprinted by permission.

"John Proctor and the Crucible of Individuation in Arthur Miller's *The Crucible*" by Michelle I. Pearson from *Studies in American Drama, 1945–Present* 6:1 (1991). Copyright 1991 by the Ohio State University Press. Reprinted by permission.

"Re(dis)covering the Witches in Arthur Miller's *The Crucible:* A Feminist Reading" by Wendy Schissel from *Modern Drama* 37:3 (Fall 1994). Copyright © 1994 by the University of Toronto. Reprinted by permission.

"Arthur Miller's 'Weight of Truth' in *The Crucible*" by Stephen Marino from *Modern Drama* 38:4 (Winter 1995). Copyright © 1995 by the University of Toronto. Reprinted by permission.

Index